# PREFACE

This book was originally intended especially for freshmen students of English at American colleges and universities. It will therefore also be appropriate for University undergraduates reading English, whose school training does not ordinarily include specific study of English as a language or of linguistics. It presents sufficient fact and theory about the language to serve as a background for literary study, which nowadays often engages in detailed analysis of texts. It can also serve as a quick introduction to the subject for those training to be teachers of English either at the primary or at the secondary level. The suggestions for further reading after each chapter will guide prospective teachers in their further study of English linguistics. Finally, it is hoped that the general reader will find here some material to satisfy his perennial curiosity about his language and perhaps to whet his appetite for further reading in the field.

The last few decades have been marked by great interest and activity in English linguistics in both Britain and the United States. One of the pressing problems facing the universities and schools is how the new theories and discoveries about our common language are to be incorporated into the English curriculum. This book attempts to supply a text that will be on the one hand accurate and up to date and on the other intelligible to the student lacking previous training in linguistics It is not intended as a text for specialists in English linguistics—it is too brief and sketchy for that. But if it inspires curiosity leading to further study about the native language, one of its major aims will have been attained.

I acknowledge my debt to those who have helped me in one way or another with the book. My colleague, W. Freeman Twaddell, has read the entire manuscript and made many helpful suggestions leading to greater accuracy of statement and clarity of stlye. Other helpful suggestions have come from Albert H. Marckwardt of Princeton University who has also read the entire book in manuscript, M. H. Abrams of Cornell University, Dudley Baily of the University of Nebraska, John Fisher of New York University, and George Levine of Indiana University. As editor, John Benedict has been a constant

and challenging critic of style; every page is the better for his painstaking scrutiny. Last but by no means least is my obligation to my
student, Miss Madeline Ehrman, who not only has read both galley
and page proofs, but has also contributed many of the exercises,
especially those for Chapter Four, which are largely her work. Her
collaboration and her criticism have both been of great value.

W. NELSON FRANCIS

*January* 1967

# THE ENGLISH LANGUAGE

An Introduction

# One

# LANGUAGE AND
# THE STUDY OF LANGUAGE

## 1. The Nature of Language

This book is about the English language—its nature, its history, its vocabulary, its writing system, and to some degree its use. It differs from most books used in the broad and vaguely defined school and college subject called "English" in that its purpose is to supply information, discuss ideas, and stimulate curiosity about our language rather than give directions and advice about how to use it. It is true that people who know something about language are likely to be more thoughtful and skillful about how they use it. But it is also true that language is interesting in itself. After all, it is a universal form of human behavior, and all of us are interested in what people, including ourselves, do.

English is, of course, only one of the many languages, perhaps as many as three thousand, which are spoken today. These languages are very different one from another. Indeed, it is primarily the fact that they are so different as to be mutually unintelligible that allows us to call them separate languages. A speaker of one of them, no matter how skillful and fluent, cannot communicate with a speaker of another unless one of them, as we say, "learns the other's language." Yet these differences, great as they are, are differences of detail—of the kinds of sounds used and the ways of putting them together. In their broad outlines, in their basic principles, and even in the way they approach certain specific problems of communication, languages have a great deal in common. It is thus possible to make some observations about languages in general before we come to the specific qualities of English in particular.

In the first place, any language is **arbitrary.** This means that there is nothing—or at most very little—in the nature of the things we talk about that dictates or controls the language we use to talk about them. When we are children we do not know this. We believe that the connection between an act or an object and the word which refers to it is somehow a natural and inevitable one. If you ask a child why he calls a certain object a *clock*, he will probably answer, "Because it *is* a clock." We can see the error of this belief in this childlike form. But it is likely to persist in a somewhat more sophisticated form in the minds of those who have not thought or studied about language. All of us have heard people make statements like "The real name for these things is *crullers*, but I call them *doughnuts* because everybody else around here does." Note the assumption that there is a *real*—natural or inevitable—name for something, even though nobody uses it. Only when we learn a foreign language do we become completely disabused of this notion. When we discover that *horloge* and *Uhr* seem to other people just as natural names for a timepiece as *clock*, we come to realize that none of them is really natural, but all are arbitrary.

Primitive peoples often build much of their religious and cultural behavior on this belief in the natural relationship of word and thing. For example, they believe that to know the name of an object, person, or deity is to gain a certain control over it: in "Ali Baba and the Forty Thieves," the words "Open Sesame!" cause the stone doors of the cave to move aside. Conversely, certain powers in the universe are thought to dislike the use of their names by mortals. Words are therefore tabooed, or euphemisms and descriptive phrases are invented such as *the little people* instead of *fairies*. The Greeks came to call those vengeful mythological creatures whose "real name" was *Erinyes* (or Furies) the *Eumenides* (or "good-tempered ones").

Although we consider ourselves too civilized for such superstitious behavior, vestiges of it remain in our conduct still. Many people will not speak of "death" or "dying" but use expressions like "passing away," "going to rest." A group of words that virtually everybody knows, most of them referring to universal bodily functions, are taboo in polite society, though polysyllabic synonyms for them are quite all right. Many of us knock on wood or cross our fingers when we say certain things, pretending—usually humorously—that this conduct will counteract the risk incurred by using powerful or dangerous words. But on our rational side we know that the only real connection between the word and the thing is in the minds of the people who speak our language.

There is, of course, a small area of language which is less arbitrary than the rest because it makes use of imitation. A child may call a clock a *tick-tock* or a train a *choo-choo*. Even here, however, there is a considerable degree of arbitrariness. The pendulum clock in the room where I am writing is making a rhythmic sound, but it certainly would not be described as "tick-tock" by an impartial—Chinese or Martian—observer. And the disappearance of the steam locomotive has removed from the scene anything making a sound even remotely resembling "choo-choo." Even supposedly imitative words of this sort are usually learned from others rather than made up in spontaneous imitation of other sounds.

Secondly, language is **conventional**. Its effectiveness rests upon a kind of unspoken public agreement that certain things will be done in certain definite ways. This is one consequence of its arbitrariness. Speakers of English are agreed upon calling a certain animal a *horse*. This is an arbitrary agreement. The principal function of language, communication, would break down if everybody insisted on using his own private arbitrary names for things. It is true that the agreement is often not complete. People may argue over whether or not whales are fish or spiders are insects. Such arguments, however, are wholly within the conventional field of language. They are concerned not with the basic agreements about words but with how much of the world of things a given word can be agreed upon to cover, which, in turn, may vary with the circumstances. It suits biologists to limit the class of things which they agree to call insects to those which have six legs, but most of us in our daily lives are agreed on including the eight-legged spiders as well. It is sometimes necessary, therefore, to specify what convention we are operating under at any given time. That is, when we are using language carefully, we must define our terms.

A third important quality of language is that it is **culturally transmitted**: it is passed on from generation to generation as a form of learned, rather than physically inherited, behavior. Nobody inherits the ability to use a particular language; everybody must learn it from other people who have themselves learned it at an earlier time. This learning begins in infancy and continues in varying intensity throughout life. The biggest part of the job is done between the ages of one and six, but it is not necessary to remind students that a good part of both their formal and their informal education consists of extending and sharpening their use of language.

An important consequence of this quality of language is that since individual people differ greatly in their capacity to learn, they also differ greatly in their command of language. This is true of all culturally transmitted activities—dancing, for example, or drawing. Some people simply have more aptitude for them, or have received more training, or both. At one end of the scale are those whose use of language and interest in it are the minimum needed to get them through routine work and simple play. At the other are writers (especially poets), actors, and others for whom the elaborate and subtle use of language is the central activity of life. Most of us fall somewhere between, depending on the nature of our work and play.

A second consequence is that like other aspects of human culture, language is subject to change. Our clothes, our food, our tools, and our speech vary from generation to generation just as they do from age to age. This change is sometimes fast and sometimes slow, sometimes radical and sometimes superficial, but it goes on all the time. Its causes are many and varied, and some of them are not fully understood. There may be a kind of slow, imperceptible, glacierlike drift, such as that which has brought about the differences in pronunciation between the English of America and the English of England. Or there may be striking innovation, taken up and circulated by fashion, like that which has added such new expressions as *hipster*, *blast off*, and *astronaut* to our vocabulary. The cumulation of such changes, going on in different ways in different places, may eventually cause what were once local versions of the same language to become distinct, mutually unintelligible languages like French and Spanish, or English and German. We don't know in how many different places language began—perhaps several, perhaps only one—but we do know that the great diversity of tongues among the peoples of the world today is almost wholly due to this process of divergent change.

The fourth and last general quality of language that will be mentioned here is that it has a very complicated **multiple structure**. This is necessary if language is to discharge the most important function that is asked of it: the communication of an infinite number of different messages, made up from a small number of vocal signals which can be learned by any human of normal intelligence. Language, in other words, is open-ended; there is no limit to the number of things that can be said. This is made possible by the mathematical possibilities of combination. Out of a relatively small group of sounds—fewer than a hundred—that any normal person can learn to produce can be made hundreds of thousands of words, which in turn can be combined according to the rules of grammar into a virtually endless number of different sentences. All languages have this complex, many-layered structure. That is what makes them adequate to the needs of their users. Contrary to some popular impressions, the word and sentence structure of the language of the most primitive peoples is highly complex. Anyone who undertakes to study an American Indian language, with its long, intricately complicated word structure and its delicate nuances of grammar, many of them very different from those we are used to in English, discovers immediately how preposterous is the widespread notion that the first Americans communicated largely by grunts, by sign-language, and by smoke signals. No matter where language is used —in the jungles of Africa or South America, the mountains of Tibet, or the islands of the Pacific—it has a complex, versatile, and adaptable structure.

## 2. The English Language Today

The three thousand or so languages of the world differ greatly in practical importance, as measured by the number of people who speak them and the part they play in world affairs. Some are spoken by only a few hundred people, others by hundreds of millions. Some are dying out, either because the groups who speak them are dwindling or, more commonly, because the speakers have adopted another, more useful language and the new generation does not bother to learn the old one. This last situation is what is bringing about the rapid disappearance of many American Indian languages in our time. On the other hand, some languages are growing in importance as the people who speak them increase in number and influence in the world. English is now one of these great and growing world languages.

We whose native speech is English seldom think how fortunate we are. The speech community of English, comprising all those who use it as their regular means of communication, numbers over three hundred million persons, any one of whom can converse (admittedly sometimes with difficulty) with any other. In addition, large numbers of people whose native speech is not English go to the trouble of learning it in order to be able to communicate with the native English speakers—or in some cases, with each other.

More people learn English in India than in England, though for all
of them it is a second language, learned laboriously at school. There
are something like seventy thousand teachers of English in Japan
alone. The result of widespread use of English is that even in the
mid-twentieth-century world of international trade, cheap and
quick travel, and vast military movement, the average American
almost never finds himself in a position where he is forced to make
himself understood in another language beside English. The American tourist in France expects to get by on English, while the American shopkeeper or hotel clerk at home likewise expects to use
English with the French tourist. The American child goes to school
with his working language well under control, and usually gives no
school time to the learning of another language until eighth or
ninth grade. Compare his position with that of the Ilocano child
from northern Luzon. When he first goes to school, he starts at
once to learn Tagalog, the national language of the Philippines;
in the second grade, he begins to learn English as well; from the
fourth grade on, all his instruction is conducted in English. At an
age when most American children have seldom if ever heard a
foreign language spoken, the Indian, Swiss, or Filipino child is a
proficient speaker of one or more languages beside his own.

It is inevitable that a language like English, spoken by so many
people scattered from one end of the world to the other, should have
many varieties, differing rather widely from one another. The most
obvious varieties are regional dialects, some of which go far back
in history. When the various Germanic tribes, commonly lumped
together as Anglo-Saxons, migrated from the continent of Europe
to the island of Britain in the fifth and sixth centuries, they already
spoke somewhat different varieties of their common tongue. Since
they tended to settle in tribal groups, these differing dialects became associated with various regions of the new homeland. Differences between them increased during the Middle Ages and have
survived into our own time. As a result, the native speech of the
plain folk, especially in the country, shows great diversity within
the relatively small area of the British Isles. We can all tell a Scot
from an Irishman and both of them from a Cockney, and Americans at first may have some trouble understanding any of them.
Other varieties of English are spoken in various parts of America,
and in other parts of the world where English has been carried. All
of these regional dialects have in common most of their grammar
and vocabulary and the main features of their pronunciation;

otherwise we would have to call them separate languages rather than varieties of a single language, English. But each has its own peculiarities, which sound unfamiliar, odd, and sometimes comical to speakers of other varieties.

Another form of diversity which English shows is based on the social class and amount of education of its speakers. Even in a single area, such as London or East Anglia, there is a wide and obvious difference between the speech of the educated professional and business people and that of factory workers, farm laborers, fishermen, and the like. This kind of difference is commonly spoken of as the difference between "good English" and "bad English." Insofar as educated English has a larger vocabulary and permits the expression of more subtle and complex ideas, this value judgment is a sound one. But it should be emphasized that uncultivated English serves quite adequately to meet the more limited demands put upon it, and hence among those who use it, it is not "bad" at all.

Our language shows variety in a third way, somewhat less obvious than the first two. If we stop to think about it, we are aware that not every word, expression, or sentence pattern is appropriate to every occasion. "Dinner is served, madam," "Dinner's ready," and "Come and get it!" are all equally communicative, but each one evokes a different mental picture of the environment where it might appropriately be heard. These divergent modes of speech, ranging from the artificial "frozen" forms of prayer and legal documents, through formal, informal, and colloquial to slang, have been called **functional varieties** or **styles** of language. Each, is appropriate to the relationship existing between the speaker, the subject, and the person spoken to. The formal notice in American sleeping cars reads "Quiet is requested for the benefit of those who have already retired"; a mother says to the noisy child, "Shh! Daddy's asleep"; a student admonishes his dormitory neighbor, "Shut up, my room-mate's sacked out." Each of these, quite proper in its own situation, would seem comic or rude in another. We all have to learn, as part of our social training, which functional variety or style of language to use in any social situation. When in doubt we usually use a somewhat formalized variety of the informal style characteristic of conversation among acquaintances who are not intimate enough for easy colloquial or slang.

By now it should be apparent that what we refer to in the easy and common phrase "the English language" is a complicated thing in-

deed. Our attitude toward it will be most realistic and practical if
we think of it as the sum total of three hundred million ways of
speaking, on the one hand very different, on the other sharing
enough features in common so that any one of the three hundred
million can communicate, albeit often with some difficulty and
misunderstanding, with any other. The English language is not
to be found in dictionaries and grammar books: it is to be found
built into the brains of three hundred million native speakers. If
they and the countless millions who have learned English as a
second language were all to be wiped out, the English language
would be as extinct as the dinosaur. Books would provide valuable
fossil-like clues, permitting scholars to reconstruct many things
about it. But the language itself is alive only so long as there are
people who naturally and easily speak it when they need to communicate. Dictionaries and grammar books are nothing more than
records of certain aspects of the language at given points in its ever-
changing history.

### 3. A Preview

In this book we shall concern ourselves with five aspects of
the English language, to each of which a chapter will be devoted.
The first of these is **grammar.** Since this word is used in different
ways in different contexts, it is important at this point to make clear
what it means. From the point of view of the objective student of
language, the **linguist,** the grammar of a language is a description
of the ways in which the language uses patterns of structure to
convey meaning. In this sense, then, the student of grammar is an
observer, an analyst, and a maker of descriptive formulas. The
fact that these formulas are sometimes called **rules** or **laws** often
leads people to think of the grammarian as a legislator. But he is
not. His rules are like the "laws of nature" that scientists talk
about; they are generalized formulas based on the way things are
and happen. In his capacity as a user of an educated form of
English, the grammarian undoubtedly prefers "I haven't any" to "I
ain't got none." But as a grammarian he recognizes that the latter
statement is just as organized and patterned—hence just as grammatical—as the former.

We might clarify the grammarian's activity by an analogy to an
observer of a rather complicated game, like chess. An intelligent

observer with no previous knowledge of the game would perceive at once that a game of chess is a highly structured activity.
He would note the formal symmetry of the chessboard, and the
fact that the pieces stand in the center of the squares rather than
on the lines. He would perceive that although there are thirty-two
pieces in use, they can be classified in at least two intersecting ways
—by shape and by color. If he was present at the beginning of the
game, he would observe that the pieces were disposed on the board
in a regular and symmetrical arrangement. And as the game went
on, he would become aware of the fact that the pieces move in turn
by color, and in regular ways according to shape—some straight,
some diagonally, some over varying distances, and some only one
square at a time. If he watched long enough, he could formulate
this highly patterned behavior into a set of descriptive rules, which
would tell us how chess is played.

The grammarian works the same way. He perceives that the use
of language is a highly conventional and structured form of behavior and that it is possible to discover and describe orderly patterns of arrangement into which various kinds of units are placed.
Since these patterns occur on several levels—the levels of sounds,
of words, of phrases, and of sentences—the rules of grammar are
more complicated than those of chess. Furthermore, since there are
many varieties of the language, there may be variations in the
rules, whereas the rules of chess are universally the same. But the
principle is the same; grammar in the sense in which we understand it here is a formal description of a systematic kind of behavior.

Secondly, we shall be concerned with **history**. Since language
changes as time passes, it has a history. We are able to observe
directly only the language of our own time, but written records
give us clues to the nature of the language of earlier days. I use
the word *clues* advisedly. Systems of writing do not indicate all
the features of language. Instead, they furnish a kind of prompter
or reminder to the person who already knows the language. But
the person who does not know a language cannot read a sample
of it aloud in a way that will seem at all intelligible to a native
speaker, even though it is written in a familiar alphabet. By the
same token, though we can make shrewd guesses from the written
record as to what Old English or classical Latin were like, we would
pretty certainly be surprised if we could revive King Alfred and
Julius Caesar for a half-hour's conversation. Language historians

(or **historical linguists**) of the future will have the benefit of disc and tape recordings, provided these perishable things can be preserved without deterioration over the centuries.

A language can be said to have two kinds of history, an **outer history** and an **inner history.** The outer history deals with what happens *to* the language—primarily what happens to the people that speak it. The establishment of English-speaking colonies in the New World was an important event in the outer history of English, because it separated one group of English speakers from the rest, introduced them into a new kind of environment, and brought them into contact with speakers of previously unknown languages.

The inner history of a language, on the other hand, deals with what happens *in* the language. It is an important fact about English, for instance, that the second person singular pronouns *thou, thee, thy,* and *thine* were once widely used but were gradually given up in all contexts except prayer. Sometimes connections can be clearly seen between the outer and the inner history, especially in the field of vocabulary. The English speakers who went to the New World picked up various words from the Indians and reshaped them into forms readily pronounced by those used to English sounds—forms like *skunk, squash,* and *hickory.* But often the events of the inner history seem unrelated to the experiences which the members of the speech community are undergoing.

Our third matter of concern will be the vocabulary of English— to many people the most interesting aspect of language. Where do words come from? How do they change? What are their meanings? How can they be used? Answering these questions is the concern of dictionaries, which are among the most widely used of reference books and the only respectable linguistic texts which are steady best-sellers. In Chapter Four we shall deal with vocabulary in several of its aspects: the nature of meanings and the way they change, and the various sources from which new words come into English. Some words, as we shall see, are formed from existing word material. Others are taken from other languages and adapted to use in English. Still others are arrived at by extending the existing vocabulary into new areas of meaning by means of metaphor and other figurative uses. Finally we shall observe the processes by which words go out of use and become obsolete.

Next we shall be concerned with the two principal media through which language is communicated from one person to another:

**speech** and **writing.** Each of these media has its own system, and the two systems are closely interrelated. A native speaker learns speech first and writing, if at all, later. In this sense the speech system is more basic than the writing system. But because of its permanence and its visual appeal, writing strikes most literate people as somehow more solid and reliable than speech. In Chapter Five we shall explore the nature of the two systems and something of their history, as well as the important matter of their relationship to one another and to the central vocabulary-grammar system which both of them express.

Related to all aspects of language—grammar, vocabulary, speech, and writing—is the matter of **usage,** which will occupy our final chapter. In the broad sense, usage simply means the collection of arbitrary conventions that are the basis for all aspects of language. But in the narrower sense the study of usage deals with the selection, among various ways of using language, of the ways preferred by a given group of speakers. Usage thus deals primarily with questions of appropriateness. Is it "correct" (*i.e.,* acceptable usage) to use *disinterested* as a synonym of *uninterested?* Which is preferred, *the data is* or *the data are?* is *the man to whom I gave it* preferable to *the man I gave it to?* or does it sound too stilted and artificial? Is it better to say *eck-onomics* or *ee-conomics?* Which is the preferred spelling, *catalogue* or *catalog?*

Most usage questions like these are individual items, each of which must be separately considered. It will not be our business to legislate upon them, but to establish a background of information and rational good sense which will aid the reader to be his *own* judge of usage. The most accomplished speakers and writers seldom resort to authoritarian sources to settle their questions about usage. Instead they base their own usage on a "language sense" derived from a lifetime of intelligent observation and careful use of English.

The person who knows something about the English language— its grammar, history, vocabulary, speech, writing, and usage—is not on that account a better user of English. But he is likely to be, since knowledge of this sort leads to interest in language and respect for its wonderful capacities. Since knowledge, rather than skill, is the primary aim of this book, it seldom lays down the law about matters of language use. But the student who has acquired the kind of knowledge it deals with can become an observer and lover of language in his own right, and also can become with confidence his own arbiter of what is effective and graceful in its use.

おはな

# For Further Reading

There are coming to be a number of good introductions to the study of linguistics, on various levels of complexity and difficulty. The following are the most comprehensive and up to date:

Dinneen, Francis P., *An Introduction to General Linguistics*. New York: Holt, Rinehart and Winston, Inc., 1967.

Gleason, H. A., Jr., *An Introduction to Descriptive Linguistics*, Revised Edition. New York: Holt, Rinehart and Winston, Inc., 1961.

Halliday, M. A. K., Angus McIntosh, and Peter Strevens, *The Linguistic Sciences and Language Teaching*. London: Longmans, Green and Co., Ltd., 1964. (Especially Part I, "The Linguistic Sciences," pp. 3-134.)

Hockett, Charles F., *A Course in Modern Linguistics*. New York: The Macmillan Company, 1958.

McIntosh, Angus, and M. A. K. Halliday, *Patterns of Language: Papers in General, Descriptive and Applied Linguistics*. London: Longmans, Green and Co., Ltd., 1966. (Especially pp. 1-69 and 183-199.)

Potter, Simeon, *Modern Linguistics*. London: André Deutsch, 1957.

Robins, R. H., *General Linguistics: An Introductory Survey*. London: Longmans, Green and Co., Ltd., 1964.

# *Two*

# ENGLISH GRAMMAR

## 1. *Constructions*

1. When I turned into Second Street, a big dog ran out and chased the wheels of my car.
2. Second turned a out big at my of ran when the and wheels car chased I street dog.

These are two strings of words—the same words but in different order. Anyone who knows English will say at once that the first string makes sense, whereas the second is a meaningless list of words. What makes the difference is **grammar**. The first string is grammatical; the words are placed in patterns that belong to the grammar of English. The second string is not so much ungrammatical as totally lacking in grammar; it is a random collection of words placed in random order. The first string is like a jigsaw puzzle assembled to make a picture; the second is like the unassembled puzzle spread out on the table. Just as pieces that fit together may accidentally fall together when the puzzle is poured from its box, so some accidental groupings of words in the second string could be part of a grammatical string: *second turned a*, for instance ("The first car went straight, the *second turned a* corner."), or *ran when the* ("The little dog *ran when the* big dog came out."). But these random sets of words have to be built into larger structures before they can be said to have any grammar.

String number 2 can have little further interest for us. But even so small a sample of grammatical English as string number 1 can reveal a good many things about English grammar when studied rather intensively. Let us take a look at some of them and incidentally begin to acquire some of the technical vocabulary that grammarians use. Grammar, like any subject of human interest from nuclear physics to skin-diving, has developed a terminology of its own, whose purpose is to allow grammarians to communicate efficiently and precisely with one another. We shall use only as much of that vocabulary as we need to avoid cumbersome circumlocutions.

If asked to divide the sentence *when I turned into Second Street, a big dog ran out and chased the wheels of my car* into two meaningful parts, people who know English would all make the division where the comma appears in the written version. The six words before the comma seem to be more closely linked with one another than any of them is linked with what follows the comma, and vice versa. Yet the two parts as wholes are definitely connected. *When I turned into Second Street* is a unit which suggests a comment, a limitation, or a specification about the other unit, *a big dog ran out and chased the wheels of my car*. This kind of grammatical unit, made up of smaller units linked by a grammatical connection, is called a **construction** and the units so connected are **constituents**. The construction may be represented by a simple diagram:

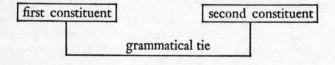

Most constructions have this very simple pattern of arrangement, though a few of them—*red, white, and blue*, for instance—have more than two constituents. This **binary** (two-part) quality of grammatical constructions is interesting not only to grammarians, but also to logicians, psychologists, and people who run digital computers. It is one of the qualities of language which give us hope that some day machines can be taught to make grammatical analyses, and hence to translate from one language to another.

Further study of the grammar of our sample of English is concerned with two matters: the nature of the grammatical tie that makes a construction out of two constituents, and the kinds of constituents that enter into constructions. We have already seen that the first constituent, *when I turned into Second Street*, suggests a comment, limitation, or specification about the second constituent. More specifically, it seems to establish the time and place of the events referred to in the second constituent. Grammarians call this kind of comment, limitation, or specification by the general

**name modification.** The constituent that does the modifying is the **modifier** or **attribute**; the constituent that is modified is the **head.** Our construction diagram can now be made more precise:

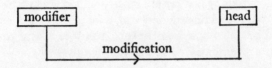

A question arises here: on what grounds can we decide which constituent is the modifier and which the head? Doesn't the second constituent of our sentence, by telling what happened at the specified time and place, also make a comment on the first constituent? The answer is to try out each constituent as a separate statement. The constituent *when I turned into Second Street* clearly cannot appear by itself as a grammatically free unit—if it is not a constituent of a larger construction, as here, or the response to a question, then it must be grammatically altered to something like *when did I turn into Second Street?* The second constituent, on the other hand, can be a grammatically free unit, in this case a sentence. The head of the construction, then, is that constituent which has the same grammatical meaning as the whole construction; and the modifier is the constituent which cannot stand by itself but which must be in the construction to have its proper grammatical meaning. All constructions of this sort are called **headed** (or, more technically, **endocentric**). Constructions whose grammatical tie is modification are nearly all headed.

Having determined that the over-all construction of the sentence we are dealing with is a modification, our next step is to examine the constituents of which it is made. Let us look first at the second of these, the head, *a big dog ran out and chased the wheels of my car.* Once again we ask what its parts are, and this time the answer may not be so immediately obvious. Two points of division suggest themselves: one between *dog* and *ran* and the other at the *and.* In either of these positions a natural break or pause might occur if the sentence were spoken or read aloud, and dividing it at either of them will leave us with orderly, grammatical sequences of words in both constituents. But a better case can be made for dividing after *dog* rather than after *out.* The phrase *ran out* and the phrase *chased the wheels of my car* both stand in the same relationship to the

phrase *a big dog*. If we divide between them, we suggest that the
first is in closer relation to *a big dog* than the second is, since our
constituents would then be *a big dog ran out* and *chased the wheels
of my car*. But if we divide first after *dog*, we show that *ran out* and
*chased the wheels of my car* are closely joined, and that taken together they make a construction with *a big dog*. This construction
is the familiar one whose constituents are **subject** and **predicate**.
We call it a **predication** and diagram it this way.

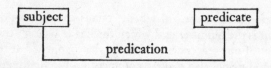

Once again we have a construction with two constituents, this
time a subject, *a big dog*, and a predicate, *ran out and chased the
wheels of my car*. Since neither of these constituents can serve the
same grammatical function as the whole construction, this construction does not have a head; it belongs to the class of **non-headed**
(or **exocentric**) constructions.

The second constituent, the predicate, now divides neatly into
two parts, *ran out* and *chased the wheels of my car*. We also have
a piece left over, the *and* which connects these two. No very good
reason can be found for putting this *and* with one part or the other.
After it has joined the constituents together, its work is finished, and
it has no further meaning or purpose in the sentence. Therefore we
can consider it as belonging not to either of the constituents but to
the grammatical tie that connects them. If we examine the two
constituents, we see that both of them conform to the definition of
**head**: either one can function in the same way as the whole
construction, that is, as the predicate in a predication whose subject is *a big dog*. Since we can readily say *a big dog ran out* and
also *a big dog chased the wheels of my car*, either constituent can
clearly be a predicate without the other, and hence either one
can be the head.

A double-headed construction like this, consisting of two grammatically equivalent constituents joined together to serve either
as a whole sentence or as a constituent of a larger construction, is a
**coordination**. Our construction uses the joining word, or **conjunction**, *and*. Since its constituents are alike, they do not need

special names; we can just call them "first constituent" and "second constituent." The construction can be diagrammed this way:

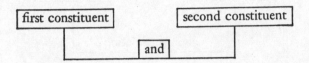

A coordination may have more than two constituents; the only requirement is that each of its constituents be able to function grammatically like the whole construction. Our sentence could just as well have read *a big dog ran out, barked loudly, and chased the wheels of my car*. This is a coordination with three constituents, the last two being joined by *and*:

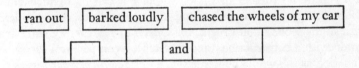

The empty box in the first section of the connecting line shows that we could also have a conjunction, in this case another *and*, between the first two constituents.

In the second constituent of our coordination, *chased the wheels of my car*, we find a construction that obviously divides into two constituents, *chased* and *the wheels of my car*. Neither of these constituents is a head, since neither one can serve the same grammatical function as the whole: a combination like *a big dog chased* is somehow incomplete, and *a big dog the wheels of my car* is impossible. *The wheels of my car* is needed to fill out or complete the meaning of *chased*. For this reason the grammatical tie of this kind of construction is called **complementation**, and the second constituent is a **complement**—in this case the kind of complement called **direct object**. Since the first constituent is now only a single word, we could simply name the word-class to which it belongs, in this case **verb**. But as will become apparent later, the first constituent of a complementation can be longer than a single word; it can be a **phrase** (a phrase is a group of words in grammatical relation to each other). So we will call the first constituent a **verbal phrase**. The general pattern for complementation is:

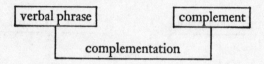

The particular pattern of *chased the wheels of my car* is:

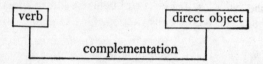

 The first of these constituents, being a single word, seems at first sight to be no further divisible. Actually it can be divided once more, into the two parts *chase* and *-d*, as we shall see. But it is clear that in the second constituent, *the wheels of my car*, we still have to do with a construction. Since *the wheels* can perform the same function as the whole construction, and since *of my car* serves to limit, comment on, or specify *the wheels*, this construction is another modification. Its basic structure is the same as that of our first construction, but it is very different in detail. The head this time comes first, so that its pattern fits this kind of diagram:

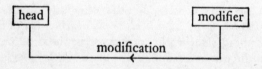

What is more, the head of this construction, *the wheels*, is another, rather special kind of modification, consisting of the head *wheels* and the modifier *the*. The word *the*, often called the **definite article**, belongs to a class of words which are called **determiners** because they indicate or determine that a noun or nominal phrase is to follow. Other determiners are *a/an*, *some*, and *no*.
 The modifying phrase *of my car* is a new type of construction, whose constituents are *of* and *my car*. Since the function of *of* is to indicate the subordinate relationship of the short phrase *my car* to the rest of the sentence—specifically to the head *the wheels*—

we call this kind of construction a **subordination**. Its constituents, neither of them a head, are a **subordinator** and its **object**:

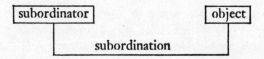

Subordinators like *of*, whose objects are usually nouns or nominal phrases, are called **prepositions**.

With the recognition that *my car* is another little modification like *the wheels*, whose constituents are a determiner and a noun, we reach the end of one branch of our analysis, since we have come down to single words. The successive constructions we have identified may be summarized in one diagram (omitting the first, overall construction and using arrowheads to indicate the direction of modification):

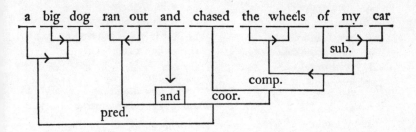

These constructions are of five main types, each with its own kind of constituents:

1. **Modification**, consisting of **head** and **modifier**.
2. **Predication**, consisting of **subject** and **predicate**.
3. **Complementation**, consisting of **verbal phrase** and **complement**.
4. **Subordination**, consisting of **subordinator** and **object**.
5. **Coordination**, consisting of **equivalent joined elements** and (optionally) a **conjunction**.

These five **major construction types** or **structures** are all that exist in English. Our sample sentence—not a very long one, but admittedly rather carefully chosen—thus includes examples of all the major construction types.

We can conclude this first essay in grammatical analysis with two general statements which are of paramount importance in English grammar:

1. Every construction found in a grammatical English sentence belongs to one of the five major construction types; it is a modification, a predication, a complementation, a subordination, or a coordination.
2. Every constituent of a grammatical construction is either a construction or a single word; no string of words not constituting a construction can be a constituent of a larger construction.

## Exercises

*I. Divide each of the following into two constituents and identify the construction type to which it belongs.*

| | | | |
|---|---|---|---|
| 1. | white house | 9. | cutting the grass |
| 2. | bought a car | 10. | cutting remarks |
| 3. | rain is falling | 11. | down the street |
| 4. | stainless steel | 12. | rain or shine |
| 5. | after dinner | 13. | walking slowly |
| 6. | peace and quiet | 14. | birds have been singing |
| 7. | have some cake | 15. | under water |
| 8. | steel bars | | |

*II. Divide each of the following into two constituents and explain why it is not possible to assign it unambiguously to one construction type.*

| | | | |
|---|---|---|---|
| 1. | flying kites | 4. | iron shirts |
| 2. | wishes help | 5. | time flies |
| 3. | like chocolate candy | | |

*III. Divide each of the following into two constituents and then divide each constituent into two. Identify all construction types involved.*

1. rolling stones gather no moss
2. peace and prosperity seldom prevail
3. exercising violently endangers health
4. people in trouble need help
5. brave men and fair women

*IV. Make a constituent diagram of each of the following.*

1. a man bought six shirts
2. playing golf requires practice
3. we took a walk along the boulevard
4. the red house by the shore was sold today

## 2. Parts of Speech

Large constructions, as we have seen, have smaller constructions as their constituents. But as we pursue our analysis, before very long we reach constituents which are single words. In fact, in the smallest constructions—like *big dog, ran out, the wheels, my car*—both constituents are single words. One of the major distinguishing marks of such minimal constructions is the selection of words that are their constituents. We can, for example, identify *ran out* as a modification, since *ran* is a head and *out* makes the kind of comment on the head that we have called modification. Other constituents could replace the head *ran* in this construction, such as *walked, fell, flew, swam, rolled*. Other constituents could replace the modifier, such as *in, up, down, away*. Putting these together in various combinations produces such phrases as *walked in, fell down, flew away*, and *swam up*, all of which are recognizably the grammatical equivalents of *ran out*, however different they may be in meaning. On the other hand, phrases like *man overboard, healthy child*, and *chasing butterflies* are different from *ran out* not only in meaning but also in grammar.

A set of words that can appear in the same position in a given construction is called a **form class**. *Ran, walked, fell, flew, swam*, and *rolled* all belong to one form class, to which *man, healthy*, and *chasing* do not belong; and *out, in, up, down*, and *away* belong to another form class, to which *child* and *butterflies* do not belong. Since *fell overboard* has the same construction as *ran out* and *fell down*, *overboard* can belong to the same form class as *out* and *down*. Its occurrence in *man overboard* puts it also into another form class, since *man overboard* is not the same construction as *ran out*. It is thus apparent that a given word may be a member of more than one form class. Actually most words can belong to many form classes. Each such membership is called a **privilege of occurrence**, and the sum of the privileges of occurrence of a word is its **distribution**. The distribution of a word like *ran*, for instance, includes constructions like *ran the machine, ran home, ran swiftly, the dog ran, ran and jumped*, and *ran wild*.

Since these are all different constructions, the membership in the form classes which make up their constituents is different, although the presence of *ran* in all of them is evidence of some overlapping. The words that may replace *ran* in *ran the machine* are *stopped, broke, built, started*, etc., while those that may replace *ran* in *the dog ran* are *barked, slept, ate, started, stopped*, etc. Notice that *started* and *stopped*, like *ran*, are in both lists. We cannot, however, find any other word that belongs to all of the form classes that *ran* belongs to. One that comes near to doing this is *went*, since we can say *went home, went swiftly, the dog went, went and jumped*, and *went wild*, but we cannot say *\*went the machine*.[1] On the other hand, we can say *started the machine, started home, started swiftly, the dog started*, and *started and jumped*, but not ordinarily *\*started wild*.

It appears, then, that in the finest analysis no two words have quite the same distribution. This is partly a matter of meaning. A word like *strolled* or *sauntered* has many of the same privileges of occurrence as *ran*; we can say *sauntered home* and *strolled away* with no difficulty, but *the dog strolled* and *sauntered swiftly*, though quite grammatical, are unlikely to occur because the meanings of their constituents don't go together. We think of strolling as an activity performed by humans, not dogs, and sauntering as a leisurely activity which cannot be done swiftly. As soon, however, as we change the other constituent of each of these phrases to one which is compatible in meaning (**lexically compatible**) with *strolled* or *sauntered*, we get perfectly acceptable phrases like *the man strolled* and *sauntered slowly*, which have the same constructions as *the dog ran* and *ran swiftly* respectively.

On the other hand, the prohibition against *\*went the machine* is not lexical but grammatical. There is no member of the form class to which *the machine* belongs in this construction that we can substitute to make this an acceptable phrase. We must conclude that while the grammatical distribution of *went* overlaps that of *ran* to a considerable degree, the overlap is not complete; *went* is simply not privileged to occur in a construction parallel to *ran the machine*.

While the borderline between these two kinds of distributional limitations, the lexical and the grammatical, is sometimes rather hazy, it is usually clear. It is also clear that if grammatical analysis is to be successful, these two kinds of restrictions must be kept separate. They belong, in fact, to two different branches of language study. The grammarian, interested in grammatical distribution, is concerned with form classes. The student of meaning (the

---

1. The asterisk is customarily prefixed to words and phrases that are non-occurrent or grammatically impossible.

**semologist**) and the maker of dictionaries (the **lexicographer**), interested in lexical distributions, are concerned with lexical classes. Each must be aware of the other's concerns, but each can pursue his analysis with considerable independence of the other. Our concern at present is with grammar, so we shall concentrate our attention on form classes.

Since the number of distinct constructions is quite large, and since every construction has at least two constituents, the number of form classes is also quite large. Just as it is convenient to class constructions together into five general construction types, so also it is useful to class words together in large form-class groups. The usual name for these is **parts of speech.** If we bring together all the words that belong to any one of the form classes to which *ran* belongs—*walked*, *strolled*, *chased*, and the rest—and also all the words that belong to any one of the form classes to which any one of these belongs, we will have a large class of words whose distributions overlap in a grammatically significant way. This large inclusive class is the familiar class of **verbs,** which has various sub-classes within it. Another large class, whose distributions overlap that of *dog* in a grammatically significant way, is the class of **nouns.** The distributions of *out* and *swiftly* can lead us to the class of **adverbs,** and the distribution of *big* to the class of **adjectives.** These are the four large form-class types which we call **parts of speech.** In addition to them, there is a smaller class of **function words,** among which we have already noticed *and*, *of*, *the*, and *my*.

The principal difference between the various sub-classes of function words on the one hand and the four parts of speech on the other lies in the fact that the parts of speech are **open** classes, whose total membership is altered frequently by the addition of new words and the dropping of old ones; while the function-word classes are **closed** classes, whose membership is much more stable and fixed. It is much easier for a new noun to win acceptance than a new conjunction. Another difference is that the grammatical significance of function words is more important than their lexical significance, which is often so general as to be very difficult to define. But only a few of them are actually wholly devoid of lexical meaning. The considerable lexical difference between the phrases *to the city* and *from the city*, which have the same grammatical construction, lies in the difference in meaning between the prepositions *to* and *from*.

## Exercises

*I. Divide the following phrases or sentences into two groups: (a) those that are ungrammatical; (b) those that are grammatical but nonsensical because of lexical incompatibility:*

1. my dog is hungrily
2. bananas grow trees
3. she was songing a sing
4. loudly sounds are unpleasant
5. loudly sounds the blanket
6. optimists can always hopeful

*II. What part of speech is* round *in each of the following constructions? In each case explain how you can tell.*

1. the fight was over in the first *round*
2. a square peg in a *round* hole
3. *round* off the end of this stick
4. come *round* and see us
5. they went *round* the corner
6. *round* the block in high gear

## 3. Morphology: Inflection

The classification of words into parts of speech in the preceding section was based wholly on grammatical distribution. Words that can enter into certain positions in one group of constructions were called **nouns**; those that can enter into certain positions in another group of constructions were called **verbs,** and so on. One consequence of this method of classification is that we cannot assign a word to its proper part of speech until we know something about its distribution. Nothing about a strange word—*pandle*, for example—tells us whether it is noun, verb, adjective, or adverb. But seeing it in just one construction may be enough to decide us. Consider the following sentences:

1. he bought a pandle
2. they pandle everywhere
3. that's a very pandle hat
4. don't come so pandle

It is clear that in sentence 1 *pandle* is a noun, like *spindle*; in sentence 2 it is a verb, like *travel*; in sentence 3 it is an adjective, like *fashion-*

*able*; and in sentence 4 it is an adverb like *early*. Even though we don't know what it means (in fact, it doesn't mean anything), we can assign it in each case to a form class on the basis of its occurrence in a construction, and very often, though not always, assignment to one form class is enough to identify a part of speech.

Once we have established our strange word as belonging to one of the parts of speech, certain consequences of this classification become apparent. We are free to extend to it many of the privileges of occurrence possessed by other members of the class. Let us say that on the basis of the sentence *he bought a pandle* we have classed *pandle* as a noun. We now know that we can make constructions like *a pandle costs money*, *the purchase of a pandle*, and *an expensive pandle*. From the point of view of grammar we can say *a liquid pandle* or *this pandle is heavy*, though if it turned out that *pandle* means "a bit of thistledown," these phrases would be nonsense because their constituents would be lexically incompatible. But there would be nothing wrong with their grammar.

Another consequence of identifying *pandle* as a noun would be that we might speak of more than one pandle, and to adjust the form of the word to fit this new notion we would add an *-s* and make *pandles*. This is a very important grammatical step. The justification for it is **analogy**. We know that almost all of the members of the class of nouns have two forms, a plain one, which is found in constructions like *this book*, and one with an *-s* ending, as in *these books*. By analogy with the multitude of nouns that follow this pattern, we decide that our new noun deserves a form in *-s* also. The analogy can be expressed as a kind of mathematical formula:

this handle : these handles : : this pandle : these X

Solving for X gives us *pandles*, which is surely the right form to use in constructions like *he bought six pandles* and *those are expensive pandles*.

The new form *pandles* thus has a different distribution from the original *pandle*. It enters into constructions with *these*, *those*, and *are*, where *pandle* cannot appear, and it cannot enter into constructions with *a*, *this*, and *is*, where *pandle* can appear. From this point of view, *pandle* and *pandles* are two separate words. But they are so much alike in form, and presumably would be in meaning if they had any, that it seems desirable to consider them simply variants of the same word. This we can do by means of the concept of **inflection**. We say that words like *books*, *dogs*, *pandles* are formed from *book*, *dog*, *pandle* by the addition of the **inflectional suffix, or** simply the **inflection,** *-s*. The plain form is the **singular,** or **un-marked,** form of the noun; the *-s* form is the **plural** form. To-gether they make up the **noun paradigm.** From the point of view of the shape, or **morphology,** of the words, we call the singular form the **stem** and the plural form the **stem + inflectional suf-fix.**

If we collect a group of nouns and list their singular and plural forms, we will find that the noun paradigm is not quite so simple as it first appears. Consider the following pairs of nouns, both as they are written and as they are pronounced:

|                 Singular | Plural                      |
|--------------------------|-----------------------------|
|          *Stem*          | *Stem + Inflection*         |
|                    book  | books                       |
|                    dog   | dogs                        |
|                    piece | pieces                      |
|                    match | matches                     |
|                    baby  | babies                      |
|                    bus   | busses                      |
|                    sheep | sheep                       |
|                    mouse | mice                        |
|                    capitalism | ———                     |
|                    ———   | scissors                    |

The first three are simple enough so far as writing goes; the in-flection is an *-s* added to the stem. In the next three, the inflection is *-es*, and in two of them—*babies* and *busses*—changes are made in the stem when the inflection is added. The next two, *sheep* and *mice*, have no inflectional suffix at all, though *mice* makes a change in the stem. Finally, *capitalism* has no plural, and *scissors* has no singular.

Similarly, variations in pronunciation become apparent when the words are spoken. Using slant lines to indicate that we are deal-ing with units of the sound system (**phonemes**) rather than letters, we can say that the inflection in *books* is /s/; in *dogs, babies,* and *scis-sors* it is /z/; and in *pieces* and *matches* it is /iz/. Selection among these variants is not haphazard but quite systematic. If the stem ends in a **sibilant** (or *s*-like) sound, the ending is /iz/; if it ends in a **voiceless consonant** like /p, t, k/, the ending is /s/; if it ends in any other sound—a **voiced consonant** or a **vowel**—the ending is /z/. But since this variation, dictated by the sound of the stem, has no effect on the meaning, we can lump these three endings together as a single linguistic unit or **morpheme**. For all purposes except pronunciation, the different variants of the morpheme, called **allomorphs**, can be treated as if they were identical. Plural forms like *sheep* and *mice*, which can be thought of as having a **zero allomorph** of the plural morpheme, are classed as **irregular**, since we cannot predict the sound of the plural on the basis of the singular. Unless we know that a word is irregular, analogy leads us to consider it regular. Assuming that our new word *pandle* is regular, we give it the /z/ allomorph, since the stem ends in the voiced consonant sound /l/. This is the way a child uses analogy in forming plurals like *mouses* and *mans*, before he learns the correct irregular plurals as separate items which do not follow the regular rules of the language.

Verbs also have inflections, which form a somewhat more complicated paradigm than that of nouns. A regular verb like *chase* has three different **marked** or **inflected** forms—*chases, chased,* and *chasing*—in addition to the plain (**unmarked**) form *chase*. A relatively small but important group of irregular verbs also have a fifth form: *drive* for example, in addition to *drives, drove,* and *driving,* has a form *driven,* whose distribution is different from that of *drove.* For this reason it is convenient to assign all verbs to a five-part paradigm, even though two of the inflections are the same for all regular verbs.

| Plain | Third Sing. | Past Tense | Past Part. | Present Part. |
|---|---|---|---|---|
| *Stem* | *Stem +{-s}* | *Stem + {-d}* | *Stem + {-n}* | *Stem + {-ing}* |
| chase | chases | chased | chased | chasing |
| turn | turns | turned | turned | turning |
| look | looks | looked | looked | looking |
| pat | pats | patted | patted | patting |
| mend | mends | mended | mended | mending |
| judge | judges | judged | judged | judging |
| watch | watches | watched | watched | watching |
| drive | drives | drove | driven | driving |
| run | runs | ran | run | running |
| know | knows | knew | known | knowing |

Just as with the plural inflection of nouns, we find that within the verb paradigm there are variants, both spoken and written. The third singular inflection is, in fact, very similar to the noun plural inflection. It has the same three sound variants (allomorphs) in the same kind of distribution. *Look* and *pat*, which end in voiceless consonants, have /s/; *turn* and *mend*, which end in voiced consonants, have /z/; and *chase*, *watch*, and *judge*, which end in sibilants, have /iz/. In writing, the ending is usually -*s*, but in some cases, like *watches*, it is -*es*. But since regular rules govern the choice of pronunciation and spelling, and since regardless of these variations the inflection has the same function, we will treat the variants as if they were all alike, and represent them by the most common written variant, {-*s*}. Letting V stand for the plain form of any verb, we have a convenient symbol, Vs, to stand for any verb in the third singular form.

There are also variants of the past tense inflection. If *chased*, *turned*, and *patted* are spoken aloud, their inflections will be heard as /t/, /d/, and /id/ respectively. All other regular verbs ending in /t/ or /d/, such as *mend*, will also have /id/; other regular verbs ending in voiceless consonants, like *look*, will have /t/; other regular verbs ending in voiced consonants or vowels, like *judge* and *try*, will have /d/. A number of other verbs have various kinds of irregularities in the past form. Some, like *drive* and *know*, form the past in the same way that *mouse* forms the plural, by a stem change and a zero allomorph of the inflection. Others, like *set*, *put*, *rid*, are unchanged in the past, just as *sheep* is unchanged in the plural. These also can be considered as having a zero allomorph of -*d*. Still others, like *creep* and *mean*, have a change in the stem and a regular or irregular allomorph of the inflection. In fact, the morphology of English past tenses has a good many irregularities. Even native speakers are sometimes in doubt and must consult the dictionary to make sure of the correct past tense form for verbs like *swing* and *strive*. There are also regional, substandard, and stylistic variants, like *dived~dove*,[2] *caught~catched*, and *dreamed~ dreamt*. But if we use {-*d*} as a general symbol for the past tense inflection, we can write Vd to mean "any verb in the past tense," including forms like *set*, *drove*, and *ran*, since this symbol does not indicate pronunciation but simply describes a class of verb forms having the same grammatical distribution.

For regular verbs like *chase* and *turn*, the past participle inflection is the same as the past tense inflection, with the same allomorphs in the same distribution. But most of the verbs that have irregular past

---

2. The symbol ~ means "varying with."

tense forms also have irregular past participles. Sometimes, as with verbs like *teach, leave, lose,* and *seek*, the past participle is the same as the past tense. In a few verbs, like *run* and *come*, it is the same as the plain form, although the past form is different. In *set, hit, put,* and others like them, both the past tense and the past participle are like the plain form. Finally, there is a group of verbs like *ride, drive,* and *know* which have -*n* or -*en* as an inflectional ending of the past participle, with or without a change in the stem. Even though this group is a small minority of the total class of verbs, it supplies us with convenient symbols: {-*n*} for the past participle inflection and Vn for any verb in the past participle form. Vn is thus a general symbol, covering *chased, turned, driven, known, run,* and all the other past participle forms.

After these irregularities, it is a relief to find an absolutely regular form. The present participle inflection has only one allomorph, pronounced /iŋ/,[3] which is attached without stem change to the plain form of any verb. The spelling rules, particularly with regard to doubling final consonantal letters and dropping or preserving final -*e*, are a bit tricky, but they also follow regular patterns. We use ŋ as the symbol for this inflection, and Vŋ to signify any verb in the present participle form. The verb paradigm thus consists of five inflectional classes: V, Vs, Vd, Vn, and Vŋ.

One very common verb, *be*, needs special notice because it not only is irregular in the five forms of the standard paradigm, but also has three extra forms. In addition to the plain form *be* and the third singular form *is*, there is a special form *am* that is used only with the subject *I*, and another present form *are*, which is used whenever neither *am* nor *is* is called for. It also has two past tense forms instead of one: *were* used with plurals and the singular pronoun *you*, and *was* used elsewhere. These forms survive from an older period when all English verbs had more inflections. Since *be* is the only verb that now has them, it is more convenient to put it in a class by itself, rather than to extend the general verb paradigm to accommodate them.

There is also an inflectional paradigm for adjectives, though unlike the noun and verb paradigms it does not apply to all members of the adjective class. Most adjectives of one syllable and many adjectives of two syllables (especially if the second syllable is not a

3. The symbol /ŋ/, derived from the International Phonetic Alphabet, stands for the final sound in words like *thing* and *song*, usually spelled *ng* in standard orthography.

suffix like *-ful* or *-less*) have **comparative** forms with an *-er* inflection and **superlative** forms with *-est*. The following are some typical examples:

| Plain (Positive) Form | Comparative Form | Superlative Form |
|---|---|---|
| *Stem* | *Stem* + {*-er*} | *Stem* + {*-est*} |
| small | smaller | smallest |
| high | higher | highest |
| simple | simpler | simplest |
| easy | easier | easiest |
| good | better | best |
| bad | worse | worst |

In the last two of these, the stem used for the comparative and superlative differs completely from that appearing in the plain form. There is no resemblance at all, in either sound or spelling, between *good* and *bet-*. Only the existence of the paradigm allows us to put them together.[4] This situation is called **suppletion,** and a paradigmatic form having a different stem from the plain form is a **suppletive form.** Another example of a suppletive form is *went* as the past form of *go*.

Other adjectives—all those with more than two syllables and many with only two, such as *hopeful* and *moral*—do not fit this paradigm. Their comparative and superlative meanings are expressed instead by constructions, in which the function words *more* and *most* are used: *more moral, most hopeful*. Even the adjectives which have the comparative and superlative inflections may use these constructions instead, when some special stylistic or rhythmic effect is desired, as in Shakespeare's "which makes thy love more strong" (Sonnet 73) or Keats's "More happy love" (*Ode on a Grecian Urn*). In Shakespeare's day it was even possible to use both the inflected form and the construction at the same time, as in "the most unkindest cut of all" (*Julius Caesar*). Nowadays, however, this is considered ungrammatical.

---

4. The paradigm is actually a shorthand form for a statement of distribution. It is arrived at by considering a set of sentences like these:

My house is *small*, but his is *smaller*.
My brother is *thin*, but his is *thinner*.
My job is *easy*, but his is *easier*.
My health is *good*, but his is———.

Any native speaker would supply *better* to fill the blank in the last sentence.

A few adverbs—those like *fast, slow, quick*, and *hard*, which have the same form as one-syllable adjectives—also use the *-er* and *-est* inflections. The comparatives and superlatives *better, best* and *worse, worst* are suppletive forms for *well* and *ill* (or, more commonly nowadays, *badly*). But these adverbs are so few that inflection is of little importance in the adverb class. Virtually all adverbs whose meanings permit comparative and superlative degrees use the *more* and *most* constructions.

One small but important group of words, which are similar in many of their grammatical functions to nouns, are the pronouns. These have inflections, but instead of distinguishing **number** (*i.e.*, singular~plural), the pronoun inflections mark **case**. That is, the pronouns have different forms to fill the constituent positions in different constructions. One form, the **nominative**, is used when the pronoun is subject in a predication; another form, the **objective**, when it is direct or indirect object in a complementation or object of a preposition. A third form, the **first possessive**, is used as a noun determiner or modifier, and a fourth, the **second possessive**, when the pronoun is acting as a substitute for the first possessive plus a noun. The following examples illustrate these four forms for the first person pronoun *I*:

| | |
|---|---|
| **Nominative:** | *I* am coming |
| **Objective:** | tell *me* the story |
| **First Possessive:** | I'll bring *my* book |
| **Second Possessive:** | you bring your book and I'll bring *mine* |

The full set of pronouns, with their four forms, appears in the following table.

| Nominative | Objective | First Possessive | Second Possessive |
|---|---|---|---|
| I | me | my | mine |
| we | us | our | ours |
| you | you | your | yours |
| he | him | his | his |
| she | her | her | hers |
| it | it | its | (its) |
| they | them | their | theirs |
| who | whom | whose | whose |

A few points about this paradigm should be noted:

1. Compared with the noun, verb, and adjective paradigms, it is very irregular. There is suppletion in *I~me, we~us*, and

*she~her*, and not many of the other forms can be clearly analyzed as stem + inflectional suffix.

2. Because of its irregularity, the paradigm must be memorized item by item by anyone who is learning English. Analogy is a wholly unreliable guide, though certain substandard forms like *his'n* and *ourn* (formed like *mine*, by adding -*n* to the first possessive) show the results of analogy.

3. The second possessive *its* is rare, though it occasionally occurs.

4. The objective *whom* is pretty well confined to educated formal and written style.

5. Another pronoun, whose forms are *thou, thee, thy, thine*, no longer exists in live present-day standard English, though it is used in the special formal language of prayer and similar contexts. It survives in some rural dialects of the north of England.

6. All of the pronouns except *who* combine with the noun *self* (plural *selves*) to make a set of compound pronouns, sometimes called **reflexive** or **intensive** from their grammatical functions. *I*, *we*, and *you* use the first possessive in this compound (*myself, ourselves, yourself, yourselves*); *he* and *they* use the objective (*himself, themselves*); *she* uses the form *her*, which is both first possessive and objective (*herself*); and *it* uses the plain form *it* (*itself*). Once again analogy has produced substandard forms like *hisself* and *theirselves*.

What has been said about inflection in this section may now be briefly summarized:

1. Nouns are inflected for **number,** the singular form being the plain or unmarked one. The noun paradigm is N~Ns.[5]

2. Verbs are inflected for **person, tense, phase,** and **aspect.**[6] The verb paradigm is V~Vs~Vd~Vn~Vŋ. The verb *be* has further person forms *am* and *are*, and is inflected for **number** in the past tense.

3. Some adjectives and a few adverbs are inflected for **degree,** and fit the paradigm A~Aer~Aest. Constructions with *more* and *most* supply the same meaning categories for uninflected adjectives and adverbs.

5. The possessive marker{*'s*} (or sometimes just '), often treated as an inflection, is better considered as a syntactic, rather than a morphological, marker, since it can be attached to phrases (as in *the mayor of Boston's car*) as well as to words. It is thus an enclitic, rather than a suffix.
6. These terms will be discussed in the treatment of verb phrases, below.

4. Pronouns are inflected for **case**. The pronoun paradigm does not lend itself to easy symbolic representatition, since there is a great deal of allomorphic and suppletive variation in it. It can, however, be represented as P~Pm~Pr~Prs.

## Exercises

*I. Give the* Vd *and* Vn *forms of the following verbs as you customarily use them (Example:* fall, fell, fallen).*Then check your forms against those given in a dictionary.*

| | | | |
|---|---|---|---|
| 1. ride | 6. shine | 11. swing | 16. flee |
| 2. bite | 7. heave | 12. see | 17. cast |
| 3. hide | 8. drag | 13. throw | 18. seek |
| 4. dive | 9. wake | 14. snow | 19. lean |
| 5. strive | 10. prove | 15. leap | 20. lie |

*II. Divide the following list of adjectives into three groups: (a) those with which you would use the suffixes* -er *and* -est *but not the* more *and* most *constructions; (b) those with which you would use only the* more *and* most *constructions; (c) those with which you might use either. Then check your usage with a dictionary.*

| | | | |
|---|---|---|---|
| 1. old | 4. incompetent | 7. pleasant | 10. high |
| 2. clumsy | 5. easy | 8. superficial | 11. gauche |
| 3. helpless | 6. friendly | 9. childish | 12. subtle |

## 4. Morphology: Derivation

Speakers of English are aware that each individual word is not always a unique string of sounds unrelated to any other, but that words often are grouped in families which have a central core of both meaning and form. Consider, for example, the italicized words in the following set of sentences:

1. that is a *tight* connection.
2. use a wrench to *tighten* the bolt.
3. the *tightness* of his collar bothered him.
4. tie it *tightly*.

In the first sentence, *tight* is a modifier of *connection*, and it could have the inflections -*er* and -*est*; therefore it is an adjective. In sentence 2, *tighten* is clearly a verb. In sentence 3, *tightness*, following the determiner *the*, is a noun. Finally, *tightly* in sentence 4, acting as modifier of the phrase *tie it*, is an adverb. Yet though they all belong to different parts of speech, these four words have the common formal element *tight* and a common semantic element which relates to firmness or absence of room for movement.

Further search through the word-stock of English turns up many words analogous to these. Like *tighten*, for instance, are *whiten* and *broaden*, both of which add *-en* to an adjective to make a verb. Like *tightness* are other nouns ending in *-ness*: *whiteness* and *happiness*. The addition of *-ly* to an adjective as in *tightly* creates adverbs like *safely* and *easily*. This process by which words are fitted to different grammatical categories by formal additions to a basic stem is called **derivation**.

In English, derivation is most commonly effected by means of **derivational suffixes** added to a stem, like the *-en*, *-ness*, and *-ly* of our examples. Just as with inflectional variants, these derivational variants can be grouped into paradigms:

| Adjective | Noun | Verb | Adverb |
|---|---|---|---|
| *Stem* | *Stem* + {*-ness*} | *Stem* + {*-en*} | *Stem* + {*-ly*} |
| tight | tightness | tighten | tightly |
| white | whiteness | whiten | whitely |
| steep | steepness | steepen | steeply |

There are, however, several important differences between inflectional and derivational paradigms:

1.  Derivational paradigms do not usually apply as widely as inflectional ones. Almost all nouns fit into the singular-plural paradigm, but only a small group of adjectives can be turned into verbs by adding *-en*: we do not have verbs like \*greenen, \*wisen, or \*beautifulen.

2.  Alternative derivational paradigms can effect the same kind of changes. Adjectives can be turned into nouns not only by adding the *-ness* suffix of our sample paradigm, but by adding *-th* (often with stem change), as in *wide—width*; *-ion*, as in *composite—composition*; or *-ity*, as in *responsible—responsibility*.

3.  A word can have no more than one inflectional suffix at a time, but derivational suffixes are not so restricted. A word which already has a derivational suffix can become the stem to which another is added, and this process may continue until four or five derivational suffixes have been strung together:

nat- + -ure    nature (noun)
nature + -al    natural (adjective)
natural + -ist    naturalist (noun)
naturalist + -ic    naturalistic (adjective)
naturalistic + -al    *naturalistical (adjective)
*naturalistical + -ly    naturalistically (adverb)

We do not often put together this many derivational suffixes, and when they reach the extent of *honorificabilitudinous* the effect is comic.

4. An inflectional suffix can be added to a derivational one, but the reverse is not possible. A noun like *tightness* can add the regular plural inflection to make *tightnesses*, but we cannot add -*ness* or -*ly* to an inflected form like *tighter* to make *\*tighterness* or *\*tighterly*. A consequence of this rule and of the rule that a word can have only one inflectional suffix at a time is that an inflectional suffix is always the last morpheme in the word to which it belongs.[7]

5. The stem to which an inflectional suffix is added is always a word in its own right,[8] while the stem to which a derivational suffix is added need not be an independent word (in linguistic terms, a **free form**). This is illustrated by *nature*, which we represented above as made up of the stem *nat-* and the derivational suffix -*ure*. This analysis is justified by the fact that both of these elements occur in other combinations and hence have status as separate morphemes. The suffix -*ure* appears in words like *stature* and *posture*, and the stem *nat-* in words like *native* and *nation*. A stem which cannot be subdivided into smaller morphemes is called a **base**. If it is also a word in its own right, like *tight*, it is a **free base**; if it must always be combined with another morpheme, like *nat-*, it is a **bound base**.

These differences usually make it easy to distinguish between inflectional and derivational suffixes. But occasionally ambiguity arises because two suffixes, one inflectional and one derivational, are **homophonous**—that is, alike in sound (and often in spelling). We have seen that -*ing* is one of the verb inflections, added to the verb stem to make the present participle. But there are two other -*ing* suffixes which are derivational. One of them forms adjectives when it is added to verb stems and other bases. It is true that words like *interesting* and *charming* originated as present participles, but their

---

7. *Brother-in-law*, plural *brothers-in-law*, is not a word but a fixed phrase; hence it does not violate this rule.

8. A few exceptions to this, such as *trousers* and *scissors*, are unimportant.

use in constructions like *a very charming girl* and *this book is more interesting than that* mark them as true adjectives. Similarly, words like *building*, when they follow determiners or take the plural inflection, as in *the buildings are tall*, must be considered nouns, formed by adding the third -*ing* suffix to verb stems. Many words like these must be seen in constructions before they can be identified, even though they have derivational suffixes. *Stranger* and *rounder*, for instance, are ambiguous—either comparative adjectives or nouns in -*er*—though *stronger* on the one hand and *builder* on the other are not.

In addition to suffixes, which always follow the stem to which they are attached, English also makes use of **prefixes,** which precede the stem. There are not so many of these as there are suffixes, and they are all derivational. As with derivational suffixes, a word may have more than one prefix, up to a usual practical limit of three, as in *irreconcilable*, which has the bound base *cil*, the derivational suffix -*able*, and the prefixes *ir-* (a variant of *in-*), *re-* and *con-*. Since most prefixes have been brought into English as parts of words borrowed entire from Latin or French, only a few of them, such as *un-* (which was not so borrowed) can be more or less freely attached to existing words. In contrast, a good many suffixes, like the -*ly* that makes adjectives into adverbs, can be extended by analogy rather freely. A paradigm of this sort, which lends itself easily to the analogical creation of new words, is called **productive.**

## Exercises

I. List four derivational suffixes which form nouns from adjectives (e.g., -ness : white>whiteness), and give an illustration of each. Which of these suffixes are productive?

II. List four derivational suffixes which form adjectives from nouns (e.g., -en : wood>wooden), and give an illustration of each. Which of these suffixes are productive?

III. Analyze the following words into their constituent morphemes and classify each morpheme as base, prefix, or suffix.

1. unfriendly
2. hopelessly
3. notification
4. reclassify
5. immovable
6. unimaginativeness

IV. By using derivational prefixes and suffixes, make as long a list as you can of words derived from the base organ. When your list is as *long as you can make it, check it against an unabridged dictionary and add further words you find in the dictionary (distinguish these from those on your own original list).*

## 5. Noun Phrases

In the sentence we analyzed at the beginning of this chapter, we identified certain phrases—*a big dog* and *the wheels of my car*—as belonging to the general construction type of modification and having nouns as head. Phrases of this sort are **noun phrases.** They are of great importance, since they may appear in various constituent positions: as subject in a predication, as complement in a complementation, and as object in a subordination. They also may vary widely in the complexity of their internal structure.

The smallest and simplest kind of noun phrase, the irreducible minimum, is a noun by itself, such as *dogs* in the predication *dogs bark.* More commonly, however, a noun phrase has at least one modifier of the head, a **determiner,** as in *a dog barks, the dogs are barking.* Determiners like *a* (*an* before words beginning with a vowel sound) and *the* always indicate that a noun is going to appear; they are the most common first elements in noun phrases. But often the determiner is separated from the noun which is the ultimate head of the construction by other modifiers of various sorts.

The most common modifiers of nouns are **adjectives.** The pattern **determiner + adjective + noun** is a very familiar kind of noun phrase:

a tall tree
the old house
that beautiful woman
my unusual friend

Nor is a noun phrase limited to one adjective; there may be two or more. In that case, the two adjectives may make up a little coordination construction, modifying the noun head as a unit, or they may act consecutively. Compare the phrases in the A column with those in the B column:

| A | B |
|---|---|
| this hopeless, impossible mess | a new blue dress |
| a tattered, ragged coat | my dear old friend |
| the red and black flag | his charming little daughter |

In the A group the adjectives are either joined by *and* or separated by a comma which could be replaced by *and* without changing the meaning. Furthermore, the order of the adjectives could be reversed; it is just as grammatical to say *this impossible, hopeless mess* or *a ragged, tattered coat*. But we cannot do the same with the pairs of adjectives in the B list. We do not ordinarily say *my dear and old friend* or *a blue new dress*. What this means is that we have to analyze the two sets of phrases differently. Each phrase in the A group consists of a noun head modified by a coordination whose constituents are adjectives, while each phrase in the B group consists of an adjective modifying a head which is itself a modification having another adjective as modifier and a noun as head. Diagrams make the difference clear:

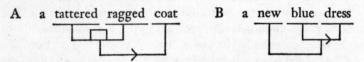

This distinction is important. For one thing, it is a guide to punctuation: if the adjectives are coordinate, they have a comma between them, but if they are consecutive they do not.

One further possibility is that an adjective modifying a noun head may itself be the head of a small modification construction:

my very dear friend
a rather old house
this extremely pretty girl

Once again the diagram makes clear the grammatical structure:

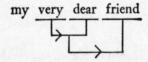

Words like *very* and *rather*, which customarily modify adjectives, are **qualifiers**; words like *excessively*, which also may have this function, belong to the general adverb class.

Between the adjective or adjectives, if any, and the head there may be one or more nouns acting as modifiers. A noun in this position is called a **noun adjunct**, and the construction consisting of a noun head modified by another noun is called a **noun-adjunct construction**. It is very common in English:

**an** army colonel
**a** wax model
**the** chemistry laboratory
**that** government clerk

As with adjectives, there may be more than one noun adjunct in a noun phrase. If there are two, either they are consecutive, or they make up a smaller noun-adjunct construction which acts as a unit modifier of the head. Compare the following sets of noun phrases and the illustrative diagrams:

| A | B |
|---|---|
| the chemistry department office | the chemistry storage shelves |
| a spring-water bottle | a spring water carnival |
| our highway safety program | the state highway patrol |

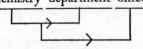 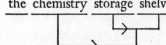

A hyphen is sometimes used to join two nouns forming a single modifier, as in *a spring-water bottle*. Consistent hyphenation would provide a means in written English of avoiding the ambiguity which can occur in constructions of this sort. *The state highway patrol* was classed above with the phrases having consecutive, rather than coordinate, noun-adjunct constructions, which means that it is to be translated as "the state-administered patrol of the highway"—but it could be put into the other group, in which case it would mean "the patrol of the state highway(s)," and might well be written *the state-highway patrol*.

When a noun phrase consists of **determiner + adjective + noun + noun,** there also are two possibilities, depending on whether the adjective modifies (A) the whole noun-adjunct construction or (B) just the first noun.

| A | B |
|---|---|
| an old Ford car | an old style car |
| a red traffic signal | a red cedar shingle |
| a foreign ocean liner | a foreign make automobile |

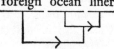 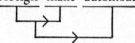

Once again the judicious use of hyphens in writing may resolve the ambiguity of such phrases as *an American army colonel*: thus *an American-army colonel* clearly means "a colonel in the American-army"; without the hyphen it would mean "an army colonel who is American."

In addition to nouns and nominal phrases, various other kinds of elements may be used in the adjunct position. Though, as we shall see, the usual position in noun phrases for adverbial modifiers is after the noun head, adverbs may occasionally appear as adjuncts: *the then king, the above example*. Verbs in the plain form, rather than in the participial forms (Vn and Vŋ) which are the usual noun-modifying verb forms, are sometimes used as adjuncts, especially in colloquial speech: *a real go team*. Prepositional phrases, whose position is normally after the noun, are put into adjunct position for special effect: *an on-the-spot check*, *an off-the-cuff opinion*. Some of these lose the determiner before the noun object and become compounds like *offhand*, *undercover*, and *downhill*; it is a little difficult to know what part of speech to assign these to, though they most resemble adverbs (dictionaries also may classify them as adjectives). Various other kinds of phrases and clauses that can be used as adjuncts are:

- a *know-it-all* expression on his face
- a *no-good* rascal
- a *pay-as-you-go* tax program
- a *devil-may-care* fellow

Finally there is a group of morphemes which seem to be intermediate between prefixes and full adjectives, such as *ex*, *pseudo*, *quasi*, and *pro*. Most of these can be used as free forms, at least in colloquial style (*his sophistication is pseudo, arguments pro and con*), but they more often appear as adjuncts. Usually in written English they are hyphenated to the noun head, as in *ex-President*, *pro-Communist*.

Two other kinds of modifiers also appear in noun phrases. Their position is between the determiner and the first adjective, if there is one. Nearest to the determiner is the position for **quantifiers**, a group of modifiers which includes words like *few* and *many* as well as all the numbers. Between them and the adjectives is the position for a small group of **particularizers**, like *certain*, *other*, and *particular* itself. Most of the particularizers can also be adjectives;

| | Predeterminer | Determiner | Quantifier | Particularizer | Adjective | Adjunct | Head |
|---|---|---|---|---|---|---|---|
| 1. | all | | | | | | dogs |
| 2. | | the | | | | | dogs |
| 3. | | | ten | | | | dogs |
| 4. | | | | other | | | dogs |
| 5. | | | | | big | | dogs |
| 6. | | | | | | hunting | dogs |
| 7. | | | several | more | | | dogs |
| 8. | not all | my own | six hundred | | very hungry | coon-hunting | dogs |
| 9. | | my son's | | | old | track | shoes |
| 10. | | my | | | old | fireman's | shirt |
| 11. | both | the | two | other | friendly | army | colonels |
| 12. | | John's | three | different | new | tan leather | jackets |

when they are they have a different meaning. Compare:

| A | B |
|---|---|
| a certain favorite spot | a certain conclusion |
| a particular street corner | a fussy, particular old man |

Note that in the B phrases, *certain* and *particular* can be modified by qualifiers or moved to predicate position after *be*, both of which are marks of adjectives:

the conclusion is certain
the old man is very particular

Not so the phrases in the A group; we do not say:

*a very certain favorite spot
*the street corner is very particular

Completing the list of modifiers which can precede the noun head in a noun phrase is a small group of **pre-determiners**, which, as the name indicates, come before the determiner. The most common pre-determiners are *all*, *both*, and *half*. But we can also put into this group certain stereotyped expressions, originally constructions but now best considered **fixed phrases**, such as *a lot of*, *a number of*, *lots of*, etc.

Six kinds of modifiers, then, may precede the noun head in a noun phrase. The presence or absence of any of these is largely independent of the presence or absence of any other, though there are rather complicated restrictions upon co-occurrence which are too involved to be treated in a grammar as short as this one. Two of the types of modifiers—adjectives and adjuncts—may be represented more than once in the same noun phrase. Not only single words but small constructions can appear in each position. It is possible, though unusual, for all six kinds of modifiers to be present in the same phrase, as in *all the ten other big hunting dogs*. The chart on page 41 shows the six positions and a number of noun phrases made up of various combinations of modifiers. Observe that nouns with the possessive enclitic *'s* may appear in either the determiner or the adjunct column, but with different meaning: *a new boy's shirt* means "a new shirt suitable for a boy," but *a boy's new shirt* means "a new shirt belonging to a boy."[9] Only in the deter-

---

9. *A new boy's shirt* can also mean "a shirt belonging to a new boy." In this case, *new boy's* is a construction acting as a unit modifier in the determiner position.

miner position do "possessive" nouns actually indicate possession.

Three other kinds of modifiers which may appear in noun phrases follow the noun instead of preceding it. These are adverbs, prepositional phrases, and subordinate clauses (the clauses we will consider in our treatment of transformations later on). Adverbs, as we have seen, make up a quite diversified class of words, only a relatively small number of which can modify noun heads—adverbs of place (including direction) and time, whose position is immediately following the noun.

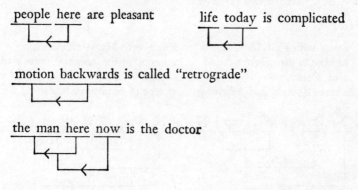

Prepositional phrases, which, as we have seen, are subordination constructions whose constituents are a preposition and (usually) a noun phrase as object, also come after the noun, and after any adverb that may follow the noun. They tend to follow the same order rule as adverbs—place before time—but this rule is by no means rigorously binding:

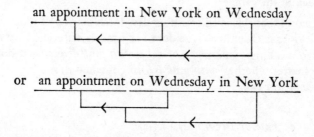

Prepositional phrases also have other kinds of meanings beside place and time, including description, ownership, constitution, and so on:

a dress with a white collar
the home of my family
a commentary on the Bible
a house of cards

When two prepositional phrases come in succession after a noun head, there is always a possibility of ambiguity. Since the object of the first preposition is usually a noun phrase, it is possible for the second prepositional phrase to modify its head only (A), rather than the whole preceding noun phrase (B). The two situations may be schematically represented this way:

|                              A |                                        B |
|--------------------------------|------------------------------------------|
| a date with a girl like Mary   | a date with Mary on Tuesday              |
| a house in the neighborhood of Boston | a house in the country with a big yard |
| a list of doctors in the vicinity | a piece of candy in a box            |

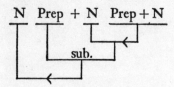     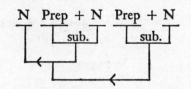

Usually it is possible to tell from the meaning which construction is intended. But sometimes ambiguity is complete:

there is a picture of a dish on a table [is the picture or the dish on the table?]
the house had a garage with big doors in back [are the doors in the back of the garage?]

One reason that this kind of ambiguity doesn't strike us more often than it does is that there is seldom very much difference between the two meanings. In *a piece of cake with pink frosting*, it doesn't much matter whether *with pink frosting* is taken to modify *a piece of cake* or just *cake*.

## 6. Other Nominal Phrases

We have seen that noun phrases of various kinds and degrees of complexity, from *a dog* to *both the two other fierce hunting dogs here in the pen*, are all modification constructions with nouns as their ultimate head and various modifiers built up in layers, sometimes with smaller constructions—other modifications, coordinations, or subordinations—within them. But there are other types of phrases, not so constructed, which appear in the characteristic noun positions of subject, complement, and object of a preposition. Because they are performing characteristically nominal[10] functions, these are called **nominal phrases**. It is not possible for us to go into detail about a large variety of them here, and some of them will be dealt with as transformations later on, but a few of the important ones may be briefly mentioned. For example, some kinds of complementation constructions may be nominal phrases. It will be remembered that the constituents of a complementation are a verbal phrase and a complement; *chased the wheels of my car* is an example. This kind of complementation cannot function as a nominal phrase. But if the verb is changed to either the **infinitive** form (*to chase*) or the **present participle** (in this case sometimes called the **gerund**) form (*chasing*), then the complementation construction can be a nominal phrase:

**Subject:** *chasing the wheels of my car* was a dangerous thing for that dog to do
**Object of Preposition:** the dog went away after *chasing the wheels of my car*
**Complement:** that dog likes *to chase the wheels of my car*

Various kinds of subordinations can also be nominal phrases. The larger ones—various kinds of **noun-clauses**—will be treated later as the product of transformations. But we may note here that even prepositional phrases may occasionally perform nominal functions:

**Subject:** *over the fence* is out
**Object of Preposition:** he came up from *under water*

Only in quite colloquial usage, however, do we find a prepositional phrase as a complement:

he likes *in town* better than *in the country*

In more formal usage, this sentence would have a noun or gerund, such as *life* or *living*, as the complement, modified by the prepositional phrase:

he likes living in town better than living in the country

10. *Nominal* is the adjective related to *noun*.

## Exercises

*I. Divide the following into two groups: (a) those in which the modi-
fier nearest to the noun head is an adjective; (b) those in which it is an
adjunct.*

1. a loud noise
2. the community chest
3. nylon stockings
4. rainy weather
5. an emergency exit
6. our considerate neighbor
7. his summer vacation
8. a steel bridge
9. a flat tire
10. the school picnic

*II. For each of the following noun phrases, indicate whether the first
immediate constituent division follows the first or the second modifier.
For those in which either is possible, state the difference between the
two constructions in meaning. (Example: old | vacuum cleaner; old
time | religion; red | brick house or red brick | house).*

1. old style clothes
2. a gray stone house
3. a new transistor radio
4. the electric appliance industry
5. that hungry old man
6. a modern jazz festival
7. heavy duty equipment
8. a heavy iron stove
9. structural steel girders
10. her new blue dress

*III. Make a table with seven columns, headed as in the table on page
41. Then write each of the following noun phrases on a separate line,
putting each modifier in the correct column of the table.*

1. the cloudy sky
2. all my six brothers
3. two other green boxes
4. my son's new leather jacket
5. every important policy decision
6. both those friendly Navy lieu-
tenants

*IV. In the table on page 41, any combination from none to all six of
the modifiers in examples 1–6 may be present, making 64 possible
phrases. Write them all out.*

## 7. Verb Phrases

The simplest form of English sentence is a predication,
whose constituents are a subject and a predicate. The subject is
always some kind of nominal, most commonly a noun phrase of
one of the types discussed above in section 5. The other constituent,
the predicate, is a **verbal phrase,** which may be a simple verb (as
in *dogs bark*) or an elaborate construction involving modifiers,
complements, or both. But no matter how elaborate it may be, the
verbal phrase always has as its core a verb or **verb phrase.**

It is important to distinguish between the two rather similar expressions: **verbal phrase** and **verb phrase**. A **verbal phrase** is any constituent, from a single verb to an elaborate construction, which exercises the predicate function. A **verb phrase**, on the other hand, is a special kind of construction made up of a **main verb** and certain other elements from a limited list of **auxiliaries**. In the sentence *The dog should not have chased the wheels of my car*, the whole predicate *should not have chased the wheels of my car* is a verbal phrase, while the verb phrase at its core is *should . . . have chased*.

The purpose of verb phrases is to restrict or qualify the general meaning of the main verb in certain specific ways. Some languages —Latin, for example—convey many of these restrictions and qualifications by means of complicated inflections attached to the verb itself. Such a Latin form as *amavissemus* conveys not only the principal meaning "love" (in the stem, *ama-*), but also the meanings of "perfect" (action in the unspecified past influencing the present), of "past time," of "subjunctive" (unreality, uncertainty, or contingency of statement), of "active" (subject acting rather than being acted upon), and of "subject in the first person plural." Such a verb form can itself be a sentence, since its personal ending (*-mus*) indicates that its subject is "we," and no further subject need be expressed.

English, however, has only four inflections that can be attached to the verb: third singular (*-s*), past tense (*-d*), past participle (*-n*), and present participle (*-ŋ*). The further restriction that there can be only one inflection on any single word—in contrast to at least four on *amavissemus*—means that the inflectional system is not adequate to express many limitations or qualifications on the meaning of the main verb. But these limitations and qualifications do not on this account go unexpressed. In place of the elaborate inflections of languages like Latin, English makes use of an ingenious and complicated system of special function words called **auxiliaries** to build verb phrases capable of expressing many fine shades of verbal meaning. Thus Latin *amavissemus* can be translated into English not by a single word but by some such phrase as *we might have loved*. Here the same ideas of perfect phase, past tense, subjunctive mood, and active voice are included, but they are signaled by various parts of the verb phrase. The number and person of the subject are not indicated in the verb phrase at all, but by the separate pronoun subject *we*. The idea of "perfect" is expressed by the auxiliary *have*; the idea of mode (contingent rather than definite action) by the auxiliary *might*; the idea of "past" by the selection of *might* rather than *may*, and the idea of "active" by the absence of the specific indicator of passive—the auxiliary *be* with the Vn form of the main verb. The Vn form of the main verb does appear, but the auxiliary *have* immediately precedes it. So the whole verb phrase, quite different in structure from the inflected Latin verb, conveys much the same group of meanings.

English verb phrases like *might have loved, was being chased,* or *will have been telling* may seem to be rather loose, disorganized strings of verb elements, but actually they are constructed according to very strict rules of selection and arrangement. The main controlling principle is that of **marking** the phrase in a particular way for the presence of a certain restriction on the meaning of the verb, and leaving the phrase **unmarked** in that particular way if that restriction does not apply or is not to be indicated (it may still apply, even if it is not indicated). The markers used may be inflections, or they may be separate words—in this case, auxiliaries. The most general, unrestricted form of the verb is the totally unmarked, or plain, form, *love*—the form that is entered in dictionaries. With the marker *to* it becomes the **infinitive**, *to love*, which is used in many constructions where we wish to name this verb without restricting its meaning in any way. But if we wish to build the verb into a predication, we must make a series of decisions as to whether or not to mark it for one or another of the various restrictions that may be put upon it.

The first such decision is whether or not to mark the verb for **tense.** The tense marker is the past inflection {-d}; if it is used, the verb is restricted to either a statement about the past, or a statement in contradiction of reality, both of which express a degree of remoteness.

**Past time:**  I *loved* her for a long time
he *came* to see me yesterday

**Unreal:**  if I *loved* her, I wouldn't do it [the assumption is that I do not love her]
I wouldn't care if he never *came* to see me [the assumption is that he did or will come or that someone thinks he ought to]

There is nothing particularly "past" in time about the last two sentences; in fact the presence of *would* gives a vague suggestion of the future to the final one.

If a verb is not marked for tense, we must decide whether or not to mark it for **person** by means of the {-s} inflection. What controls the decision here is not an optional restriction on the meaning of the verb, but an automatic selection dictated by the subject. If the subject is *he*, *she*, *it*, a singular noun, or a complex nominal not having a plural noun or a coordination of nouns as head, the verb must have the person marker {-s}; otherwise it must be unmarked.

**Marked for Person:**   he *loves* his children
                           the boy *tells* the truth
                           walking in the rain *gives* me pleasure

**Unmarked:**   they *love* their children
              the boys *tell* the truth
              singing and dancing *give* me pleasure

The next decision concerns **mood** or **mode.** If some doubt or contingency is to be cast on the verb phrase, so that its assertion is not outright but in some way or another qualified, dependent, or tentative, one of a group of **modal auxiliaries** is inserted into the phrase. If, on the other hand, the assertion is definite and outright, the phrase is not marked for mode. The modal auxiliaries are:

| Present Form | Past Form |
|---|---|
| will | would |
| shall | should |
| can | could |
| may | might |
| must | |
| ought (to) | |
| need | |
| dare | |

The first four of these have past tense forms; the last four do not.[11] This means that if the modal auxiliary selected is *must*, *ought*, *need*, or *dare* the verb phrase cannot also be marked for tense, since if a modal auxiliary is used in a verb phrase, it is what carries the tense-marking inflection. The modal auxiliaries never have the person-marking {-s} inflection.

11. *Dare* and *need* can also act as full verbs, in which case they have Vs, Vd, Vn, and Vŋ forms. They seem to be losing their status as modal auxiliaries in today's English. *Should* in its most common meanings is a present form.

Now we must decide whether the verb is to be marked for **phase**. The phase-marker is the auxiliary *have* followed by the Vn (past participle) form of the next element in the verb phrase. If a modal auxiliary is also present, the plain form of *have* is used; if there is no modal auxiliary, the form of *have* appropriate to the tense or person is used. Some phase-marked verb phrases are:

(you)  have loved
(he)  has loved
(they)  had loved
(we)  might have loved

In general we mark a verb for phase to show that the effect of the action it describes is still influential, even though it happened in the past. *The sun rose* simply tells us that at some time in the past the sun came up; it may since have gone down. But *the sun has risen* tells us that the effect of this past happening is still with us; the sun is still in the sky. When the perfect phase is combined with the past tense, as in *the sun had risen*, the significant continuing influence of the action is moved to a specific point in the past, as in *when the sun had risen, it was light*; or it is given the "unreal" meaning of the past form, as in *if the sun had risen it would be light*.

The next decision we must make relates to **aspect**. The marker in this case is the auxiliary *be* followed by the Vŋ (present participle) form of the next element in the phrase. If the auxiliary *be* comes first in the phrase (as it will if mode and phase are unmarked), it must appear in the form appropriate to the selected tense and to the person and number of the subject—unmarked for tense: *am* if the subject is *I*, *is* if the subject is *he*, *she*, *it*, or a singular noun or nominal, *are* in other cases; marked for tense: *was* for singular subjects (except *you*) and *were* for plural. If the auxiliary *be* is preceded by a modal auxiliary, it must be in the plain form, and if it is preceded by *have*, it must be in the past participle form *been*, since the auxiliary *have* is always followed immediately by a past participle. Examples of aspect-marked verb phrases are:

(I) am talking
(they) are singing
(he) is walking
(he) was thinking
(they) were riding
(she) could be coming
(we) have been reading
(you) should have been working

We mark a verb for aspect to indicate that the action of the verb covers a limited span of time. *They sang a song* simply tells us that this action took place some time in the past, but *they were singing a song* (*when I entered the room*) indicates that at a given time, and for a limited time before and after, the action was going on.

Finally we must decide whether or not to mark a verb phrase for **voice**. The marked, or **passive**, form makes use of the auxiliary *be* followed by the Vn form of the main verb. Once again the form of *be* selected depends on what precedes it in the phrase, or if nothing precedes it, what the subject is. The following are all passive-marked verb phrases:

(the house) was destroyed
(the job) can be done
(the bridge) has been built
(the windows) were being washed
(the door) should have been closed

The passive form is usually selected in order that the receiver of the action of the verb will be the subject—perhaps for emphasis, perhaps because the performer of the action is unknown or irrelevant.

These various choices in all their combinations make possible 123 different verb phrases with the same main verb, ranging from the simple unmarked form *love* to wholly marked phrases like *could have been being loved*. Admittedly, phrases like the latter are rare, but they conform accurately to the rules, and they are acceptable to speakers of English as grammatical and meaningful. In contrast, phrases strung together in violation of the rules, like *could being told* or *have ought being telling* are immediately perceived to be ungrammatical, hence meaningless, by the native speaker.

The rules for constructing grammatical verb phrases in English can all be summed up in the following table (Ø means no element present):

|  | Tense | Mode | Phase | Aspect | Voice | Main Verb |
|---|---|---|---|---|---|---|
| Marked | -d | Modal Auxiliary | *have* -n | *be* -ŋ | *be* -n | *love*, etc. |
| Unmarked | -s, ø | ø, *do* | ø | ø | ø | ø |

Observe that in each of the "Marked" positions except Mode and also in the "Unmarked" position for Tense there are inflections, indicated by the hyphen. These are to be attached to the end of the *next following* element in the verb phrase, whatever it may be. In the case of the {-*n*} inflection in the Voice position, the next element must be the main verb. But in all the other cases the next item may be the main verb or it may be an auxiliary. A verb phrase marked for tense, phase, and aspect and unmarked for mode and voice would begin as:

$$| \text{ -d } | \varnothing | \text{ have -n } | \text{ be -ŋ } | \varnothing | \text{ love}$$

Transferring the inflections to the end of the next following element, we get:

$$\text{have -d } | \text{ be -n } | \text{ love -ŋ}$$

In standard form:

had been loving

There are a few restrictions, which have already been mentioned, on the free choice of marked or unmarked forms on this chart. If the modal auxiliaries *must, ought, dare,* or *need* are used, tense cannot be marked. Normally, singular subjects select the -*s* form if unmarked for tense, but if the next element is a modal auxiliary, they take the zero form, and if the next element is *be*—either as full verb or as auxiliary—various special rules govern the choice among *am, is,* and *are* in the unmarked row or *was* and *were* in the marked row. Otherwise this chart may be applied quite mechanically and it will always produce a legitimate, grammatical verb phrase.[12]

The foregoing description of English verb phrases may appear unorthodox to those accustomed to the more traditional treatment in terms of present, past, and future tenses with perfect and progressive counterparts to account for phase and aspect. Actually the traditional presentation is not an accurate description of the situation in English at all. Except for the so-called progressive forms, which we have here described as marked for the aspect of limited duration, it is nothing but a translation of the tense system of Latin. By exaggerating the importance of tense and omitting consideration of all the modal auxiliaries except *will* and *shall*, it fails to indicate

---

12. The appearance of *do* in the unmarked position for Mode will be explained below.

the actual patterns of structure and meaning that characterize the remarkable and unique verb system of English. The description presented here, which owes much to some distinguished modern grammarians,[13] is intended to focus attention on the English verb system as it actually is, rather than as a partial copy of the quite different system of Latin.

## Exercises

*I. Make a table with six columns, headed respectively Tense, Mode, Phase, Aspect, Voice, Main Verb. Using a separate line for each, place the constituents of the following verb phrases in the proper columns, following the model on page 51. Put a zero (Ø) in the unmarked positions.*

1. (he) has departed
2. (we) must be going
3. (the story) has been told
4. (the accident) should have been reported
5. (you) must have been running
6. (we) may be being ignored
7. (you) should have been being paid

*II. Choose one of the modal auxiliaries and from your reading collect examples of phrases in which it occurs. On the basis of these examples, as well as of your own usage, list the various meanings this auxiliary can have. Check your analysis against that of a large dictionary such as Webster's New International or the Oxford English Dictionary.*

*III. Read pages 6-12 of The English Verb Auxiliaries by W. F. Twaddell, 2d ed. (Providence: Brown University Press, 1963); then write an explanation in your own words of his terms current relevance and limited duration.*

*IV. Compare the structure of the English verb system with that of some other language you have studied, such as Latin, French, German, or Spanish.*

## 8. Negatives and Interrogatives

Often it is desirable to make a statement in the **negative** —to reverse the meaning of a statement so as to deny or exclude its

13. Especially W. F. Twaddell, Martin Joos, and Noam Chomsky.

C

normal meaning. We do this in English in two ways: (1) by including somewhere in the total sentence a negative word such as
*no, nobody, nowhere, never, none;* (2) by expressly negating the
verb phrase by means of the function word *not* or its reduced form
*n't* (pronounced /ənt/or/nt/).[14] In modern standard English these
two methods are mutually exclusive: we say either *he has found
none* or *he hasn't found any,* though older standard English and
present-day substandard English gain extra negative emphasis by
using both, as in *he hasn't found none.* On the infrequent occasions
when both are used in the same construction in standard English,
the effect is to negate the negation and return it to a kind of positive:
*he couldn't have gone nowhere* in effect means *he must have gone
somewhere.*

The rule for negating a verb phrase in English is a simple one: we
simply insert *not* or its reduced form *n't* after the first auxiliary in
the verb phrase. This is the modal auxiliary if one is present, *have* if
there is no modal but the verb is marked for phase, and *be* if neither
modal nor *have* is used. The following examples illustrate these
various possibilities:

| | |
|---|---|
| he could ∧ go | he couldn't go |
| he should ∧ have gone | he shouldn't have gone |
| he has ∧ gone | he hasn't gone |
| he has ∧ been telling | he hasn't been telling |
| he is ∧ telling | he isn't telling |
| he is ∧ being told | he isn't being told |
| he was ∧ told | he wasn't told |

In each example the caret indicates the position following the first
auxiliary, which is where the *not* or *n't* is inserted in the negative
form. The one problem in this system is posed by verbs which are
unmarked for mode, phase, aspect, and voice and therefore have no
auxiliary for the *not* to follow. Older English simply put the *not*
after the main verb or its complement. But except for archaic formulas like *she loves me; she loves me not,* we do not do this in modern
English.[15] Instead, we put in the dummy auxiliary *do* for the *not*
to follow. Since this *do* is followed by the plain form of the main

14. Slants / / are used to enclose material in phonemic transcription, for
which see Chapter Five. The character /ə/, called *schwa,* represents a mid
central vowel like that of *but* or the first syllable of *about.*

15. If the main verb is *be,* however, this kind of inversion is obligatory, and
if it is *have,* it is optional: *he isn't here; I haven't any ~ I don't have any.*

verb, it fits more easily into the unmarked position in the modal auxiliary column of the chart on page 51. And since it is always the first (because the only) auxiliary in its verb phrase, the inflectional markers for tense and person are attached to it:

| | |
|---|---|
| they come | they don't come |
| he comes | he doesn't come |
| we came | we didn't come |

This auxiliary *do*, unlike all the others we have discussed, has no effect on the meaning of the verb phrase. It simply makes possible a consistent pattern for negative phrases by filling the otherwise empty auxiliary position and supplying an auxiliary for *not* to follow.

Another change, more technically called a **transformation,** that affects verb phrases is the **interrogative** or question-asking transformation. One of the standard ways of asking a question in English is to **invert,** or reverse the position of, the subject and the first auxiliary of a statement:

| | |
|---|---|
| he can come | can he come? |
| he has come | has he come? |
| he is coming | is he coming? |
| he was told | was he told? |

Again a problem arises if there is no auxiliary, since the older practice of inverting the subject and the main verb is no longer followed.[16] Browning's famous line, "Irks care the crop-full bird; frets doubt the maw-crammed beast?" indicates how strange this construction sounds today (as indeed it did in Browning's day). Again we use the dummy *do* as an empty auxiliary to invert with the subject:

| | |
|---|---|
| they speak | do they speak? |
| he eats | does he eat? |
| the boys came | did the boys come? |

These two optional transformations can both be applied to the same verb phrase, producing the **negative-interrogative** construction. There are actually two forms of this construction, differing in

16. Except when the verb is *be* or *have*.

the position of the *not*. Thus if the interrogative transformation is made first, the *not* will follow the first auxiliary immediately:

he has come → has he come? → hasn't he come?

But if the negative transformation is made first, the *not* will follow the subject:

he has come → he has not come → has he not come?

This last type of negative-interrogative verb phrase is characteristic of more formal written style, rather than ordinary spoken English. It cannot employ the reduced form *n't*, since this must always immediately follow an auxiliary.

The empty auxiliary *do* has one more use. Occasionally a special emphasis or contrast causes us to put a stronger stress on an auxiliary than on the main verb:

I didn't say I *will* do it, I said I *can* do it

If there is no auxiliary in the verb phrase to carry this stronger stress, *do* fills the gap:

I told the truth                        I *did* tell the truth

## Exercises

*I.  Transform the following statements to questions. Then write a concise paragraph describing how you would teach this part of English grammar to a foreigner learning English.*

1. he is coming
2. the book must be returned
3. the sun shines
4. he is here
5. he has been here
6. you have time to study
7. he needs some help
8. he did his work
9. he came

*II.  Compare the English manner of negating a verb with that of Latin, French, or German.*

*III.  From your reading in Chaucer, Shakespeare, or other older literature, find examples of "double negative." What seems to be the meaning of double and multiple negatives in older English?*

## 9. Verbal Phrases

What we have called **verbal phrases** are constructions which involve a verb phrase as a major constituent and which act as the predicate constituent of predications. One type of verbal phrase is a modification in which the verb phrase is head and the modifier or modifiers are **adverbials**—that is, either adverbs or other elements in adverbial position and function. Apart from adverbs themselves, the most common adverbial elements are prepositional phrases.

Adverbs in English are a rather complex set of words, both in form and in distribution. Some are clearly marked by derivational suffixes, the most common of which is *-ly* added to adjectives. Others—*fast, hard, slow, up, down*—have no such indicator. Furthermore, the positions of adverb modifiers of verb phrases vary considerably. Some adverbs, especially the *-ly* group, can appear before the verb phrase, after it (the most common position for adverbs), or even in the middle of it, producing a split constituent:

    he frequently has spoken
    he has spoken frequently
    he has frequently spoken

Other adverbs, such as *away* or *back*, can appear after the verb phrase only: we say *he has run away* but not *\*he away has run* or *\*he has away run*.

Just as in the case of adjective modifiers in noun phrases, more than one adverb can appear in a verbal phrase. Careful examination will show that unless the adverbs are coordinate (as in *walked slowly and carefully*), the verb phrase and its nearest modifier make up a modification construction which itself becomes the head of a larger modification, and so on until the last adverb has been included.

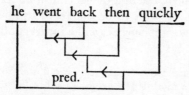

This sentence illustrates the usual, though not absolutely obligatory, order of adverbs according to meaning: place or direction first, then time, and finally manner.

Prepositional phrases as modifiers of verb-phrase heads follow patterns similar to those of adverbs, except that they seldom occur before or in the middle of the verb phrase. Again the usual order is place, time, manner, though exceptions to this order are more common in the case of phrases than in the case of adverbs. The usual order would thus be *he went to the city on Wednesday*; but *he went on Wednesday to the city* does not strike us as being so unusual as to be ungrammatical.

The other common type of verbal phrase is the **complementation**, which, it will be remembered, has as its constituents a verb or verb phrase and some sort of **complement**. Complement constructions are of four kinds, depending on the type of verb used and the number and kind of complements.

1. If the verb is *be* or one of the small group of verbs that can replace *be* (such as *seem, become, remain*) and the complement is either a nominal phrase or an adjectival phrase, the construction is called **linking** or **copulative,** and the complement is called a **subjective complement.** The following are typical linking constructions:

he was a good doctor
he became a doctor
she is very beautiful
the day dawned fair and cool

2. If the verb cannot replace *be* and the complement is a single noun or nominal phrase, the construction is **transitive** and the complement is a **direct object:**

he sold his house
the dog chased the cat

3. If the construction is transitive and there are two complements, both nominal, the first of which can be transformed into a prepositional phrase with *to* or *for* (or occasionally some other preposition), the complements are the **indirect object** and **direct object** respectively:

he sent her some flowers [*cp*. he sent some flowers to her]
he got his son a football [*cp*. he got a football for his son]

It is sometimes possible to have an indirect object without a direct object, but only if the direct object can be easily inferred from the immediate context. In answer to *Have you heard the news?* one might answer *Yes, John told me*, where the direct object *the news* (or the substitute *it*) can be easily inferred following the indirect object *me*.

4.  If the verb is transitive and there are two complements, the first a nominal and the second either a nominal or an adjectival, and if the first complement is characteristically a direct object, the second complement is called an **objective complement**:

> he painted the barn red
> they considered the painter a genius

Since the complementation constructions described in 3 and 4 may both take the form of a verb phrase followed by two nominals, a possibility of ambiguity arises. Usually the kind of verb used prevents this ambiguity. In *he gave his wife a present* there is no doubt about which construction is involved: it can be transformed into *he gave a present to his wife* but not into *he gave his wife to be* (or *as*) *a present*; *his wife a present* is thus the indirect object—direct object construction. On the other hand, *they believed the soldier a hero* transforms into *they believed the soldier to be a hero* but not into *they believed a hero for the soldier*. But some verbs can enter into both types of construction, in which case the intended meaning is usually made clear either by the larger context or by inherent probability. *They named Mr. Jones a director* would ordinarily be taken as the equivalent of *they named Mr. Jones to be a director*, though the other meaning, *they named a director for Mr. Jones*, is not impossible. With *they named the corporation a director*, the double possibility still exists, but the probabilities are reversed: *they named a director for the corporation* is the more probable meaning.

Since both modification and complementation may be involved in the same verbal phrase, and since both the modifiers and the complements which are among their constituents may themselves be rather elaborate constructions, verbal phrases may be very complicated structures indeed. There is not space here to explore their complexities. But by careful and precise analysis we can reduce them to the basic constructions that we have briefly dealt with here. We simply proceed, as we did at the beginning of this chapter, from the large, all-embracing construction to its constituents, and thence to their constituents, until we finally reach the single words and morphemes which are the ultimate constituents of the most complicated grammatical structures.

## Exercises

*I. Separate the following into five groups:* (*a*) *intransitive constructions containing adverbial modifiers;* (*b*) *linking constructions;* (*c*) *transitive constructions with single (direct) object;* (*d*) *transitive constructions with indirect and direct objects;* (*e*) *transitive constructions with direct objects and objective complements* (*note that some ambiguous constructions may belong in both of the last two groups*).

1. (the troops) held their fire
2. (a tadpole) becomes a frog
3. (the train) runs on a track
4. (the engineer) runs the train
5. (he) found himself a seat
6. (he) found himself an outcast
7. (he) bought his wife a present
8. (he) sent away for a new book
9. (we) expect a good return on the money
10. (we) have been talking about two different things
11. (it) has been a great help to us
12. (you) surely can't consider that a friendly thing to do
13. (I) got my new car a set of seat covers
14. (the food) tastes very good
15. (the court) appointed John Smith a guardian

## 10. Simple Sentences

Words, then—or, more precisely, morphemes—are the ultimate grammatical constituents, the smallest units with which grammar concerns itself. At the other end of the scale come sentences, the largest linguistic structures which grammar deals with. It is true that sentences in connected discourse are linked together by various means, some of which are very similar to the grammatical links which tie together the constructions within the sentence. But at least at the present stage of the study of grammar, we do not attempt to deal with units larger than sentences.

Just what is a sentence? Are there any clear-cut, objective criteria which allow us to distinguish one string of words as a sentence and another as a non-sentence? Or must we depend upon some vague, intuitive "sentence sense" to make this distinction?

Many answers to these questions have been put forward, usually in the form of definitions of the sentence. But most of them are unsatisfactory. Take, for instance, the familiar definition "A sen-

tence is a group of words expressing a complete thought." This
raises as many problems as it solves. When is a thought complete? A
writer may need a paragraph, a chapter, even a whole book to
express a thought with what he considers completeness. Each sentence in his discourse will contribute a part, but none of them will
express his complete thought.

Yet there is a germ of truth in this definition. A sentence is a
*grammatically complete construction*; it does not need the help of
other constructions to make its grammatical meaning clear, though
its total meaning may depend heavily on the context in which it
appears. This is what the linguist Leonard Bloomfield means by his
statement that "each sentence is an independent linguistic form, not
included by virtue of any grammatical construction in any larger
linguistic form."[17] This is not an infallible criterion which can
separate sentences from non-sentences, and it, too, raises many questions. While it is not an air-tight definition, it is a useful statement
about sentences and it goes about as far as a short statement can. A
completely accurate definition would have to be a detailed description, considerably longer than this chapter or even this book, of all
the kinds of grammatical constructions that native speakers of
English accept as sentences. It is more effective, instead of attempting a short definition, to approach the sentence from the point
of view of structure.

The basic pattern for English sentences is a predication, with a
nominal phrase as subject and a verbal phrase as predicate. Since
we have already gone into some detail about these two kinds of
phrases, it is not necessary here to analyze these constituents further. But we might remind ourselves that, owing to the great diversity of these phrases in length and structure, what are called **simple
sentences** may range from truly simple ones like *Dogs bark* to quite
long and complicated ones like *The three large dogs in the next
street are always barking at the wheels of passing cars*. No matter
how long it may be, a sentence containing only one predication is
still considered a simple sentence.

Certain grammatical consequences arise from combining a
nominal phrase and a verbal phrase into a predication. These may
be thought of as the elements in the construction that belong to the
tie linking the constituents, rather than to the constituents themselves. The first element is **word order**. In the overwhelming ma-

jority of statement sentences in normal speech or written prose, the subject precedes the predicate. So dominant is this pattern that the native speaker always considers the first noun phrase in a sentence the subject unless there are very strong clues that it is not. This has caused a curious historical change in the grammar of sentences like *He was given the prize,* which, looked at closely, doesn't appear logical—after all, it was *the prize* that was given, not *he.* This type of sentence actually developed from an older form equivalent to *Him was given the prize,* with *the prize* as subject and *him* as indirect object, but in inverted order. But so strong was the feeling that the nominal preceding the verb, *him,* should be the subject, that its case was changed to the nominative form. Grammarians therefore have invented the term **retained object** to account for the construction of *the prize.*

As we have seen, when a statement is transformed into a question, the subject is inverted with the first auxiliary of the verb phrase in the predicate, thus usually splitting the predicate into two parts and producing a **discontinuous constituent.**

A second grammatical element in the constructional tie of predication—the requirement, already mentioned in our discussion of verb phrases, that different forms of the verb must be selected to go with different kinds of subjects—is an example of **concord.** When the verb is not marked for tense, singular subjects (except *I* and *you*) require the verb phrase to carry the *-s* marker for number; plural and compound subjects and the pronouns *I* and *you* require the unmarked verb form.

A third grammatical consequence of linking a nominal and a verbal phrase in a predication is the possibility—in some cases the requirement—of substituting a pronoun for a noun in the predicate. If we use the nominal *John* as subject and the verbal phrase *bought John a book*—assuming that *John* refers to the same person both times—we change the second *John* to the **reflexive pronoun,** *himself.*

John bought John a book → John bought himself a book

Or if the predicate contains a noun or noun phrase with the possessive particle {*'s*} which repeats the subject, it is changed to the first possessive form of the pronoun:

John brought John's friend → John brought his friend

Sometimes the predication at the core of a simple sentence is the head of a modification construction. The modifier, usually an adverb or adverbial phrase, is then called a **sentence modifier**. Most commonly it comes first in the sentence:

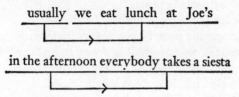

Many of the expressions used to make transitions between sentences or to link them together are sentence modifiers of this sort:

on the other hand, this policy is dangerous
as a result, the battle was lost

Certain of these transitional sentence modifiers may come after a part of the main predication, splitting it into two parts:

the law, however, will not permit this policy

## 11. Compound and Complex Sentences

Sentences containing more than one predication are traditionally classed as **compound** if the over-all construction is a coordination of two or more simple sentences, and as **complex** if one of the predications is some kind of subordinate element—a modifier, subject, or complement. Insofar as it calls our attention to the distinctive nature of the coordination construction, this distinction is of some value. But the really important fact about both compound and complex sentences—as well as some simple sentences—is that their structure can best be considered to be the result of combining two or more simple sentences into a larger structure. A recent school of grammarians has called the rules governing these combinations **generalized transformations.** This simply means that the rules governing the changes that must be made in the constituent sentences when they are combined can be stated in general terms. We shall not here state the rules with the precision which characterizes more detailed transformational grammars; instead we will simply examine a few of the generalized transformations that produce the more common types of compound and complex sentences.

When two or more simple sentences are combined by a generalized transformation into a larger sentence, five kinds of grammatical change may take place:

1. The order of the elements may be altered.
2. Certain specific morphemes or function words may be added (but not **lexical words**—words from the general vocabulary, rather than the limited lists of function words).
3. Certain elements may be deleted.
4. Certain substitutions, such as pronouns for nouns, may be made.
5. Changes may be made in the morphology of some words.

It should be emphasized that these changes are not random or casual but quite systematic; they are part of the grammar of English.

The simplest way in which two sentences can be combined is by **coordination.** The sentences are simply put side by side, as it were, and by punctuation (if in writing) or by intonation (if spoken) the fact is established that they are to be taken together as one sentence. Frequently, though not always, one of the class of function words called **coordinating conjunctions** is used to establish the fact of coordination more firmly:

the heavens opened
the rains fell  } → the heavens opened and the rains fell

When the two constituent sentences have one or more elements in common, the later appearance or appearances of the element or elements may be deleted. The result is a sentence which is theoretically simple, because it has been reduced to a single predication, but which contains a coordination testifying to its compound origin:

the sun reached the horizon
the sun finally set  } → the sun reached the horizon and ~~the sun~~ finally set →
the sun reached the horizon and finally set

Instead of being dropped, a repeated element may be replaced by a substitute—by a pronoun, if it is a noun or nominal, or by some other element, such as the verb substitute *do*, if it is another type of constituent:

John was in a hurry
John stopped to say "hello"  } → John was in a hurry but *he* stopped to say "hello"

I didn't speak  
John spoke  } → I didn't speak but John *did*

In the event of a large amount of duplication between the predicates of the two constituent sentences, the second one may be reduced, by deletion, to a part of the verb phrase, perhaps to as little as a single auxiliary, which serves as a **pro-predicate:**

I have never taken a jet plane trip to San Francisco  
My sister has taken a jet plane trip to San Francisco  } → I have never taken a jet plane trip to San Francisco, but my sister *has*

A second important generalized transformation makes one of the constituent sentences into a **relative clause,** which can then serve as a modifier in a noun phrase. In order for this transformation to take place, there must be a noun which appears in both constituent sentences. In the second sentence, this noun is replaced by a **relative pronoun** (*who, which, that*), which is shifted to the beginning of the clause:

I saw a tall man  
the man was running away  } → I saw a tall man who was running away

he sent me a letter  
I read the letter hastily  } → he sent me a letter I read which hastily →  
he sent me a letter which I read hastily

In certain cases the relative pronoun, if it is not the subject of its clause, can be deleted:

I gave it to a man  
I know the man  } → I gave it to a man I know whom →  
I gave it to a man ~~whom~~ I know →  
I gave it to a man I know

If the repeated noun or nominal in the second sentence refers to place or time and is the object of certain prepositions, the whole prepositional phrase may be replaced by *where* or *when*:

he never left the house  
he lived in the house  } → he never left the house he lived in which → he never left the house in which he lived →  
he never left the house where he lived

The relative transformation is a very important one in English and has ramifications far beyond what we have space to discuss here. According to one theory of grammar it accounts, by deletion and inversion, for all adjectives used as modifiers in noun phrases.

At any event, it is responsible for one of the most useful and versatile of grammatical elements, the relative clause.

A third type of generalized transformation changes one of the constituent sentences into an **adverbial clause** by prefixing to it a **subordinating conjunction** (*as*, *before*, *since*, *if*, *when*, *because*, etc.). The sentence changed may be either the first or the second. In either case, it becomes a modifier of the other constituent, and hence a form of sentence modifier:

it rains
we won't have the picnic } → if it rains, we won't have the picnic

The model sentence with which we began this chapter demonstrates such a transformation following a coordinating transformation:

a big dog ran out
the dog chased the wheels
  of my car } → a big dog ran out and ~~the dog~~
chased the wheels of my car
I turned into Second Street } →
when I turned into Second street a big dog ran out and chased the wheels of my car

As before, elements which are common to both constituent sentences can be deleted from the one which is transformed into an adverbial clause. This deletion produces what is commonly called an **elliptical clause**:

he was working
he was singing a happy song } → while ~~he was~~ working he was
singing a happy song →
while working he was singing a happy song

A fourth generalized transformation—or rather a whole set of them—accounts for **nominalizations**, by which constituent sentences are transformed into various kinds of nominals, which then are able to occupy positions as subjects, complements, and other nominal elements in the main sentence. The simplest of these produces **noun clauses** by prefixing *that* to the constituent sentence:

I know X
he did it } → I know that he did it

Under certain circumstances, the function word prefixed to the noun clause may be one of those that in other contexts (by simple transformations) produce questions: *how, what, who, when,* etc. The resulting noun clause may occupy any position which a noun phrase may occupy:

**Subject:** why he did it is a mystery
**Direct Object:** he told me when to go
**Indirect Object:** give whoever is there the message
**Objective Complement:** he made me what I am today
**Subjective Complement:** the fact is that I am hungry

Other nominalizing transformations may produce **infinitive phrases,** as in

$$\left. \begin{array}{l} \text{he told me X} \\ \text{I must go} \end{array} \right\} \;\rightarrow\; \text{he told me to go}$$

**Or gerund phrases,** as in

$$\left. \begin{array}{l} \text{he likes X} \\ \text{he swims in cold water} \end{array} \right\} \;\rightarrow\; \text{he likes swimming in cold water}$$

Not all grammarians agree that these last kinds of nominal constructions are to be accounted for by generalizing transformations. For this reason, and because the rules of alteration and deletion are rather complicated, we do not go into them here.[18] But they are of interest as showing how one theory, at least, accounts for the creation of English sentences of great complexity by the successive combining of simple sentences no more involved than those in a child's primer. Some such process must be at the bottom of our miraculous ability to produce new sentences, never before spoken or written, in complete confidence that they are grammatical English. And the reverse—some mode of analyzing a complicated structure into its simple components—no doubt accounts for our ability to understand the new and unique sentences produced by others. It is this close relationship to the fundamental workings of the mind which makes grammar the fascinating subject it is.

18. The most complete statement in precisely formulated terms so far published is to be found in *The Grammar of English Nominalizations* by R. B. Lees (Bloomington, Indiana, 1960).

# For Further Reading

There are all kinds of grammars of English, from brief sketches to compendious treatises in many volumes. They vary not only in length but also in their underlying grammatical theory. The following brief list is intended to reveal some of this variety and to suggest profitable areas of exploration for students interested in English grammar.

Curme, George O., *English Grammar*. New York: Barnes and Noble, 1947.

Fries, Charles C., *The Structure of English*. New York: Harcourt, Brace & World, Inc., 1952.

Gleason, H. A., *Linguistics and English Grammar*. New York: Holt, Rinehart & Winston, 1965.

Jespersen, Otto, *Essentials of English Grammar*. London: George Allen, 1933.

——, *A Modern English Grammar on Historical Principles*, 7 vols. Copenhagen: Einar Munksgaard, 1909-49.

Lees, Robert B., *The Grammar of English Nominalizations*. Bloomington, Indiana: Indiana University Research Center in Anthropology, Folklore, and Linguistics, 1960.

Long, Ralph B., *The Sentence and Its Parts*. London: The University of Chicago Press, 1961.

Mittins, W. H., *A Grammar of Modern English*. London: Methuen & Co., Ltd., 1962.

Palmer, Harold E., and F. G. Blandford, *A Grammar of Spoken English*. 2d ed. Cambridge: W. Heffer & Sons, Ltd., 1939.

Poutsma, H., *A Grammar of Late Modern English*, 5 vols. Groningen: P. Noordhoff, 1926-29.

Strang, Barbara M. H., *Modern English Structure*. London: Edward Arnold, Ltd., 1962.

Sweet, Henry, *A New English Grammar, Logical and Historical*, 2 vols. Oxford: Clarendon Press, 1898.

Zandvoort, R. W., *A Handbook of English Grammar*. 5th ed. Groningen: J. B. Wolters, 1953.

# *Three*

# THE HISTORY OF ENGLISH

## 1. *Language and History*

The essence of history is change taking place in time. Anything which endures in time has a history, because in this world of flux anything which endures in time suffers change. But if history is to be meaningful, there must also be continuity. A people, a nation, or a language may change over a long period so greatly as to become something vastly different from what it was at the beginning. But this great change is the cumulation of many small changes. At any stage in its history, the people, nation, or language is fundamentally the same entity that it was in the immediately preceding stage, albeit changed in detail. It has preserved its identity.

The preservation of identity through continuity of change, then, characterizes things which have a history. It is easier to see this in the case of concrete objects, like the Great Pyramid or Keats's Grecian urn. Their continuity is physical; the actual stuff of which they are made has endured through centuries. Their history is primarily what has happened to them and around them; the change they have suffered has chiefly been change of environment, rather than change of their own nature. Indeed, what fascinated Keats about the urn was its placid unchangingness in the midst of changing generations of men. Its history is entirely what can be called "outer history."

But what do we mean by "preservation of identity" when we are speaking of peoples, institutions, organizations? Unlike the pyramid and the urn, they usually do not preserve physical identity. But we can still speak, for example, of "the history of the United States Senate," even though there is nothing physical to link the people who now comprise that body with the Senate of 1790. What does link them is a continuity of function and purpose, an orderly progression of change. One Senator replaces another, the numbers change, the mode of election changes, the place of meeting changes, but still from year to year it is the same institution.

The history of a language is of this latter sort. At any given moment, the identity of a language is the sum total of the speaking habits of all the people who use it. These habits change from year to year, even from day to day, and therefore the language also changes. But the people still know they are speaking "the same language." Its identity persists in spite of change through the generations. After a while the accumulated changes may become so great that it almost seems like a wholly new language. But the continuity is such that very few people are aware of the changes that occur even in their own speech from year to year. During the fifteen hundred or so years of its recorded history, English has changed so greatly that its earliest form is unintelligible to modern speakers of English. But at no time was the language of the father unintelligible to the son. There has been unbroken continuity from generation to generation.

To the linguist, the most important aspect of the history of English is its "inner history": the succession of gradual changes over the years which have brought about the great differences between our speech and that of King Alfred. But English has had an interesting outer history as well. It has been uprooted and transplanted; it has had to compete with other languages, once or twice for its very existence; it has been carried all over the world and has taken root in lands and climates very far and very different from its original home. Let us first survey this outer history before we come to consider the nature and order of the changes which constitute its inner history.

## 2. The Outer History: Indo-European, Germanic, and Old English

English belongs to the Indo-European family of languages, as do most of the languages of modern Europe. A family of languages is a group of languages which have enough in common in their grammar, sound structure, and vocabulary to support the belief that they all are divergent variants of the same original language. The continuous but gradual changes which constitute the inner history of a language may proceed in various directions. Therefore, if two groups of speakers of a single language are separated and kept from communicating with one another, each group will eventually develop its own distinctive version of the language. Each version will preserve its identity through continuity of change, but after a sufficient time has gone by, the two versions will be so different from each other that they will be for all practical purposes separate languages. By this time each will usually have acquired a name of its own, and the original language will no longer exist. The process is like the division by which one-celled organisms multiply. When an amoeba has split into two, each of the resulting amoebas continues the original, but neither can claim to *be* the original. It is in this sense, rather than the genealogical one, that we can say that one language is "descended" from another. It is in this sense that English—as well as German, French, Russian, Greek, Persian, Hindi, and many other languages—is descended from a hypothetical Proto-Indo-European language, spoken some four or five thousand years ago in north-central Europe.

Since the people who spoke Proto-Indo-European, whoever they may have been, had no writing system, there are no records of what the language was like. But scholars have been able to reconstruct many of its features by studying and comparing the oldest surviving records of the various languages making up the Indo-European family. This laborious and painstaking task of **comparative reconstruction** is one of the great accomplishments of nineteenth and twentieth century linguistics. It is still continuing, as new evidence comes in from the decipherment of hitherto unreadable writing systems like Hittite and Minoan. But it is certain that we will never have direct evidence of Proto-Indo-European itself.

Nor will we ever know very much about its speakers. But we do know that the language came to be spoken over an area too large to permit close intercommunication among all its speakers.

There resulted regional variations, local dialects, and eventually distinctive languages, many of which themselves split up into language families. There are eight principal language families within the larger Indo-European family, all of them represented by living languages. They are the following:

1. **Indo-Iranian,** which includes the classical Vedic and Sanskrit literary languages, as well as many of the living languages of Persia and India. Another large and important group of languages spoken in India, the **Dravidian** family, are not Indo-European in origin, but represent a survival of languages spoken before the Indic version of Indo-European spread to India.

2. **Hellenic,** which includes the ancient and modern languages and dialects of the Greek mainland, Crete, Rhodes, islands of the Aegean, and Greek-settled areas of southern Italy and Sicily.

3. **Italic,** whose principal member is Latin and the family of languages, called the **Romance** languages, which have developed from the spoken Latin of various parts of the Roman empire.

4. **Celtic,** whose modern members are the non-English languages of Ireland, Wales, and the Highlands of Scotland, and the non-French language of Brittany. Gallic, the language of Caesar's Gaul, was a Celtic language which has no modern descendant.

5. **Balto-Slavic,** including the Baltic languages of Latvia and Lithuania, and the Slavic group of Polish, Czech, Russian, Bulgarian, and Serbo-Croatian. Some scholars prefer to consider these two separate families.

6. **Germanic,** the family to which English belongs, as well as standard German, Dutch, Flemish, Danish, Norwegian, Icelandic, and Swedish, and many local dialects spoken in Scandinavia, Germany, Austria, and the German-speaking part of Switzerland.

7. **Armenian,** a language and group of dialects spoken in what is now a part of the Soviet Union.

8. **Albanian,** the language of Albania and of small groups or pockets in southern Italy.

In addition to these languages and families which survive into modern times, many have died out altogether: their continuity has been broken, and their identity has perished. Some of these, such as Tocharian (apparently a separate family), the Oscan and

Umbrian members of the Italic family, and the Gothic member of the Germanic family, we know about from written records that have survived. A few names of persons and places are all that is known about others, like Gallic. Doubtless many others have perished without a trace, either because their speakers were annihilated by war or other calamity, or because they abandoned their native language in favor of another, as many American Indian tribes are doing today.

Our concern here is with the Germanic family, which includes English and its nearest relatives. The hypothetical source language from which the various Germanic languages have developed is called **Proto-Germanic,** or simply **Germanic.** Since its speakers had no writing system, we know nothing directly about Proto-Germanic. But by the first century after Christ, when the Germanic tribes touched the fringes of the Roman empire, we begin to get historical information about them. The divergent change which was ultimately to produce the contrasting Germanic languages of today had begun to appear in the dialects of this period. About this time, too, Germanic people in northern Italy, far from their north European homeland, came in contact with alphabets and devised the earliest Germanic writing system, the **futhork,** or **runic alphabet.** Unfortunately for linguistic history, they used it very sparingly, mostly for ritual and magical purposes, so that only small inscriptions on stone monuments and metal weapons survive from as early as the third century after Christ. Germanic languages did not adopt writing in the usual sense until Christianity introduced them to Latin and the Roman alphabet.

The first extensive written record of a Germanic language is the translation of part of the New Testament into Gothic by Bishop Ulfilas in the middle of the fourth century. By this date, the original Proto-Germanic had divided into three sub-families, each itself in the process of differentiating into distinct languages and dialects. Gothic belonged to the East Germanic family, now extinct. A North Germanic group, derived from a parent Old Norse, now includes the Scandinavian languages. The rest of the Germanic languages—notably English, Dutch, and German—belong to the West Germanic sub-family. The various branches of

Germanic are shown in their family relationships in the chart on page 75.

At the time that Ulfilas was carrying out the notably Christian task of translating the Bible into his native East Germanic tongue, the speakers of the language which was to be English were living beyond the farthest reach of the Roman dominion in what is now Denmark and northern Germany. They were rugged seafaring folk, pagan in their religion, and had no political organization larger than the large tribe or small kingdom. For some reason—most likely because they were themselves being pushed from the east—they were restless and unstable. The green island of Britain across the North Sea, the farthest outpost of Roman conquest and settlement, attracted them. Their ships had been there, and some of their warriors had fought there. Finally, some time in the latter half of the fifth century, they began to go there in large numbers to stay. The first major event in the outer history of the English language was under way.

The Anglo-Saxon invasion of Britain was one phase of the barbarian invasions that brought about the downfall of the Roman empire. Julius Caesar had scouted the island in 55 and 54 B.C., but his rather ambitious efforts at military conquest were frustrated by the fierce resistance of the inhabitants and by a rebellion in recently conquered Gaul, which drew Caesar back to the continent. It was not until a century later, in A.D. 43, that Britain was successfully annexed to Rome by the Emperor Claudius.

The inhabitants of Great Britain at the time the Romans took it over were of various Celtic strains, who had themselves invaded and conquered the island at an earlier date. During the four centuries that separated the Roman conquest from the coming of the Anglo-Saxons, the Celtic Britons adopted Roman civilization and eventually Christianity. Even today, towns like Bath and St. Albans preserve extensive Roman ruins, and the many English towns whose names end in -chester, -cester, and -caster remind us of the ubiquitous posts or camps (Latin castra) of the legionaries. When the legions were withdrawn to meet invaders nearer home, the untrained British were at first no match for the rugged Germanic invaders.

These invaders traditionally are assigned to three groups. The

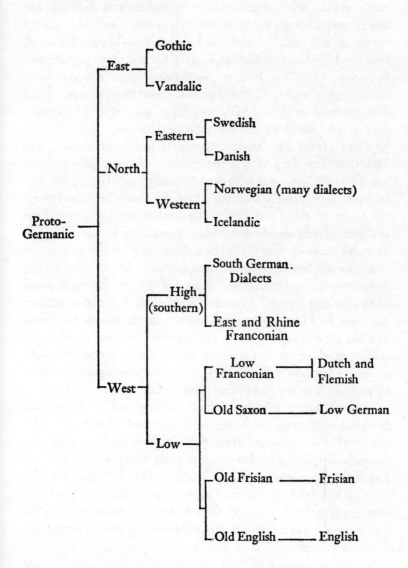

Angles, whose European home was probably modern Denmark—both the peninsula of Jutland and the islands to the east—eventually settled what is now northern and central England and southeastern Scotland. Their name was early extended to the whole of the island except the fringe areas—Wales, Cornwall, and the Highlands of Scotland—held by the surviving Britons, Scots, and Picts. The land was soon being called *Englalond* and its language *Englisc*. The Saxons, who came from Schleswig and Holstein in what is now West Germany, took over the southern part of the island except the extreme southeast. The counties of Essex (from East Saxon), Sussex (from South Saxon), and Middlesex, and the southwestern region of Wessex carry on their name. Finally the Jutes, who may originally have come from Jutland but more recently were inhabiting the North Sea coast around the mouth of the Rhine, settled the southeastern county of Kent and parts of the central southern coast, including the Isle of Wight. Probably some of their Frisian neighbors came with them.

As the shiploads of warlike invaders continued to pour in, the British resisted as well as they could, but they missed the support of the Roman legions. At that, the conquest was not a swift or easy one. Not for two hundred years were the British, the Scots, and the Picts really subdued. For a period of some years in the middle of the sixth century, the British almost turned the tide, under the leadership of a shadowy general whom legend was later to magnify into the great King Arthur. But ultimately the Celtic peoples withdrew into the mountainous regions of Wales and Scotland and across the water to Ireland and to Brittany. And the Anglo-Saxons turned from fighting them to fighting among themselves—petty kingdom against petty kingdom. Every now and then a powerful man like Penda or Offa of Mercia would succeed in establishing himself as dominant ruler over the other regional kings. But England did not begin to become a unified nation until it was faced with another powerful outside threat, the marauding Danes.

Before the coming of the Danes, however, there was another event which was of great importance to the history of the language—the Christianizing of England. As we have seen, the Angles, Saxons, Jutes, and Frisians were pagans. Their kings claimed direct descent from Woden, the ruler of the Germanic pantheon. But they had had some contact with Christianity, both on the Continent and in Britain. Some of their rulers had married Christian princesses. When the missionaries came during the latter part of the sixth century, both from Ireland in the north and from Rome in the south, many of the rulers and their people were ready for the new religion. By the middle of the seventh century the conversion was complete, superficially at least. Pagan ideas and customs survived, as some of them do to this day, but they were often incorporated into the framework of the new religion. Sometimes even the names were preserved with a new meaning: The old pagan spring festival of *Easter* gave its name to the Christian feast of the Resurrection.

But Christianity had another important linguistic effect. It brought England into an international community whose working language was Latin. From this period begins the characteristic English habit of word-borrowing. Latin *monachus* and *monasterium, episcopus* and *presbyter* were taken over, eventually to become our modern words *monk* and *minster, bishop* and *priest.*

There had undoubtedly been at least minor dialectal differences in the speech of the various tribes even before they migrated to England. After the settlement and the establishment of regional kingdoms, dialectal differences increased. We can recognize four main dialect areas, each of which undoubtedly had local variants within it, though we do not have enough material from specific localities to know what they were (see the map on p. 78). The Anglian region, greatest in area, included two dialects: Northumbrian, covering the north of England and the Lowlands of Scotland, and Mercian, spoken in a broad band across the center of the country. In the Jutish settlements in Kent, Surrey, and the southern coast, the Kentish dialect prevailed. The rest of England south of the Thames spoke West Saxon.

Survivals of these dialect differences persist to this day in the local speech of plain folk in different parts of England. What we now think of as standard British English comes primarily from the speech of London, which was just about at the meeting point of Mercian, West Saxon, and Kentish, and preserves features of all three. But in the earlier part of the Old English period, espe-

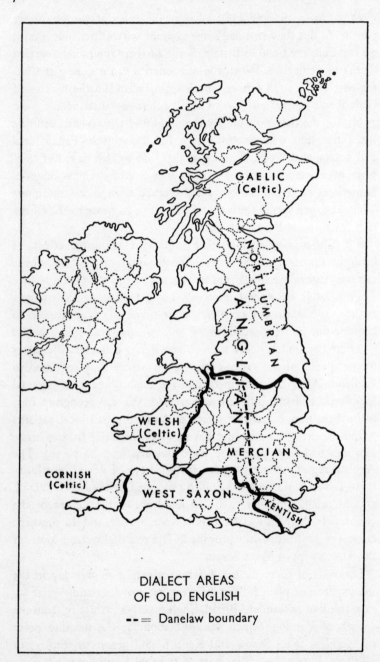

DIALECT AREAS
OF OLD ENGLISH
- - = Danelaw boundary

cially the eighth century, the dominant language of literature and culture was Northumbrian. The major cause of the political and cultural shift from Northumbria to Wessex was the Danish invasions. This accounts for the fact that virtually all surviving Old English literature is in West Saxon.

The Danish Vikings who began their devastating raids on Britain during the early ninth century were former neighbors of the Anglo-Saxons on the Continent. They, too, were pagan seafarers, whose long ships were capable of crossing the Atlantic. During the course of the ninth century they almost succeeded in conquering the whole island. But they were opposed by King Alfred, the great leader of the West Saxons, who fought them to a standstill, though he could not succeed in driving them out entirely. In the treaty of Wedmore in 878, and in a subsequent agreement in 886, Alfred concluded an arrangement with Guthrum, the principal Danish leader, by which England was divided by a line running roughly from northwest to southeast across the middle of the island (see map). This line created a southwestern English area and a northeastern Danish area called the Danelaw.

Within the Danelaw, the new inhabitants seem to have settled down fairly peaceably alongside the English. The linguistic consequences of this invasion are important and interesting. As Scandinavians, the Danes spoke various dialects of Old Norse, the ancestor of the modern Scandinavian languages. But their language was by no means so different from Old English as modern Swedish or Danish is from modern English. The Danes seem to have adopted English, but they carried over into it many words from their native Norse. Many of these words, like *sky* and *gait*, and even the pronouns, *they*, *their*, and *them*, have since become standard English. And many **isoglosses**, lines separating dialect features, still follow closely the thousand-year-old boundary of the Danelaw.

After a century of peace, there were more Viking raids, and for a time England even had a Danish king, the famous Canute. But the next event of major influence on language was the conquest of England by William of Normandy in 1066–1069. The Normans were descendants of Vikings who had settled in Normandy, just across the English channel from the south coast of

England, at about the same time that their kinfolk were settling in Britain. They, too, had given up their native speech and adopted that of their new home, a dialect of French. By the time of William, they were thoroughly French in most ways, including at least nominal adherence to Christianity. But they also preserved the rugged fighting qualities of their Viking ancestors.

William had a very tenuous claim to the English throne, but it served him as a pretext for invading and subjugating the country. The Norman Conquest was a military and political one, like that of the Romans a thousand years before, rather than a mass invasion like those of the Anglo-Saxons and the Danes. William attacked and subdued the English ruling class and largely replaced them with Norman henchmen and allies. But there was no great influx of settlers in the wake of his armies, so that although the business of government and law was conducted in Norman French, the masses of the common people continued to speak English. In effect, the language "went underground" for about a century and a half after the Conquest. There are written records from this period, but very little literature was written in English. With the conservative forces of educated and literary usage in abeyance, the language changed more rapidly than it otherwise would have. By the time it again emerged as a literary language, about the year 1200, it was so changed that we give it a new name, Middle English. The Middle English period lasted until another time of extensive change in the fifteenth century.

## 3. The Outer History: Middle English

The four centuries included in what students of the English language call the Middle English period embrace the high point and subsequent decline of the Middle Ages. Politically they mark the first stages of the development of government by Parliament and law, an art which England was to perfect in subsequent centuries. In terms of social organization, this period marks the transition from the feudalism established by William the Conqueror to the combination of bourgeois town-dwellers and free tenant farmers which formed early modern society before the Industrial Revolution. The incessant efforts of English kings of this period to hold or regain their Continental possessions, culminating in the intermittent warfare with France in the fourteenth and fifteenth centuries known as the Hundred Years' War, failed of their objective. With the loss of their holdings in France, the English kings and great barons became English in fact. The contrast is striking between Richard I, the Lion-Hearted, ruling at the end of the twelfth century, who spent less than a year of his ten years' reign on English soil, and Elizabeth I, four hundred years later, who never left England. During that four-hundred-year period, England changed from an overseas possession of Dukes of Normandy and Anjou to an independent and fiercely patriotic nation.

It is not necessary here to trace the details of this development. Our concern is with history as it affected the English language, which means that certain aspects of English medieval history take on special prominence in our eyes. Certainly one of the most important facts about English history since the Norman Conquest is that England has never again been invaded or conquered from outside by a people speaking another tongue. There have been serious threats of such invasion at intervals of roughly one hundred and fifty to two hundred years: by the French in the reign of John (1215) and again in the reign of Richard II (1385), by the Spaniards in the reign of Elizabeth I (1588), by the French again under Napoleon (1804), and by the Germans under Hitler (1941). But all of these were either repulsed or frustrated before coming to the ultimate attempt.

English thus did not have to compete with a new invading language. But during the first two centuries of the Middle English period, it was in competition with French. During the twelfth and most of the thirteenth centuries, French was the language of the king's court—which was, in effect, the government—the schools and newly founded universities (when they did not use Latin), the magnates of the realm, both ecclesiastical and lay, and undoubtedly the well-to-do tradesmen and merchants of the towns. Even those whose native speech was English, if they were to assume a position in these circles, early had to learn French and virtually abandon English as a means of communication with their peers. Only the ordinary people, in country, village, and town, used English freely and exclusively. Since they outweighed the

French speakers in numbers, if not in wealth and power, they forced bilingualism upon their superiors. The linguistic effects of that bilingualism were far-reaching.

The causes of the ultimate emergence and total victory of English in this battle of the tongues seem obvious enough. The constant warfare with France and the ultimate total loss of French-speaking lands on the one hand encouraged a growing English nationalism and, on the other, made French less important to the magnates of the realm than it had been when half of their vassals lived in France and spoke French. National pride both fosters and is fostered by possession of a national language, as the artificial and politically stimulated revival of Erse in Ireland and Hebrew in Israel has demonstrated in our day. The beginnings, however slow, of opportunities for schooling, and the founding of the universities of Oxford and Cambridge during the thirteenth century opened one channel through which humble folk could rise in the world to positions of power and responsibility in church and state. By the early fourteenth century, the universities were passing regulations forbidding their members to speak English—a sure sign that many university students found it easier to do so than to use French or Latin.[1]

The turning point seems to have been around the year 1300. By that date, literary works in English, many of them translated from French originals, were beginning to be produced in some numbers. Soon after the middle of the century the law courts (1362) and the Parliament (1363) were conducting their business in English. John Gower, writing during the last third of the century, played it safe (as he thought) by writing three long poems, one each in Latin, French, and English. But his great contemporaries Chaucer, Langland, and the unknown author of *Sir Gawain and the Green Knight* staked all on English and showed that it could be the vehicle of great poetry. During this period also the followers of the reforming theologian, John Wyclif, produced the first major Bible translation since Old English times. By the time of Chaucer's death in 1400, the language of England was unquestionably English.

1. See A. C. Baugh, *History of the English Language*, 2d ed. (New York: Appleton-Century-Crofts, 1957), pp. 165f.

But it was still several kinds of English. The dialectal divergence which we have already remarked in Old English increased during the early Middle English period, when the restraining and standardizing forces of schooling and literature in English were well-nigh nonexistent. Since most speakers of English did not often move very far beyond the villages of their birth, local dialects could develop uninhibited by the need for broad regional inter-communication. In fact, circumstances were ideal for greatly increased dialectal differentiation.

By the age of Chaucer, when English emerged as the language of literature, government, and education, five major dialect areas can be recognized, with much local variation within each of them (see map, p. 84). The Northern dialect covered about the same area as the Northumbrian dialect of Old English: England north of the Humber and the Lowlands of Scotland as far as the Firth of Forth. The Old English Mercian area was now divided into a West and an East Midland area, the latter including also East Anglia and the so-called "Home Counties" surrounding London north of the Thames. The Southern dialect covered the old West Saxon area, and Kentish carried on Kentish Old English. The major difference between the Middle English dialect pattern and that of Old English thus was the split of the Midland area. A major reason for this becomes clear when we observe that the boundary between East and West Midland runs close to the boundary of the Danelaw, which separated Danish from English territory in A.D. 900.

Even as this dialectal variation reached its peak, forces tending to counteract it were growing. The result was not so much to reduce or do away with dialectal differences—they remain strong in uneducated country speech to this day. What happened instead was that the speech of London and the London area came to be thought of as standard, or at least preferred for cultivated use. Chaucer is sometimes given credit for influencing this choice, but the truth is more likely the other way about. Chaucer was a Londoner born and bred, and he wrote the colloquial and educated speech of his native town. Modern readers, inheritors of the standard English tradition, find it much easier to read Chaucer's poetry than that of Langland, tinged with his native southern West Midland, or that of the *Gawain* poet, who, though a courtly gentle-

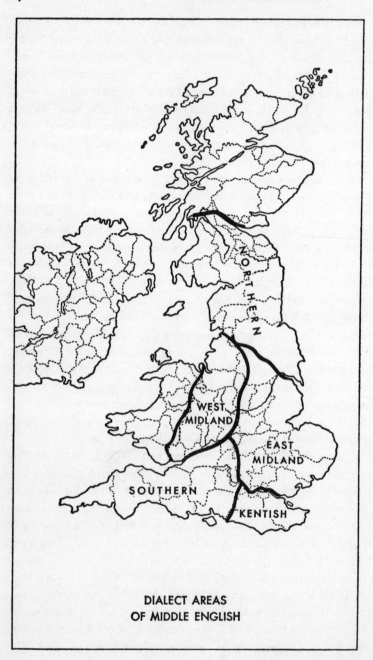

DIALECT AREAS
OF MIDDLE ENGLISH

man, used the dialect of his native region in the extreme northern part of the West Midland area. On the other hand, the York-shire-born Wyclif, who lived much of his life in Oxford and London, and Kentish John Gower both wrote in the new stand-ard dialect of London.

The reasons that London dialect became the standard are largely political and economic. As the center of government, the meeting place of Parliament, and the largest commercial center and seaport in the country, London was a center to which most people of importance found it necessary to travel and where they met others from "every shires ende of Engelond." It also hap-pened to be on the southern edge of the Midland area, and its speech was midway in many features between the North and the South. The standard dialect that evolved there was predominantly East Midland, but it incorporated some Northern features (the pronouns *they*, *their*, and *them*, for example) and some Southern ones (such as third person singular verbs in *-eth*).

Since virtually all our evidence about dialect differences and the emergence of standard is derived from written records, it is not always easy to decide how much the standardization of written materials actually reflects the adoption of standard pro-nunciation as well. The great differences between regional vari-eties of English pronunciation in our own time are concealed by the fact that we all—Scotsman and Londoner, Bostonian and Georgian alike—use the same standard writing system, with only minor regional variations. This kind of standard did not exist to so great an extent in Old English and earlier Middle English, though there is evidence to show that there were conventional standards that persisted after sound changes had taken place. There were also local standards, to which scribes more or less closely adhered, but there was still room for the individual to spell as he spoke, to some degree at least. The beginnings of the modern standard system for all writers lie in the age of Chaucer, and they were greatly strength-ened by an event of major importance in the succeeding century. In 1476 William Caxton set up his press at the sign of the "Red Pale" in Westminster and began to issue the editions of late Middle English classics which were the chief product of his press. Printing,

D

the first industry to engage in mass production, with its ability to spread identical copies of the same text over the whole country, made a standard writing system both desirable and feasible. The English writing system used since 1500 reflects little regional variation (except for the special case of Scots, as written off and on since the fifteenth century). And while the pronunciation of English has changed extensively since Caxton's time, the writing system has changed very little.

## 4. The Outer History: Modern English

The Old English period saw the establishment of English in its new island home and its development from the language of pagan warriors and pirates to the language of a civilized and Christianized society. During the Middle English period, English, temporarily eclipsed in the upper levels of society by French, reshaped itself grammatically, enriched its vocabulary by extensive borrowings from its rival, and emerged as a national language equal to the needs of one of the greatest of poets. The next chapter, the modern English period, is marked by two major developments: (1) the continued growth of the language in versatility, variety, and wealth of vocabulary as it became the vehicle for one of the richest and most extensive of literatures, and (2) the spread of the language into many new parts of the world and the rapid growth of the English-speaking community into a position of world-wide influence and importance. These two developments are not unconnected; each reinforced the other.

During the first hundred years or so of the modern period—roughly from the establishment of Caxton's press in 1476 to the publication of Spenser's *Shepherdes Calender* in 1579—English faced in Latin another formidable rival as the language of literature, learning, and education. The Latin of this period was no longer the workaday language of the medieval church and university, but a revival of the highly cultivated language of Cicero and Virgil. The humanistic Renaissance, which had been flourishing in Italy for a century or more, reached England during the latter part of the fifteenth century. Under the patronage of the young Henry VIII, an educated man and a poet in his own right,

English scholars like John Colet and Thomas More, as well as international figures like Erasmus, encouraged the study of the "three tongues"—classical Latin, ancient Greek, and Biblical Hebrew. The language in which they wrote not only their learned works but also their private letters to one another was Latin. The best literary works of the period, such as More's *Utopia* and Erasmus' *Praise of Folly*, were in Latin. Children learned Latin at school, where, once they had learned to read it, English was neglected as a subject of study.

Once again English emerged successfully from this temporary eclipse. It had continued to be the language of government, law, and commerce, so that its position in the nation had not been threatened. Influenced by the fierce patriotism of the Tudor age, the powerful advocacy of scholars like Sir Thomas Elyot and Roger Ascham (the tutor of Queen Elizabeth I) and schoolmasters like Richard Mulcaster, and the brilliant performance of great writers, English won a high place in the world of learning and literature. It is true that the ancient languages, especially Latin, enjoyed great prestige in educational and scholarly circles down to the nineteenth century. But the appearance of three of the greatest English poets, all of whose careers fall within less than a century, established English once and for all as a great literary language. Of the three, Spenser was the most self-conscious advocate of English. In his *Shepherdes Calender*, *Faerie Queene*, and other works, he consciously attempted to supply English with a body of poetry to rival that of Homer and Virgil. Shakespeare, writing for the popular theatre, had no alternative to English. Milton, the most scholarly and learned of the three, wrote in Latin and Italian almost as fluently as in English, but used English as the medium for his great epic. Since the work of these men, no one has questioned the suitability of English as a literary language. The subsequent tradition, carried down to our own time by Dryden, Pope, Johnson, Wordsworth, Tennyson, Yeats, and Eliot, has proved again and again the versatility of English as a medium for poetry.

The expansion of English as a world language has matched its literary development. Compared with Spain and Portugal, England came late to the enterprise of exploration and discovery which so greatly enlarged the known world in the sixteenth century. Not until the very end of the century did England turn from the piratical harassment of Spanish overseas possessions to the task of establishing some of her own. But during the seventeenth century, she established colonies on the eastern coast of North America so firmly that English ultimately won out as the speech of most of the middle part of the continent, between French-speaking Canada on the north and Spanish-speaking Mexico on the south. So firmly did English become entrenched in North America that it withstood peaceful "invasions" far more massive than those of the Danes or Normans had been. Dutch, Swedes, Germans, Welsh, Poles, Czechs, Russians, and many others emigrated to the New World, both before and after it became a nation. Usually they hastened to learn the language of their new home, so that a generation or so after their arrival their descendants were added to the growing number of English speakers. A few built self-centered societies that preserved the language as well as the customs of the old country. But the overwhelming majority were assimilated rapidly into the culture and speech community established by the English.

Meanwhile English was expanding elsewhere on the globe. In India the English governors, traders, and settlers were outnumbered many times by a native population speaking many languages, both Indo-European and Dravidian. English became the language of government and business, but never that of the whole people. But in Australia, New Zealand, and Canada beyond the French settlements, the situation repeated that in what became the United States: a primitive and relatively sparse native population was overwhelmed by English-speaking settlers. The result of this great expansion of English during the seventeenth to nineteenth centuries has been to create three types of English-speaking areas. In countries like the United States and Australia, English is the native speech of all but a very small minority of the population. In other areas, like India, Pakistan, and the new countries being created from the former African colonies of Britain, English is a second language for almost everybody, but it serves as the common medium of government and business among people whose native languages are mutually unintelligible. Finally, in countries like Japan, which do a great deal of business with the United States and the United Kingdom, English is a second language of commercial utility and social prestige.

One result of this spread of English around the world has been the establishment of various regional standards whose speakers view their own kind of English as being just as good as, if not better than, that of southern England. The Scots have always maintained their native standard, though in the eighteenth century in particular many Scotsmen, like James Boswell, labored hard to acquire the standard speech of southern England. But even in Boswell's day patriotic Scots, predecessors of the great Burns, were writing poetry in the dialect of the Lowlands. Nowadays only the most reactionary Briton questions the right of Scottish, American, Canadian, and Australian versions of English to be standard in their own lands. And as speakers of these varieties of English become more and more involved in the vast enterprise of teaching English as a second language throughout the world, the prejudices against them as inferior forms of English are disappearing.

Before concluding this hasty survey of the outer history of English, we should take account briefly of three other important trends during the modern English period. The first of these is the growth of mass education, and the consequent spread of literacy to virtually all native speakers of English. This has had profound effects on the language and its speakers. In the age of Chaucer, and even in that of Shakespeare, literacy was an attribute of a special minority. Today it is the illiterate person who is the exception, and the ability to read and write with some skill is a requisite for all but the most menial employment.

A second phenomenon of modern times which has had a great effect on the language is the accelerating revolution in all fields of knowledge, but especially in science and technology. This has affected all the languages of the civilized world, not just English. One consequence has been the building up of a large common vocabulary of science, in which the same words appear in many languages, only slightly adapted in spelling and pronunciation.

A third important development has been the extensive and intensive study of the language itself. The study of English grammar, both contemporary and of older periods, began in the sixteenth century, but has been greatly intensified since the middle of the eighteenth. The same is true of lexicography, the making of dictionaries, which began long before the days of Samuel Johnson but received a strong impetus from his great dictionary of 1755. Our schools today universally teach facts and theories about the English language, as well as give practice in the skills of using it. This kind of study about language has considerable influence upon people's attitudes toward language and hence has a feedback effect on the language itself.

In the course of its fifteen-hundred-year history, beginning as the language of a few thousand Germanic tribesmen in northern Europe and ending as a great world language, English has passed through many phases and vicissitudes. While its circumstances were changing, its internal nature was changing as well. Let us next take a look—again inevitably hasty and superficial—at this "inner history" of English.

## 5. The Inner History: Indo-European to Old English

The changes which constitute the inner history of a language usually affect, in varying degrees, all three major aspects of the language: vocabulary, grammar, and pronunciation. Evidence for all three kinds of change prior to the earliest surviving documents is entirely indirect: it is derived by reconstructing the original forms from which divergent known forms are most likely to have evolved. Since changes in grammar and pronunciation usually affect not individual items but groups of similar items, it is possible to make general statements that cover these systematic changes. Changes in vocabulary are more likely to be individual, though even here some generalizations can be made, especially about change of meaning.

After the dates when documents become available, the evidence for changes in grammar and vocabulary is direct. But the only direct evidence for pronunciation would be audible recordings of speech, which did not exist before the present century.

So the reconstruction of older pronunciation must be based upon the skillful interpretation of written evidence. As we know from the situation in the English of our own time, spelling is not always a very accurate guide to pronunciation. But combined with the evidence of comparative reconstruction and some direct comments on and descriptions of pronunciation by earlier writers, the written records can lead to at least a plausible reconstruction of older pronunciations.

Since the speakers of the Indo-European parent language had no writing system, all the evidence about its nature is indirect. The branch of linguistics which deals with the reconstruction of this language on the basis of comparative study of its descendants is known as **Indo-European philology**, and it is highly detailed and technical. For our purposes it is enough to observe certain broad features of hypothetically reconstructed Proto-Indo-European, and to note how some of them became modified in the course of the development of Germanic and later of Old English.

In pronunciation, Proto-Indo-European seems to have had a system of strong accents, whose position in the word shifted when various affixes appeared, and in so doing affected the sound of vowels. This same phenomenon, known by both the German name **ablaut** and the English name **gradation**, also characterizes modern English, in contrast to a language like French or Spanish, where the vowels have the same value whether accented or not. Thus in English the syllabic of the accented first syllable of *native* is a long vowel, /e:/, but that of the unaccented first syllable of *nativity* is a much shorter and weaker central vowel, /ə/. Similar vowel contrasts in Proto-Indo-European account for the still existing variation in some irregular verbs, such as *ride*, *rode*, *ridden*. Sets of words with similar root meanings, like *sit*, *sat*, *set*, *seat*, *settle*, also show survival of Indo-European ablaut variation in modern English.

Another characteristic of the Proto-Indo-European sound-system was the existence of three sets of stops, the kind of consonants made by a temporary complete interruption of the air-flow. In modern English the /k/ sounds at the beginning of *cat* and *quarter* and following the /s/ in *skit*, though phonetically quite a bit different, are to all significant purposes the same. But in Proto-Indo-European they were separate sounds, which had different subsequent development in different languages. Thus English *wheel* and Greek *kyklos* (from which English subsequently borrowed *cycle*), though now very different, go back to a common Proto-Indo-European original which began with a lip-rounded kind of /kʷ/ sound. Germanic preserved the lip-rounding, as /w/, while Greek preserved only the /k/.

The most sweeping changes in the sound-system, as one branch of Indo-European developed into Germanic and subsequently into Old English, were in the consonants. Systematic correspondences, such as the contrast of English *father* and *foot* with Latin *pater* and *pedem*, illustrate the effect of these changes, which were worked out and formulated by nineteenth-century linguists under the misleading titles of Grimm's and Verner's "Laws." They are not laws in the usual sense at all, but simply general statements describing systematic changes in pronunciation.

In its grammar, Proto-Indo-European was very much a **synthetic** language, that is, one which depended heavily on morphological markers, especially inflections, to indicate grammatical relationships and meanings. Thus its nouns seem to have had as many as eight cases to express meanings conveyed in modern English by prepositions, word order, and other devices characteristic of **analytic** languages. In the course of the development of Germanic and Old English, several of these cases (such as the **locative** and the **ablative**, both of which survived in Latin) disappeared, probably because sound changes caused their inflections to become identical with those of other cases. By Old English times only four cases—**nominative, accusative, genitive,** and **dative**—are common to all nouns, with traces of a fifth, the **instrumental,** surviving. Modern English has preserved a combined dative-accusative only in pronouns, and the genitive survives as the possessive marker, -'s.

Another feature of Proto-Indo-European nouns was **grammatical gender:** the assignment of nouns to different classes based originally on some aspect of meaning. In spite of the terms **masculine** and **feminine** applied to two of these genders, the original distinction does not seem to have been based on sex. One theory holds that it was based on a contrast between individual (masculine) and type (feminine). In any case, grammatical gender carried with it the requirement of **agreement** between noun and adjective: adjectives had distinctive forms to be used with the different genders. Anyone who has studied Latin has become familiar with agreement in gender. Both gender and associated agreement were preserved in Germanic and Old English, and have persisted in German to the present day, though modern English has discarded them.

The verb system of Proto-Indo-European seems to have included both aspect and tense, with distinctive endings also for person. There were probably five tenses: present, imperfect, perfect, aorist, and future. In Germanic and subsequent Old English the tenses were reduced to two, the present and the past, or preterit. Proto-Indo-European had four moods: indicative (for statements), imperative (for commands), subjunctive (for unreal statements), and optative (for wishes). In Germanic the last two of these fell together (as they also did in Latin); the resulting subjunctive appears in Old English and survives in a few vestiges in modern English. But the elaborate development of modal auxiliaries, which now express many of the shades of meaning formerly expressed by moods, occurred in Germanic and later in English.

Another morphological complexity of Proto-Indo-European was an inflected passive, which almost totally disappeared in Germanic and shows only vestiges in Old English. Old English developed instead the phrasal passive (*be* with the past participle) which we use in modern English. Proto-Indo-European also had a set of dual number forms, both in nouns and verbs, which survived in Greek and Gothic but disappeared in West Germanic except for a few pronoun forms. In sum, the principal grammatical development as the Germanic branch of the Indo-European family diverged from the others was a tendency to reduce the number of grammatical categories marked by distinctive inflections, and thus to carry out to a considerable degree the change from a synthetic to an analytic language which has been the continuing trend of English grammar.

Although the English vocabulary will be taken up in detail

in Chapter Four, one point ought to be considered here: the distinction between **native** and **borrowed** words. Native words are those which can be shown to have come down in the direct line of descent from the oldest known form of the language, which in the case of English is Proto-Indo-European. Borrowed words are those which have been adopted into the language from an outside source. A borrowed word, once it has been adapted to the uses of the borrowing language, usually becomes so thoroughly naturalized that only scholars know about its foreign origin. The notion sometimes put forward that somehow "native Anglo-Saxon" words are better than those borrowed from other languages has no basis in fact. Certainly *table* and *chair*, for all they were borrowed from French, are just as good words as the native *board* and *stool*.

To the historian of language, however, the distinction is important because he bases his inferences about earlier states of the language upon a knowledge of the sources of its words. Thus a pair of words like *chalk* and *calcium* is interesting because, while both are borrowed from Latin *calcem*, the appearance of the initial *ch*-sound in *chalk* shows that it was borrowed before the so-called palatalization of initial /k/ in early Old English. This instance also illustrates the fact that, when a borrowed word has become naturalized, it is subject to the same sound-changes which affect the pronunciation of native words.

In general a word is considered to be a native Indo-European word if it exists in two or more of the main Indo-European families, without evidence that it was borrowed from one into the other or others. Thus English *father*, which is paralleled not only by German *Vater*, but also by Latin *pater*, Sanskrit *pitā*, and others, is clearly a native word.

One use to which the study of the native Indo-European vocabulary has been put is to supply evidence for speculation about the culture of the original speakers of Proto-Indo-European and the location of their homeland. Thus the fact that there are native words for *cow* and *wheel* but not for *plow* has been taken as evidence that they were herdsmen, possibly nomadic, rather than tillers of the soil. The existence of common words for *winter*, *snow*, *beech* (tree), and *salmon* has been considered to prove that their home was in north-central Europe. But such evidence is risky and cannot be carried too far, since even though common words may exist in several languages, their meanings may be so different as to make it impossible to be sure of the meaning of the Indo-European original.

In general the vocabulary of Germanic and hence of early Old English was principally made up of native Indo-European words. Already the Germanic fondness for compounding as a source of new words was strongly in evidence. Early contact of the Germanic tribes with Roman traders had given rise to some borrowing of Latin words, such as *wine* and *kettle*, both of which go back to pre-Anglo-Saxon Germanic. But the great influx of foreign borrowings which was later to characterize the English vocabulary had not yet begun.

## 6. The Inner History: Old English to Middle English

The passage of Old English given with its translation on pages 96-97 is a sample of the language as it was at the end of the ninth century. It is the beginning of the Preface to Pope Gregory's book called *Pastoral Care* in an English translation made for or perhaps actually by the great King Alfred, about the year 890. After the devastating wars with the Danes had been halted by Alfred's agreements with Guthrum (see above, p. 79), the king set out to restore learning and culture in his kingdom. Part of his program was to prepare a translation of this manual for parish priests and to send a copy to each of the bishops in England. Our passage is quoted from the copy destined for Wærferth, Bishop of Worcester, which is now in the Bodleian Library at Oxford.

At first sight the passage seems so strange as not to bear any relation to English at all. But upon closer examination, especially after a few adjustments to the spelling are made, familiar words begin to appear. The character ð is used as we use *th* in modern English, and *æ* spells the sound of *a* in *cat*. Knowing this we can

## from ALFRED'S *PREFACE* TO GREGORY'S *PASTORAL CARE* †

Ælfred kyning hateð gretan Wærferð biscep his wordum
luflice & freondlice; & ðe cyðan hate ðæt me com swiðe oft
ón gemynd, hwelce wiotan iu wæron giond Angelcynn, ægðer
ge godcundra hada ge worul[d]cundra; & hu gesæliglica tida
5 ða wæron giond Angelcynn; & hu ða kyningas ðe ðone ónwald
hæfdon ðæs folces [on ðam dagum] Gode & his ærendwrecum
hersumedon; & hie ægðer ge hiora sibbe ge hiora siodo ge hiora
ónweald innanbordes gehioldon, & eac út hiora eðel gerymdon;
& hu him ða speow ægðer ge mid wige ge mid wisdome; & eac
10 ða godcundan hadas hu giorne hie wæron ægðer ge ymb lare
ge ymb liornunga, ge ymb ealle ða ðiowotdomas ðe hie Gode
[don] scoldon; & hu man utanbordes wisdom & lare hieder ón
lond sohte, & hu we hie nu sceoldon ute begietan gif we hie
habban sceoldon. Swæ clæne hio wæs oðfeallenu ón Angel-
15 cynne ðæt swiðe feawa wæron behionan Humbre ðe hiora
ðeninga cuðen understondan ón Englisc, oððe furðum án
ærendgewrit óf Lædene ón Englisc areccean; & ic wene ðæt[te]
noht monige begiondan Humbre næren. Swæ feawa hiora
wæron ðæt ic furðum anne ánlepne ne mæg geðencean besuðan
20 Temese ða ða ic to rice feng. Gode ælmihtegum sie ðonc
ðæt[te] we nu ænigne ón stal habbað lareowa. & forðon ic
ðe bebiode ðæt ðu dó swæ ic geliefe ðæt ðu wille, ðæt ðu
ðe ðissa woruldðinga to ðæm geæmetige swæ ðu oftost mæge,
ðæt ðu ðone wisdom ðe ðe God sealde ðær ðær ðu hiene
25 befæstan mæge, befæste.

---

recognize *ðæt* as *that*. Other words that look much like their
modern descendants are *wordum* (*word*, with dative plural ending), *freondlice* (*friendly*, with -*e* ending to mark it as adverb),
*folces* (*folk*, with genitive singular ending), *wisdom*, and many
others. Some have passed through sound changes which have

† MS Hatton 20, Bodleian Library, ed. H. Sweet, EETS, O.S. 45, 1871.

King Alfred bids greet bishop Wærferth with his words
lovingly and friendlily; and I let thee know that it very often
came to [my] mind what wise men formerly were throughout
England, either of the sacred orders or the secular; and how
happy times then were throughout England; and how the
kings that then had rule of the folk in those days obeyed God
and his ministers; and they maintained their peace, their moral-
ity, and their control within the country and also enlarged
their domain outside; and how they then prospered both with
war and with wisdom; and also the sacred orders how eager
they were both with teaching and with learning and concerning all the services that they ought to do for God; and how
people from outside [the country] sought wisdom and teaching here in this land, and how we now would have to get them
from outside if we were to have them. So complete was its falling off in England that there were very few this side of Humber
who could understand their liturgies in English, or translate
a letter from Latin into English; and I believe that there were
not many beyond Humber. So few of them there were that I
cannot think of a single one south of Thames when I came to
the throne. To God Almighty be thanks that we now have any
teachers in the place. And therefore I bid thee that thou do as
I believe thou will, separate thyself from these worldly matters as often as thou canst, that thou apply the wisdom that
God gave thee wherever thou mayest.

---

been reflected in altered spellings; thus the combination *æg* became in Middle English a diphthong *æy*, which is illustrated
in *mæge* (modern *may*) and *ægðer* (modern *either*). Actually
more than half the words in this passage are still in use, though
altered in shape, pronunciation, and sometimes in meaning.
As an illustration of some of the grammatical features which

Old English inherited from Indo-European but which have since passed out of the language, consider the clause *hu ða kyningas ðe ðone ónwald hæfdon ðæs folces on ðam dagum Gode & his ærendwrecum hersumedon*, which we may represent word for word as "how the kings that the rule had the folk's on those days God and his ministers ['errand-workers'] obeyed." The word order is clearly not that of modern English, and in the modern English rendering is ambiguous. But the Old English is not ambiguous, because the grammatical function of virtually every word is marked by inflectional endings. Even the function word that serves the purposes of both definite article and demonstrative takes on different forms—*ða, ðone, ðæs, ðam*—in agreement with the noun it modifies. *ða kyningas* could be either nominative (hence subject) or accusative (hence direct object), but since the verb *hæfdon* is plural and *ðone ónwald* is accusative singular, we know that the passage means "the kings that had the rule." The noun phrase *ðæs folces* is separated from *ónwald*, to which it is closely related, by the verb, but since it is doubly marked as a genitive, we know that this phrase is to be read "rule of the people." Following the preposition *on* we have the dative *ðam dagum* for "those days"; if it were subject or direct object, it would be *ða dagas. Gode & his ærendwrecum* are the nearest nouns preceding the verb *hersumedon* ("obeyed," plural), which would mark them as its subject in modern English, but because they are marked as datives by the ending *-e* (singular) and *-um* (plural) respectively, we know that they are objects (*hersumian* is one of a group of verbs whose direct objects are in the dative rather than the usual accusative). When all these markers are taken into account, there is only one thing the passage could mean: "how the kings who had the rule over the people in those days obeyed God and his ministers."

Preservation of Germanic grammatical gender is illustrated in this passage by pronoun reference. Thus in line 14 the pronoun *hio* is feminine and thus refers all the way back to the feminine noun *liornunga* in line 11. In line 24, the pronoun *hiene* is masculine singular accusative and refers back to the masculine noun *wisdom* earlier in the sentence. In modern English, which has switched from grammatical to semantic gender, we would use *it* to refer to both *learning* and *wisdom*, unless we were personifying these abstractions as feminine goddesses.

Even in this short passage there is much more to be observed. But enough has been said to illustrate the major grammatical difference between Old and Modern English—the dependence on inflectional markers rather than word order to indicate grammatical relationships. The contrast in pronunciation could only be brought out clearly by reading the passage aloud, though the spelling is often a signal that the sound was quite different. All three of these aspects—grammar, pronunciation, and spelling—underwent gradual change during the two centuries following Alfred, and more rapid and sweeping change during the two centuries following the Norman Conquest. Let us next look at a passage of Middle English from about the year 1200 to see what some of those changes were.

The brief passage printed with its translation on pages 100-01 is from the opening chapter of *Ancrene Riwle*, or *Rule for Anchoresses*, which was written sometime between 1175 and 1200, probably in the southwest of England. Our selection is taken from the manuscript known as Cotton Nero A.xiv (after its seventeenth-century owner and his shelf-mark), now in the British Museum. The manuscript was copied as much as fifty years after the book was written, and therefore may include some scribal changes. But it is a good sample of English of the early part of the thirteenth century. It shows some features of the dialect of its region, inherited from the West Saxon of Alfred but not continuing in standard English, which as we have seen derives from the dialect of London.

A few points about the spelling will reduce the unfamiliar look of the text considerably. In addition to the ð, which we encountered in our selection from Alfred, there are two unfamiliar letters. The first of these, ȝ (called "yogh"), is here used where modern English uses an initial *y*, as in the pronoun *ȝe* (the old nominative form of *you*). Later this letter was also used after vowels to spell the velar spirant (like German *ch*), which even later came to be spelled *gh*. But in this manuscript the Old English spelling of this sound with *h* still persists, as in *mihte* (*might*) and *þuruh* (*through*). The runic letter "thorn," þ, which was also from the *ANCRENE RIWLE* †

Nu aski ʒe hwat riwle ʒe ancren schullen holden. ʒe schullen
allesweis mid alle mihte & mid alle strencðe wel witen þe inre,
& te vttre vor hire sake. þe inre is euere iliche, þe vttre is
misliche. vor eurich schal holden þe vttre, efter þet ðe licome
5 mei best mid hire serui ðe inre. nu þeonne, is hit so þet alle
ancren muwen wel holden one riwle? *quantum ad puritatem
cordis circa quam uersatur tota religio.* þet is, alle muwen &
owen holden one riwle, onont purte of heorte, þet is cleane,
schir inwit, wið vte wite of sunne þet ne beo þuruh schrift
10 ibet. ðis makeð ðe leafdi riwle, ðe riwleð & rihteð & smeðeð
ðe heorte, & tet inwit of sunne. vor nout ne makeð hire woc,
bute sunne one. Rihten hire & smeðen hire is of euch religiun,
& of efrich ordre þe god & alðe strengðe. þeos riwle is imaked
nout of monnes fundleas, auh is of godes hestes. for þi heo is
15 euer on, & schal beon wið vte monglunge & wið vte chaungunge, & all owen hire in on euer to holden.

---

used in Old English (though not, as it happens, in our selection
from Alfred), is here used interchangeably with ð where we use
the digraph *th*. The usage of *v* and *u* differs from modern practice: instead of *v* being restricted to the consonant and *u* to the
vowel, both are used for both consonant and vowel, the *v* being
used at the beginnings of words and the *u* elsewhere. Thus in
*vttre*, *v* is the vowel, but in *vor* it is the consonant; and in *eurich*,
*u* is the consonant but in *schullen* it is the vowel. This practice
prevailed into the seventeenth century. We might also note that
the aspirated *w*-sound is spelled *hw* as in Old English, rather than
*wh* as in modern English.

In vocabulary, this passage is interesting because it shows the
beginning of the influx of French words which was to become

† MS Cotton Nero A.xiv, f. 1 verso, ed. M. Day, EETS, O.S., 225, 1952.

Now you ask what rule you anchoresses shall hold. You shall always with all [your] might and with all [your] strength well keep the inner [rule] and the outer for her [*i.e.*, its] sake. The inner rule is ever alike; the outer is different, for every [one] shall hold the outer according as the body may best with it serve the inner. Now then, is it so that all anchoresses may well hold one rule? "with regard to purity of heart, about which all religion is concerned"—that is, all may and ought to hold one rule concerning purity of heart, that is clean, pure conscience, without reproach of sin that be not bettered through shrift. This the lady's rule brings about, which rules and corrects and smoothes the heart and the conscience of sin. For naught makes it crooked but sin only. To correct it and smooth it is of each religion and of every order the good and strength of all. This rule is made not by man's invention, but is of God's commandment. Therefore it is ever one and shall be without mingling and without changing and all ought as one ever to hold it.

---

a veritable flood as the thirteenth and fourteenth centuries progressed. There are six words of French origin in our brief passage: *riwle, serui, purte, religiun, ordre,* and *chaungunge* (modern *rule, serve, purity, religion, order,* and *changing*). According to the Oxford Dictionary, four of these—*riwle, purte, ordre,* and *chaungunge*—make their first appearance in written English in this text. The others first appeared not long before. The word *ancre* itself (of which *ancrene* is a genitive plural) first appeared as a borrowing from Latin in Old English, but it had very little use before this very widely circulated book made it popular.

Except for these seven words, the vocabulary of this passage is all native. It is of interest to note some of the words which were later to be replaced by borrowings from French and hence to become obsolete or archaic:

| witen : obey | schrift : confession |
| schire : pure | fundleas : invention |
| inwit : conscience | hestes : commandments |
| wite : fault | |

Other native words have been supplanted by words themselves
native, as *licome* by *body* and *woc* by *crooked*. Even though
the Norman occupation was more than a century old, the re-
making of the English vocabulary which was one of its consequences had barely begun when the author of the *Ancrene Riwle*
wrote.

In grammar, however, we can see many changes in the direction of modern English, particularly in word order. A word-for-
word "translation" does not produce the ambiguities which resulted from a similar treatment of the Alfred passage, though in
a few places the order is not that of today's English. Thus in the
first sentence the inversion of verb and subject after the initial
adverb (*Nu aski ʒe . . .*) is no longer current, and the moving
of the past participle of a passive verb to the end of the clause in
*þat ne beo þuruh schrift ibet*, though possible in today's English,
is less common. On the other hand, verb phrases with modal
auxiliaries, as in *schullen holden, muwen wel holden*, are in the
modern order, rather than the inverted order of Alfred's *habban
sceoldon* ("should have"). And since the characteristic case inflections of Old English have virtually disappeared, such grammatical functions as direct object are indicated by position, as
in *alle ancren muwen holden one riwle*. But some relationships
which must today be indicated wholly by order could still be
indicated by inflections: the singular-plural distinction is still
preserved in the auxiliaries *mei–muwen* and *schal–schullen*, where
modern English has lost the distinctive plural forms.

One feature of Old English grammar that is still evident in this
text is grammatical gender, as it is revealed by pronoun reference.
The word *riwle* derives from Old French *reule*, which in turn
comes from the Latin feminine noun *regula*. The author of the
*Ancrene Riwle* regularly uses the feminine pronoun (nominative *heo*, genitive, dative, and accusative *hire*) to refer to *riwle*.
But by this time the definite article has ceased to be inflected

for gender and case, and has become the unchanging *þe* (or in one case *te*) as in modern English.

Once again little can be said about pronunciation without an oral rendering. But some features of the spelling indicate changes that had occurred in pronunciation during the three centuries since Alfred. The making of new diphthongs is illustrated by *mei*, which we saw as *mæge* in the Alfred passage. Spellings like *heorte* and *beo*, though seeming to preserve Old English diphthongs, are probably here intended to represent a rounded front vowel (as in German *hören* or French *boeuf*), which was a normal West Midland feature. The change of Old English *ā* to an *ō* sound (probably like the *au* of modern English *taut*) is shown in *holden* (Anglian Old English *haldan*) and *on*, *one* (Old English *ān*). The change of initial *f* to *v* in *vor* (*for*) and the *u*-spelling in *sunne* (*sin*), representing a rounded front vowel as in German *dünn*, are characteristic of the southwest Midland dialect of this manuscript.

In sum, then, we may conclude that this sample of early Middle English, though it still looks very much like a foreign language at first glance, is perceptibly less so than the English of Alfred, especially in its grammar. The next two centuries, during which English re-established itself as a language of literature and culture worthy of the art of a Chaucer, were to see sweeping changes in vocabulary, and in the century following Chaucer the pronunciation was rather radically altered while the spelling remained relatively fixed. It is in this late Middle English and early modern English period that the language becomes recognizably the language we know in the literature since Shakespeare.

## 7. *The Inner History: Middle English to Modern English*

The passage on page 104 is from William Caxton's preface to his second edition of Chaucer's *Canterbury Tales*, printed in 1484. It is obvious at once that the language has changed greatly, especially in vocabulary, during the three centuries since the *Ancrene Riwle* was written. Although the spelling is different from modern practice in minor ways and there are a few gram-

## from CAXTON'S *PREFACE* TO CHAUCER'S *CANTERBURY TALES*, 2nd Ed., 1484 †

Grete thankes laude and honour / ought to be gyuen vnto the clerkes / poetes / and historiographs that haue wreton many noble bokes of wysedom of the lyues / passions / & myracles of holy sayntes of hystoryes / of noble and famous Actes / and faittes / And of the cronycles sith the begynnyng of the creacion of the world / vnto thys present tyme / by whyche we ben dayly enformed / and haue knowleche of many thynges / of whom we shold not haue knowen / yf they had not left to vs theyr monumentis wreton / Emong whom and inespecial to fore alle other we ought to gyue a synguler laude vnto that noble & grete philosopher Gefferey chaucer the whiche for his ornate wrytyng in our tongue may wel haue the name of a laureate poete / For to fore that he by hys labour enbelysshyd / ornated / and made faire our englisshe / in thys Royame was had rude speche & Incongrue / as yet it appiereth by olde bookes / whyche at thys day ought not to haue place ne be compared among ne to hys beauteuous volumes / and aournate writynges / of whom he made many bokes and treatyces of many a noble historye as wel in metre as in ryme and prose / and them so craftyly made / that he comprehended hys maters in short / quyck and hye sentences / eschewyng prolyxyte / castyng away the chaf of superfluyte / and shewyng the pyked grayn of sentence / vtteryd by crafty and sugred eloquence / of whom emonge all other of hys bokes / I purpose temprynte by the grace of god the book of the tales of cauntyrburye / in whiche I fynde many a noble hystorye / of euery astate and degre / Fyrst rehercyng the condicions / and tharraye of eche of them as properly as possyble is to be sayd / And after theyr tales whyche ben of noblesse / wysedom / gentylesse / Myrthe / and also of veray holynesse and vertue / wherin he fynysshyth thys sayd booke / whyche book I haue dylygently ouersen and duly examyned to thende that it be made acordyng vnto his owen makyng /

---

† Sig. a ij recto. Ed. W. J. B. Crotch, EETS, O.S. 176, 1928, p. 90.

matical differences, this is recognizably modern English. The
modern reader needs no translation.

Although, as Caxton remarks in another preface, the language
has changed considerably from that of Chaucer, Caxton's spelling is essentially the same as that of Chaucer's day. It is true that
the alphabet has been revised by dropping ð, þ, and ȝ in favor of
the rather more clumsy modern use of *th* and *gh*. But Caxton uses
the same vowel characters as Chaucer, although his pronunciation, especially of long vowels, was probably quite different. For
example, Chaucer pronounced *name* as *na:m* or *na:mə*, while
Caxton, although using the same spelling, probably pronounced
the word to rhyme with modern *ham*. Further change since Caxton's time has produced the modern pronunciation /ne:m/ with
the long vowel as in *may*. This freezing of English spelling according to the conventions of the early fifteenth century in spite of subsequent changes of pronunciation is one of the principal causes of
the difficulties and inconsistencies of modern English spelling.

But Caxton's spelling is still not as rigorously standardized as
that of today. He is free to spell *book* alternatively with or without a final -*e*, and the plural appears once as *bokes* and once as
*bookes*. The latter point raises the question as to whether the
plural ending still had syllabic value for Caxton, or whether it
had been reduced to /s/ or /z/ except after sibilants, as in present-
day English. Spellings like *clerkes, actes, thynges*, and *monumentis*
seem to indicate a distinct syllable, but *passions, maters*, and
*condicions* argue for a non-syllabic ending. It is probable that
his usage was about the same as ours, and that the -*es* and -*is*
spellings are conventional survivals from a time when the ending
was pronounced as a separate syllable.

Caxton's grammar shows further development in the direction
of modern English, though in some places his word order is not
ours. Where he has *monumentis wreton*, we would have *written
monuments*. It is still possible for him to invert verb and subject
in a statement beginning with an adverbial modifier, as in *in
thys Royame was had rude speche*. In modern English if we wish
to put the subject after the verb, we supply an **expletive** or
temporary subject, *it* or *there*, in the normal subject position:
"**in this realm there was rude and incongruous speech.**" **Note**

that we only use the passive of *have* in some special idioms, like the traditional country newspaper expression, "a good time was had by all." In other respects Caxton's verb phrases have characteristically modern structure, as in *ought to be gyuen, shold not haue knowen*. But he still uses the *-th* form of the third person singular, which was to be largely supplanted during the next century by the *-s* form, derived from Northern dialect.

One or two other grammatical points are worthy of notice. As in Chaucer's English, Caxton commonly uses *that* with subordinating conjunctions: compare the conjunction *to fore that* ("before") with the preposition *to fore*. He uses *the whyche* as a relative pronoun referring to a personal noun and *whom* referring to an impersonal one (*writynges*). Forms like *thende, tharraye*, and *temprynte* indicate elision of the unstressed vowels of *the* and *to*, which is no longer characteristic of standard English. He uses the *th-* forms of the third plural pronoun, which were borrowed from Old Norse into the Northern dialect, in all three cases (*they, theyr, them*), in contrast to the practice of Chaucer, who uses the native English forms in *h-* in the possessive and objective cases. In general Caxton's grammar, though unmistakably of an older day, presents no problems to the modern reader.

But it is in vocabulary that Caxton's English shows the greatest change from that of the *Ancrene Riwle*. The great enrichment of the English vocabulary by borrowings from French, which took place during the period from 1250 to 1400, is very apparent in this passage. If we exclude function words, more than half the words are of French origin. Of sixty-one French words in the passage, only eleven were in the language when the *Ancrene Riwle* was written. Nine more appeared in the thirteenth century, thirty-eight during the fourteenth, and three in the fifteenth. Thus, exclusive of the function words, almost all of which are native, more than a third of the vocabulary of this passage came into the language during the two centuries before Caxton wrote. It is no wonder that he considered pre-Chaucerian English "rude and Incongrue."

The importance of this addition to the vocabulary is emphasized by the fact that almost all of the French borrowings in this passage are still in use, though sometimes with altered meanings.

A few, such as *historiograph*, *royame*, *incongrue*, and *gentylesse*, have yielded to the closely related forms *historiographer*, *realm*, *incongruous*, and *gentility*. But the rest are still with us. Nor are they all literary or high-flown words like *superfluity* and *embellish*. Many have become essential items in the workaday vocabulary, where they have replaced or supplemented Old English words of similar meaning. Such are *poet*, *saint*, *famous*, *act*, *present*, *labour*, *rude*, *appear*, *place*, *very*, *virtue*, *finish*, *duly*, and *examine*. Our vocabulary would indeed be impoverished without words of this sort. Often the retention of the Old English word alongside the French import has given us pairs of near-synonyms with delicate differences of meaning, as in

|          |          |
|----------|----------|
| deed : act   | work : labour   |
| stead : place | seem : appear  |
| end : finish  |               |

Caxton, who, to judge by his prefaces, thought and worried quite a bit about the state of English in his day, was aware of this great change in its vocabulary. In the preface to one of his translations from French, he describes his effort to strike a mean between the "rude" old words of the older English and the "curious" new vocabulary borrowed from French. It is interesting to note that he describes the French words as "the comyn termes, that be dayli vsed."

One more three-hundred-year leap forward brings us to the language of the later eighteenth century. The passage on page 108 is from Boswell's *Life of Johnson*, first published in 1791. Even though Boswell was a Scotsman, he had mastered standard English, and this passage may be considered a fair sample of the more formal literary English of the period.

It is apparent at once that the spelling is completely standardized and is almost exactly that of our own day. The only exception in this passage is the *-ck* ending of *characteristick*. Punctuation has changed somewhat since Boswell's time, mostly in the direction of fewer and less strong marks. We would not use the colons in lines 9 and 18, but most likely a comma in the first case and no mark at all in the second. A good many of Boswell's from BOSWELL'S *LIFE OF JOHNSON* †

That superiority over his fellows, which he maintained with
so much dignity in his march through life, was not assumed from
vanity and ostentation, but was the natural and constant effect
of those extraordinary powers of mind, of which he could not
but be conscious by comparison; the intellectual difference, which
in other cases of comparison of characters is often a matter of
undecided contest, being as clear in his case as the superiority
of stature in some men above others. Johnson did not strut or
stand on tip-toe: He only did not stoop. From his earliest years,
his superiority was perceived and acknowledged. . . . His school-
fellow, Mr. Hector, has obligingly furnished me with many par-
ticulars of his boyish days: and assured me that he never knew
him corrected at school, but for talking and diverting other boys
from their business. He seemed to learn by intuition; for though
indolence and procrastination were inherent in his constitution,
whenever he made an exertion he did more than any one else. In
short, he is a memorable instance of what has been often observed, that the boy is the man in miniature: and that the distinguishing characteristicks of each individual are the same,
through the whole course of life. His favourites used to receive
very liberal assistance from him; and such was the submission
and deference with which he was treated, such the desire to ob-
tain his regard, that three of the boys, of whom Mr. Hector was
sometimes one, used to come in the morning as his humble at-
tendants, and carry him to school.

---

commas would be omitted in modern practice. Apart from these
points, however, the conventions of the writing system are modern and standardized.

Boswell's grammar, also, is little different from ours. The use
of the empty auxiliary *do* in the modern way, which was worked
out in the eighteenth century, is illustrated in the negative verb

† Ed. G. B. Hill and L. F. Powell, 1934, p. 47.

phrases *did not strut* and *did not stoop*. Not illustrated in this passage but occurring elsewhere in the work is the verb phrase marked for aspect (e.g., "When he and I were travelling"), which, though going back in its origins to Old English, became much more frequent in the seventeenth and eighteenth centuries. The catenative verbs, characteristic of modern English, are illustrated by *seemed to learn* and *used to come*.

Some of Boswell's turns of phrase, though perfectly in accord with modern English grammar, have an old-fashioned ring. Thus "he never knew him corrected at school, but for talking" would nowadays be something like "he never knew him to be corrected at school except for talking," and we might render "three of the boys, of whom Mr. Hector was sometimes one" as "three of the boys, sometimes including Mr. Hector." But these differences are more stylistic than grammatical. Perhaps the principal difference in grammar between Boswell's English and ours is the relative scarcity of the noun-adjunct construction. There is no example of it in this passage, and (excluding a few compounds) there are only three—*gunpowder plot, Christmas exercise*, and *college vacation*—in a ten-page passage of which this is a part. Again the noun-adjunct construction was perfectly grammatical in Boswell's day, so we must attribute its increased frequency in present-day English to a stylistic rather than a grammatical change.

Boswell's vocabulary reflects the increase in the number of words of Latin and sometimes Greek origin which was a result of the Renaissance revival of the classical languages. This passage contains twelve words which entered the language after Caxton's preface, our last sample. These words, with the dates of their earliest citation in the Oxford Dictionary, are *superiority* (1526), *obligingly* (1654), *intuition* (1497), *indolence* (1603), *procrastination* (before 1548), *inherent* (1578), *exertion* (1677), *miniature* (1586), *distinguish* (1561), *characteristic* (1664), *favourite* (1583), and *deference* (1647). In addition, five words— *character, particular, constitution, individual*, and *attendant*— though they were in the language in 1484, are here used in meanings or functions which they acquired later. It is interesting to note that in this passage Boswell does not use a single word which had been in the language less than a hundred years. This is evidence of the fact that the influx of classical borrowings was a phenomenon of the period roughly from 1550 to 1675. On the whole the eighteenth century was a period of stabilization of the vocabulary—a good time for the development of lexicography, which was crowned by the publication of Johnson's great dictionary in 1755.

As we look back over the nine hundred years separating Boswell's biography from Alfred's preface, we can see that, while the English language maintained its identity unbroken throughout this long period, it underwent changes which, though gradual, were so great as to be revolutionary. In grammar, it changed from a largely synthetic language, depending principally on inflectional markers to indicate syntactic relations, to an analytic one, depending principally on word order and function words. Its pronunciation went through two periods of radical change, which would make a speaker of Old English, if one should miraculously appear, totally unable to understand the language of Boswell's or our own day. During the first half of this period, the spelling system was adjusted from time to time to reflect the changes in pronunciation. But it became virtually fixed at a point representing the pronunciation of approximately the year 1400, so that modern spelling cannot be learned by ear. Finally, its vocabulary underwent two periods of extensive borrowing, from French in the thirteenth and fourteenth centuries and from Latin in the sixteenth and seventeenth. And even as Boswell wrote, the third period of extensive vocabulary change, resulting from the vast scientific, intellectual, and technological revolutions of the nineteenth and twentieth centuries, was beginning.

# For Further Reading

Baugh, Albert C., *A History of the English Language*. London: Routledge & Kegan Paul, Ltd., 1951.

Brook, G. L., *A History of the English Language*. London: André Deutsch, 1958 (paper, New York: W. W. Norton & Company, Inc., 1964).

Clark, John W., *Early English*. London: André Deutsch, 1957 (paper, New York: W. W. Norton & Company, Inc., 1964).

Jespersen, Otto, *Growth and Structure of the English Language*. Oxford: Basil Blackwood, Ltd., 1956.

Pyles, Thomas, *The Origins and Development of the English Language*. New York: Harcourt, Brace & World, Inc., 1964 [an accompanying exercise book, *Problems in the Origins and Development of the English Language*, by Pyles and John Algeo (same publisher, 1966), has a great many useful and stimulating exercises and problems].

Robertson, Stuart, *The Development of Modern English*. 2d ed., rev. by Frederic G. Cassidy. Englewood Cliffs, N.J.: Prentice-Hall, 1954.

Wyld, Henry C. l, *A Short History of English*. London: John Murray, 1914. (The principal emphasis in this older book is on phronology.)

## Four

# THE VOCABULARY
# OF ENGLISH

### 1. Words and Meanings

The major purpose of language is to communicate meaning. All languages accomplish this purpose by combining meaningful units, or words, into meaningful arrangements, or grammatical constructions. The total meaning of a sentence thus has two parts: the meanings of the words of which it consists and the meanings of the constructions in which the words are combined. In normal language these two aspects of meaning are closely interwoven. But it is possible to separate them artificially, or to eliminate one so that only the other remains. We did this at the beginning of Chapter Two, where the words making up a meaningful sentence were re-shuffled in order to break up the grammatical organization of the sentence. The result was a mere list of words, each of which suggested an area of meaning but contributed nothing to the total meaning of the list. In fact, the list had no total meaning.

Conversely, we can preserve the grammatical meaning of a sentence but fill its constructions with nonsense syllables rather than meaningful words, as in

The snark was a boojum.
He snaffed the frumious bandersnatch with his vorpal snickersnee.

Because of the grammatical structure of these sentences, indicated not only by the word order but also by markers like the function words *the*, *a*, *with*, *his*, the inflectional suffix *-ed*, and the derivational suffix *-ous*, they suggest considerable meaning. But only when meaningful words are inserted does normal communication take place:

The animal was a skunk.
He shot the furious elephant with his powerful rifle.

The system of grammatical constructions available for use in a given language is its **grammar.** The collection of meaningful words available for use in the grammatical constructions of a language is its **vocabulary** or, to use the more specific linguistic term, its **lexicon.** In this chapter we shall be surveying the lexicon of English with two things in mind: the sources from which words enter the lexicon, and the ways in which their meanings interact. But first we must know what a "meaningful word" is. This in turn involves us in two problems: what is a **word**? and how does it have **meaning**?

## 2. What Is a Word?

At first sight it may seem superfluous to embark on a definition of **word.** After all, everybody knows what a word is, or thinks he does. This is true for the informal purposes of ordinary conversation. But when this rough and ready notion has to be made precise—as, for instance when one is writing a telegram or when an author is being paid "by the word" for a magazine article—some problems arise. Is *don't* one word or two? If *going to* is two words, does it remain two when pronounced *gonna*, as it frequently is even by educated speakers? What about *instead* and *inside*? *set-up* and *upstart*? *hotbed* and *blackboard*? *brother-in-law* and *great-grandmother*? *drug store* and *court martial*? Cases like these make it clear that our ordinary notion about what a word is, which is based partly on meaning and partly on the way we write, is rather fuzzy. It would be well to sharpen it a bit.

Let us begin with a large class of linguistic forms which can be called **lexical units.** Under this term we include any freely movable segment of language whose meaning cannot be deduced from a knowledge of its parts and the way they are put together. Take *court martial.* Although we can recognize two familiar parts in this segment of English—*court*, meaning "a place where law cases are tried, or a king rules, or a game like basketball or tennis is played," and *martial*, meaning "warlike, pertaining to war"—we are still very far from deducing that when combined in this order these familiar items together mean a "formal military tribunal or a case tried before such a tribunal."

Similarly, *bláckboàrd* must be counted as a single lexical item, since there is no way to tell that these items in this arrangement (note that the pattern of stress is part of the arrangement) mean "a smooth, flat surface of slate or other material, supported in a vertical position to be written upon with chalk." On the other hand, *blàck boárd* is not a single lexical unit, since anyone who knows *black* and *board* and the normal adjective-noun modification pattern can deduce that it means "board colored black." (Some *bláckboàrds* are green, but all *blàck boárds* are black!) By the same criterion, *black market* ("illegal sales or other transactions involving either restricted kinds of merchandise or prices other than those fixed by law"), even though it has the normal modification pattern including stress, must be considered a single lexical unit, in contrast to *meat market* or *flower market*, whose meanings are readily deducible.

The class of lexical units clearly includes a wide variety of things, ranging from word-sized units like *tree* and *kangaroo* to rather complicated phrases like *the man in the street* (meaning "the average citizen"). Even whole sentences like *Don't count your chickens before they are hatched* ("don't be overly optimistic about the outcome of an uncertain venture"), insofar as they consist of a fixed arrangement of unchangeable parts having an accepted meaning different from that deducible from the parts and their arrangement, must be classed as single lexical units.

The smallest meaningful units of language—those which cannot be subdivided into smaller meaningful units—are called **morphemes**. In Chapter Two this term was used to describe inflectional suffixes like *-ed* and *-ing*. But the term has a wider application. It refers to any segment of language which has meaning and which cannot be divided into smaller units all of which also have meaning. *Hat* is a single morpheme; and so is *kangaroo*. Neither of them can be shown to be made of smaller parts that also have meaning. On the other hand, *hats* and *rooster* are both made up of two morphemes: *hat* + *s* and *roost* + *er*.

In combinations like *rooster, greenness, lucky, widen,* and *strongly,* all of which are made up of two morphemes, one morpheme carries the principal part of the meaning of the whole. This is called the **base** (or sometimes the **root**). The bases in the examples are *roost, green, luck, wide,* and *strong.* These particular bases are capable of standing by themselves and of entering rather freely into grammatical combinations. For this reason they are called **free bases.** Other bases cannot stand alone or enter freely into grammatical constructions but must always appear in close affiliation with other morphemes. These are called **bound bases.**

We can recognize a common base *turb* in such words as *disturb*, *perturb*, and *turbulent*; it never stands by itself as the *green* of *greenness* does, so it is a bound base.

The third kind of morphemes are those like *-ness*, *-en*, and *dis-*, which are not bases, since they do not carry the principal meaning of the combinations into which they enter. These are called **affixes** (p. 34). They are always bound, either to a base or to a combination containing a base. It is important to distinglish, as we did in our discussion of grammar, between **derivational** and **inflectional affixes.** Derivational affixes, it will be remembered, usually affect the grammatical category and the total meaning of the words in which they appear. Inflectional affixes (all of which are suffixes in English) are markers of grammatical functions but do not change the part of speech or basic meaning of the words to which they are attached. In fact, we usually consider two forms which differ only in their inflectional affixes as mere variants of the same word, rather than as separate words: *love, loves, loved,* and *loving* are **inflectional variants** (more technically **allologs**) of one word, *love*; but *lover, lovable,* and *lovely*, which have different derivational suffixes, are different words, having different meanings and belonging to different parts of speech.

All lexical units in English are made up of combinations of these various types of morphemes. A few examples of each may help keep them in mind:

Bases
    Free: *green, monkey, kangaroo, macaroni*
    Bound: *turb, cred, tele, philo*
Derivational Affixes
    Prefixes: *re-, dis-, un-, retro-*
    Suffixes: *-en, -ly, -able, -ity*
Inflectional Suffixes
    *-s, -ed, -en, -ing*

On the basis of this morphemic structure, it is convenient to divide lexical units into three groups, which we can call **simple words, compound words,** and **idioms.** Any lexical unit can be assigned to any of these three groups. Furthermore, any grammatical utterance larger than a single lexical unit is composed of constructions of which lexical units are the constituents. The sum total of lexical units makes up the lexicon of the language. Let us take a brief look at each of the three classes.

1. **Simple Words** are the lexical units which contain only one base. The simplest consist of nothing but a single free base with possible inflectional variants. Any free base, therefore, can be a simple word.

Still simple words, but somewhat more complex in their structure, are those consisting of a base—free or bound—and one or more derivational affixes. Since derivational affixes, especially suffixes, can pile up to the number of four or five without becoming too unwieldy, some simple words of this type are quite long. But since they contain only one base, they still are simple words. Examples of words of this sort with free bases are *unkind, friendly, enliven, likelihood,* and *unsuitability*. Examples with bound bases are *propel, credible, disturbance, spectator, stabilization,* and *inseparability*.

2. **Compound Words** are lexical units that have more than one base, with or without derivational affixes, and a pattern of arrangement which is not a normal syntactic construction. The difference may lie in the way the bases or simple words which are the parts of the compound are stressed. In *blackboard*, the stronger stress is on the first element, *black*, while in a normal construction consisting of adjective and noun the stronger stress is on the noun head, as in *black board*. Therefore *bláckboàrd* is a compound word while *blàck boárd* is a construction of two simple words. Like *bláckboàrd* are *bluebird, sunlamp,* and *drug store* (note that some compound words are written as if they were constructions).

The arrangement of the constituents of a compound word may differ from the normal syntactic patterns in order also. Both *court martial* and *downfall* illustrate this, since adjectives like *martial* normally precede their noun heads, while adverbs like *down* follow the verbs they modify. Other examples are *housekeep, by-pass, up-bringing*. Many compound words bring together simple words which cannot be the constituents of a normal syntactic construction in any order or with any stress pattern: *baby-sit, vacuum clean, overcoat, runway*. Finally, some compounds bring together two or more bases at least one of which is bound. This pattern also contrasts with normal syntactic constructions, since elements which enter into syntactic constructions are usually free forms. Examples of two-base compounds with one bound and one free base are *telegraph, multiply, huckleberry, andiron, cheeseburger, iconoclast*. Examples with two bound bases are *isotherm, microcosm,* and *homeopath*. Many of both types—as indeed of all kinds of compounds—may add further complications to their structure by taking on derivational affixes, as in *multiplication, iconoclastic,* and *isothermal.*

3. **Idioms.** Lexical units which consist of two or more simple or compound words put together in a normal syntactic pattern are **idioms.** What makes them lexical units (rather than ordinary constructions) is the fact that they must be learned—and hence defined in dictionaries—as wholes. Knowing the meanings of the words and the meaning of the grammatical construction in which they occur does not make it possible to figure out the meaning of the whole idiom. Otherwise they are similar in grammatical arrangement to normal syntactic constructions. *First base* as used in baseball is an idiom because it has a special and restricted meaning. But in a sentence like *Stop at the first base you come to,* the combination *first base* is an ordinary modification, whose meaning is clear to anyone who knows the meaning of *first* and *base* and the meaning of the modification construction

A large and important class of idioms in English are the verb-adverb combinations often called **two-part** and **separable verbs.** These consist of a verb, usually monosyllabic, and an adverb from the group that also function as prepositions (*up, out, over,* etc.). English has many of these, and we rely on them heavily, especially in informal writing and speech. One group of them are called **separable verbs** because they are subject to a transformation which inserts the direct object between the verb and adverb. This transformation is optional if the object is a noun or nominal phrase but obligatory if the object is a pronoun.

a. The police *broke up* the riot.
   The police *broke* the riot *up.*
   The police *broke* it *up.*
b. The bride *put off* the wedding.
   The bride *put* the wedding *off.*
   She *put* it *off.*

The lexical unity of these separable verbs is indicated by the fact that it is usually possible to find a single word—usually of Latin or French derivation—that is closely equivalent in meaning:

The police *suppressed* the riot.
The bride *postponed* the wedding.

There are many other kinds of idioms, ranging from short phrases like *home run* and *at sea* (meaning "confused, bewildered") to longer constructions like *dog in the manger, center of gravity,* and *pay attention to.* They make up a larger part of our vocabulary than we are normally aware of, at least until we try to translate "idiomatic English" into another language. Then we find that expressions which are perfectly familiar to us as native speakers simply cannot be translated as ordinary constructions can. Instead we must treat them as indivisible lexical units, whose meanings must be expressed in some other way than by direct translation—sometimes, in fact, by finding an idiom of equivalent meaning in the language into which we are translating. English *go out,* for example, cannot normally be represented by *aller dehors* in French; instead, one verb, *sortir,* is used.

## 3. How Do Words Mean?

The world of objects, ideas, events, relationships, and emotions in which we live out our lives is, in William James's phrase, "one great blooming, buzzing confusion."[1] Only very limited parts of it divide up neatly into separate and distinct units which can be given separate and distinct names. Yet in order to talk about it in language, which is by its very nature divided into separate and distinct units, we must somehow impose an order on the chaos of experience. This imposed order is a prerequisite of **meaning**. And since it is to a large extent imposed and arbitrary rather than inherent in the nature of things, it differs from one language community to another. This is why it is often very difficult to translate from one language to another, especially if the two languages are used by people with very different ways of looking at the world.

A simple illustration of contrasting ways of organizing the outside world involves words used to describe color. The color spectrum actually shows continuous change from one end to the other. But if we are to have separate words to apply to different parts of the spectrum, it must be divided arbitrarily into sections, to each of which a word can be assigned. Speakers of English, Thai, and Japanese, given an unmarked spectrum and asked to indicate

1. William James, *Principles of Psychology*, New York: Henry Holt, 1890, vol. I, p. 488.

how they would separate and name the colors, responded as follows[2]:

| ENGLISH | violet | blue | green | | yellow | orange | red | |
|---|---|---|---|---|---|---|---|---|
| THAI | muaŋ | namŋan | faa | khyaw | lyaŋ | seed | deeŋ | |
| JAPANESE | murasaki | ao | | midori | kiiro | mikaniro | momoiro | aka |

These divisions correspond closely in some respects; one could confidently translate English *violet* by Thai *muaŋ* and Japanese *murasaki*. But observe that Japanese *ao* covers the area which in Thai is divided into two parts, called *namŋan* and *faa*. Furthermore, though English *blue* and *green* cover the same total area as Japanese *ao* and *midori*, the line of division between the members of each pair is in a different place, so that all three of the following equivalences are possible:

blue = *ao* (Thai *namŋan*)
green = *ao* (Thai *faa*)
green = *midori* (Thai *khyaw*)

Neither English *green* nor Japanese *ao* can be automatically translated into either of the other languages.

When we learn our native language, then, we also learn a way of dividing up the whole field of things to be talked about into separate chunks of meaning. Since this segmenting is a very complicated and abstract process, which everyone must do for himself on the basis of his own experience of life and language, it is inevitable that no two people do it in exactly the same way. Even in a relatively concrete area like color, speakers of the same language may disagree. A shade which one person calls *yellow* another may call *orange*. Obviously in more abstract areas, the differences may be greater. Where do we draw the line between *love* and *affection*? between *contempt* and *scorn*? between *difficult* and *impossible*?

A moment's thought about this situation leads inevitably to a conclusion of paramount importance: *words do not have meanings; people have meanings for words.* This apparently innocent and

2. This experiment was conducted by a student of Professor J. C. Catford at the University of Texas in the summer of 1960.

obvious statement goes counter to many naive notions about language and has far-reaching consequences for the study of vocabulary and meaning.

1. **Individual and Local Differences.** One obvious result of the fact that words do not *have* meanings as people *have* heads is that different people may have different meanings for the same word and different words for the same meaning. These differences may be individual or they may be associated with a particular group, class, or region. Individual differences come from differing individual experiences. They often lie in the area of **connotation**, that is, the body of emotional associations which a person has with a word. The total meaning of such a word as *brother* for any given person will depend on such matters as whether or not he had a brother or brothers, and if he did what his relations with his brothers were like. From this point of view it can be said that no two persons—except, perhaps, identical twins—have the same meanings for any word. That's why reactions to poetry, which often depends rather heavily on connotation, differ greatly from one reader to another.

But individuals, and especially social, regional, and occupational groups, may also differ in the **denotations,** or core meanings, which they have for words. Take such a simple word as *keeper*. On the basis of the morphemes of which it consists, we would expect its meaning to be something like "one who or that which keeps." But this doesn't get us very far. To a person associated with zoos, *keeper* means "one of those responsible for the care of captive animals." To a mechanic or carpenter, *keeper* may mean "a device which holds something in position," such as the striking plate of a lock, or a second nut screwed on top of the first one to prevent it from coming unscrewed. To a convict, a *keeper* is primarily an official whose duty is to prevent his escape. To a fisherman, a *keeper* is a fish that is large enough to be legally kept. In the country a *keeper* is one who is responsible for protecting game from poachers. One could cite many other specific meanings which people have for the word *keeper*.

Conversely, people from different geographical regions or different social classes may use different words to express the same meaning. In the northern part of the eastern United States a certain kind of receptacle is called a *pail*; from northern Pennsylvania south the same object is called a *bucket*. The man responsible for an

American railroad train is the *conductor;* in England the same function is performed by a *guard.* A drink made by beating up milk, flavoring, and ice cream is variously known as a *frappe,* a *cabinet,* a *frost,* or a *milk shake* in various parts of the United States. *Words do not have meanings; people have meanings for words.*

2. **Multiple Meanings.** A further consequence of this relation between people, words, and meanings is that even a single individual may have many meanings for a single word. Take the simple word *dog,* for instance. A rather casual sample of the meanings I can associate with this word includes:

1. a four-footed animal, "man's best friend"
2. a mean or despicable person
3. a horse that never wins races
4. a small lever or other mechanism that prevents a ratchet-wheel from turning backward
5. a homely or unattractive girl
6. to fasten down, as the hatch of a ship
7. to follow closely and persistently
8. to loaf, malinger, or slow down on the job

In addition I recognize it as an element in idioms like *putting on the dog,* "dressing up"; *gay dog,* "young man who is given to flirting with girls" (old-fashioned); *dog in the manger,* "selfish person who prevents others from using or enjoying something, even though it is of no use to himself"; *dog days,* "hot, sultry days of late summer." These examples are certainly enough to illustrate that to speak of *dog* as "having a meaning" is a bad misrepresentation of the situation. This word—like virtually all common words—serves many purposes in my vocabulary. I have many meanings for it.

3. **Influence of Context.** How does a hearer or listener know which of the many different meanings associated with a word is intended when the word is used? The answer usually given is "from the context." The reader selects from the set of meanings which he has for a word the one which fits best with the meanings of the other words with which it appears. This is a rather circular process, because the words in the context may also require a choice of meaning on the basis of *their* context, which includes the original word. Thus a constant process of selection and adjustment goes on in the mind of the reader or listener, as he works out the meaning

of a phrase or sentence. It is easy to select, for example, the most appropriate meaning for *dog* in each of the following sentences.

1. Our *dog* likes to chase cars.
2. Because a *dog* was broken, the brakes failed to hold.
3. The horse I bet on turned out to be a real *dog*.

The words in the environment of a given word and the grammatical structures of which it is a part make up its **linguistic context**. Sometimes we must know the **non-linguistic context** as well in order to select the appropriate meaning. The word *blow* in an utterance such as *that was a hard blow* means quite different things in the context of a boxing match or a sailing race. Many words when removed from a context can hardly be said to mean anything at all. They are meaningful only in a context which gives some clues as to which of their many possibilities is being used at the time.

**4. Change of Meaning.** Since meanings do not belong to words themselves, but are associated with words by the people who use them, it is obvious that meanings may change. More exactly stated, what happens is that people come to associate new meanings with old words, or they give up some of the existing associations. As a kind of short-cut way of talking, we say that the words *acquire* or *lose* meanings. It is all right to use this terminology if we constantly remind ourselves that it is not the words but the people that "have" the meanings, and hence the people who acquire and lose them.

From one point of view it is inconvenient that we do this with words. The word *nice*, for example, during the 700 or so years it has been in English, has been used at one time or another to mean the following: foolish, wanton, strange, lazy, coy, modest, fastidious, refined, precise, subtle, slender, critical, attentive, minutely accurate, dainty, appetizing, agreeable. Some of these are almost directly opposed to one another: "wanton" and "modest," for instance, or "foolish" and "minutely accurate." Nowadays we usually use the word to mean "pleasant or agreeable in a general way" (*nice weather*, a *nice time* at the party), or "well-bred, of superior background and moral character" (a *nice girl*), or "pleasant, affable" (a *nice chap*). But when we read older literature, we become aware that these meanings won't fit the context. When Hotspur, in Shakespeare's *Henry IV, Part I*, speaks of "the *nice* hazard of one doubtful hour," *nice* seems to mean "risky, precarious," by extension from the meaning "slender, delicate." On the other hand, in *Henry V* when the king, courting the French princess who has refused him a kiss, says "*nice* customs curtsy to great kings," *nice* means "cautious, punctilious." To supply the modern meaning would in either case cause misunderstanding.

But from another point of view, this practice of shifting the meanings associated with words is a convenient one, since it reduces the number of new words that have to be found to represent new meanings. *Coach*, for instance, has kept pace with the times by being successively applied to a horse-drawn vehicle, a kind of railway carriage, and now a kind of airplane or class of airplane travel. These changes have come about naturally and obviously; nobody finds it odd to say that he wants a *coach* ticket on a jet plane to San Francisco.

In the next section of this chapter we will take up the causes and manners of changes of meaning. For the present we simply observe once again that changes of meaning are a further consequence of the fact that meanings are not inherent in words, but are associated with words by the people who use them. When the speakers of a language consciously or unconsciously change their habits of association, the "meanings of the words" inevitably change.

5. **Problems of the Lexicographer.** Most people consider the task of the **lexicographer**—the writer of dictionaries—to be a fairly straightforward one. All he has to do is to find out "the correct meaning" of a word and list it in his dictionary. Then the person who wants to know what a word means simply looks it up, as he would look for a logarithm in a table or a telephone number in a directory. But a little consideration of the points we have been discussing will reveal how naive this attitude is. No amount of looking at the words themselves can tell the lexicographer what their "correct meanings" are. It is the people who use the words that have the meanings, and it is to them that the lexicographer must go. But because he cannot very well do so directly, he goes to the evidence of how people have used the words in published writings. He relies mainly on the relationship between the word and its context. Since it is the context that helps the reader choose among the possible meanings with which a word can be associated, the lexicographer assumes that if enough contexts can be collected for a given word, they will narrow down its possible meanings sufficiently for him to be able to describe these meanings ("define the word") by means of other, presumably familiar, words.

Suppose, for example, the lexicographer finds the following contexts for the word *pandle*:

1. He bought a new pandle for his house.
2. Don't rely on a wooden pandle; buy one of our stainless steel ones.
3. The pandle carried the name "Jones" below the number 326.
4. A lighted pandle stood beside the walk, just under the front gate.
5. It was a monotonous neighborhood of identical houses, differing only in the numbers on the pandles.

Even on the strength of these few examples, the lexicographer would feel moderately sure that he cound define a *pandle* as "a kind of sign, of wood or metal, placed near the entrance to a house and showing the street number and (sometimes) the name of the inhabitant." If he finds other contexts, such as "the ship was wrecked because of a broken pandle," he will be forced to the realization that some people have a quite different meaning for the word. He will then attempt to find enough contexts to lead him to a clear notion of this second meaning, and so on. But in no case will he consider that he is seeking the "real" or "correct" meaning of the word. He is instead attempting to find out, as accurately and objectively as he can, what people have in mind when they put this word into a context. We all do this when we hear a new word. But the lexicographer does it purposely, systematically, and on a large scale. He does our collecting and comparing for us, and tabulates the results in his dictionary, so that we can take a short cut and look the strange word up, instead of waiting until we encounter it enough times to deduce its meaning. But the authority of the dictionary ultimately rests on the practices of those who used the word in the first place, and on the care with which the lexicographer has collected and analyzed his examples.

## 4. How and Why Meanings Change

The ways in which people change the meanings they associate with words make up one of the most interesting and amusing facets of language study. The great Oxford English Dictionary, which records in detail the meanings of all English words over the last thousand years, is a fascinating book to browse in. Most of the examples used in this chapter are based on its definitions and collections of illustrative examples.

The various ways in which meanings change are of three main types: *extension*, *limitation*, and *transfer*.

1. **Extension.** In spite of the fact that new words are being added to the language all the time, people ordinarily do not make up a new word if an old one will serve. Therefore, when some new aspect of the outside world requires a new segment of meaning, an existing word often has its range of meaning extended to cover the new area. The vocabulary of railroading, for example, had to be built up quite rapidly to meet the numerous new objects, events, and occupations which this new mode of transport created. It is true that some new words, like *locomotive*, were created. But, for the most part, words which had already been in the language for a long time were simply extended to cover those new segments of meaning which most closely resembled their existing ones. For the way along which the trains traveled, the old word *road* was used. The iron *rails* took their name from similarly shaped wooden parts of a fence. Collectively they made up the *track*, whose older meaning was "a path." A place where the track divided was called a *switch*, from an old word meaning originally a long slender twig or branch. A string of cars pulled by a locomotive naturally took on the name *train* (at first *train of carriages*), extended from the meaning "a body of persons, animals or vehicles travelling together in order, esp. in a long line or procession" (OED) which it had had since the fifteenth century. Various words previously used to describe vehicles drawn by horses had their meanings extended to cover the new vehicles: *carriage, coach, car* (in America), *van* (in Britain). Places where the trains stopped came to be called *stations*, by extension of the meaning of a word already used to describe places on a highway where stage-coaches stopped to change horses or passengers. A piece of paper entitling one to *ride* on the train was called a *ticket*, a word which had been used in this general sense in the theatre since the seventeenth century. Devices used to indicate the state of the track ahead were called *signals*, a word which already had the general meaning of "indicator," or *semaphores*, a word made up of Greek roots ("sign-carrier") during the Napoleonic wars to describe a device for sending messages.

And so it went. All these extensions of the meanings of existing words did not lead to confusion or ambiguity, since it was always apparent from context when one was using the words in their new application. When one wanted to *take* a *train*, he went to the *station*, paid the *fare* and got a *ticket*, went out on the *platform*, *boarded* a *carriage*, and *rode* along the *track* to his destination. All of the italicized words were in the language long before the railroad was thought of, and the areas of meaning they were used to cover were sufficiently similar to the new meanings of railroading so that it seemed the most natural thing in the world to extend them. Since the extensions seemed so logical and obvious, people recognized the new meanings without being told. The whole process of adjusting the language would have been much more difficult if new words had had to be coined for all these new meanings.

2. **Limitation** is the opposite of extension: the number of segments of meaning a word is used to refer to becomes reduced for one reason or another. Some of the meanings of the word may cease to be needed because the objects or events in the outside world to which they refer go out of use. But since language is not restricted to dealing with the actual and the contemporary, meanings may persist after the things they refer to have disappeared. Words or meanings of this sort, often used to give historic or old-fashioned flavor, are called **archaic**. But some meanings cease to be useful even in a historical context, and thus become **obsolete**. A great part of the elaborate vocabulary of alchemy, for instance, consisted of special meanings for words like *tincture*, *elixir*, *multiplying*, *embibing*, *cementing*, and *mortify*, all of which are used in Chaucer's alchemical *Canon's Yeoman's Tale*. Except in the very special context of an account for modern readers of what the theory and practice of alchemy was like, these meanings are obsolete, and these words have thus become more limited, at least in this respect, though they may have simultaneously expanded their meanings in some other area.

More often, the meanings of a word become limited because of the extension of the meanings of other words into parts of its territory, or because of the appearance of new words which take over some of its segments of meaning. The Old English word *steorfan*, which has come down to us as *starve*, once had the general meaning "to die." But during the late Old English period, the Norse word *deyja*, our present *die*, was borrowed into English, and gradually took over the general meaning. *Starve* continued to be used, but in the special sense "die of hunger" (sometimes, especially in the north, "die of cold"). Then, since its association with the idea of hunger became very much strengthened by this limitation, its meaning was extended to cover "suffer from hunger, be inadequately fed" without necessarily implying fatal consequences. So now one can come in from a day of outdoor exercise and say "When will dinner be ready? I'm *starving*!" without requiring emergency measures to prevent immediate death.

Another familiar example of limitation is the word *meat*, and its relationship to the words *victual(s)*, *food*, and *flesh*. All of these words except *victuals* are native words, going back at least to Old English times and probably to Germanic. Originally *meat* (OE *mete*) meant "food in general ... usually, solid food in contradistinction to drink" (OED). *Food* (OE *fóda*) was nearly synonymous with *meat*, if anything rather broader in meaning: "what is taken into the system to maintain life," which is still its overriding meaning. It could apply then, as now, to the sustenance of plants as well as animals and men. *Flesh* had the general meaning then, as now, of "the soft substance, *esp*. the muscular parts, of an animal body." It could also mean "the muscular tissue, or the tissues generally, of animals regarded as an article of food." This last meaning the Oxford Dictionary calls "somewhat archaic" and the final quotation it gives illustrating this meaning is from Dr. Johnson in 1772. Meanwhile *meat* had acquired the specialized meaning "the flesh of animals used for food," which appeared as early as the fourteenth century but came into full use in the fifteenth. It was still used in the more general sense, but with diminishing frequency, until the early nineteenth century. In the early fourteenth century, also, the French word *vitaille*, later respelled *victual* and often used in the plural, *victuals*, was borrowed. Its meaning was almost synonymous with both *food* and *meat*. By the early nineteenth century, it had ceased to be used very much except in regional and lower-class dialect. The whole situation can be diagrammed somewhat like this:

| Meaning | Word | OE | 1300 | 1500 | 1800 | Present-day English |
|---------|------|----|----|----|----|----|
| "food in general" | food | ——————————————————————————— | | | | |
| | meat | ————————————————————————— ... | | | | |
| | victuals | ———————————————— . . . . . . . . . . | | | | |
| "animal flesh as food" | flesh | —————————————————— . . . . . . . . . . | | | | |
| | meat | . . . . . . ————————————————— | | | | |

It is clear that between about 1400 and about 1800, *meat* gradually limited its meaning to "animal flesh as food," partly at least because the addition of the new *victual(s)* to the existing *food* produced three near synonyms. And as *meat* increasingly took over the specialized meaning of *flesh*, that word was thrown back to its more general meaning. Meanwhile *victuals*, perhaps having helped to limit the meaning of *meat*, itself was unable to hold out against the old and unchanging *food*, and declined from reputable use. The speaker of Present-day English is left with three fairly clear-cut and differentiated words: *food*: "what is taken for nourishment, especially solid"; *flesh*: "the muscular parts of animals"; *meat*: "flesh as food."

The ultimate in limitation occurs when all the meanings of a word become obsolete, and the word ceases to be used at all, or is used in consciously archaic contexts. When streetlights came in in the seventeenth and eighteenth centuries, it was no longer necessary to have one's way lighted at night by a torch or *link*; the occupation of *link-boy* went out and with it the word. In these days of mechanized agriculture, no one sows the seed of wheat or other grains by hand, and the sower's basket and its special name *seedlip* have both disappeared from use. Articles of dress and of food, both of which are especially susceptible to changes of fashion, are very prone to becoming obsolete and taking their names with them; no one wears *stomachers* or *doublets* any more, or eats *posset* or *galingale*. The modern reader who encounters these words in older books or in the purposedly archaic language of a historical romance must go to a historical dictionary to find their meanings.

In addition to this disappearance of the referent, competition from other words is another cause of obsolescence. *Clyster* has been replaced by *enema*, *wright* by *carpenter* (Chaucer uses both, just about synonymously), the noun *hallow* by *saint* and the verb by *sanctify*, and *aerodrome* by *airport* or *airfield*. Even function words—the relatively inconspicuous words that serve primarily to indicate grammatical relationships—may become obsolete in this way. The Old English preposition *mid*, cognate with German *mit*, gradually yielded to *with*, whose original meaning was "against"—still preserved in compounds like *withstand* and idioms like *fight with* someone. The Middle English auxiliary *gan*, which was used to indicate a kind of emphatic past tense, disappeared about the time that other auxiliaries—especially *have/had* and *do/did*—were increasing in use.

Sometimes words and meanings are kept from total extinction by being preserved in the dialects or jargons of special groups. Very few Englishmen or Americans nowadays know anything about the parts of a horse's working harness, but in some rural parts of both countries there are those who still use—and hence talk about—*hames*, *girths*, *traces*, and *whiffletrees*. The special language of sailing—nowadays used almost exclusively by yachtsmen—is full of old words like *luff*, *jibe*, *halyards*, and *belay*, and of special meanings, archaic in the general vocabulary, for words like *tack*, *point*, *lay*, *wear*, *sheet*, and *yard*. Some of these special terms enjoy a life in the general vocabulary as parts of idioms like *take a new tack*, which is used by many people who have no idea what it means in nautical speech. Idioms like this originated in a metaphor, which is a common form of **transfer**, the third way in which meanings are changed.

3. **Transfer** is the process by which a wholly new meaning becomes attached to a word as a result of some similarity, association, or other relationship of the new meaning to one of the old meanings of the word. **Metaphor** is one of the commonest modes of transfer. It depends on a similarity of some sort—in shape, in size, in function, in color, or in any of hundreds of other ways—between the established referent of a word and some new referent. When a metaphor is first used, both the user and the hearer or reader are conscious of both referents and of the similarity between them that makes the metaphor apt. If I say "At the rush hour, the hungry mouths of the underground stations swallowed thousands of homeward-bound commuters," I am using *hungry*, *mouth* and *swallow* in metaphorical senses. The reader, I trust, will not think that I believe that underground stations have mouths with which they eat commuters. When a metaphor is used frequently, people begin to take it for granted, and to accept the once metaphorical meaning of a word as an ordinary meaning. To speak of the *mouth of a river* is no longer to use a metaphor, since this expression has been used so often that "the end of a stream where it flows into another stream or body of water" is an accepted meaning of *mouth*.

These **frozen metaphors**, as they are sometimes called, are very numerous in the history of language. Not only *mouth*, but the words used for other parts of the body, such as *leg*, *arm*, *hand*, *head*, and *foot*, have in the course of time acquired many new meanings by this process. Many of the words we use to describe emotions, abstractions, and complex relationships have acquired these meanings—which may now be their principal ones—by metaphor. *Depressed* ("pushed down"), *inspire* ("breathe in"), *intact* ("not touched"), and *insist* ("stand on"), for example, go back to Latin in both their original and their metaphorical meanings. Others are native words or compounds, like *upset*, (mental) *breakdown*, *fondness* (originally "foolishness"), and *insight*.

Other kinds of transfer also originate as figures of speech, whose original intent was to clarify or make more vivid the idea being dealt with. The figure **synecdoche** (taking the part for the whole) created the meaning "assistant, employee, worker" for *hand*, and the special meaning of *nose* in the expression *counting noses*. The figure **metonymy** (naming an object or idea by naming a closely related object or idea) has given *chair* the meanings "presiding officer" and "endowed professorship," and *seat* the meanings "house, estate," as in *country seat*, and "location," as in *the seat of government*. Many of the meanings of such a versatile word as *board*—such as "governing body" and "sum paid for regular meals"—have come about by this sort of transfer.

Another kind of transfer that creates new meanings—often quite unpredictable ones—results from a shortening process, by which one of the constituents of a phrase comes to stand for the whole phrase and thus takes on the meaning of the phrase. The word *transistor*, for instance, was first coined from recognizable morphemes, on the pattern of such existing words as *resistor* and *transformer*, to describe an electronic device capable of performing the functions of a vacuum tube. Since transistors are smaller than vacuum tubes, their invention made it possible to reduce the size of electronic equipment that had formerly depended on tubes. By the normal process of adjunct modification, a radio employing transistors came to be called a *transistor radio*. Then this was shortened, in popular speech, to *transistor* by dropping the noun head, which was, as it were, taken for granted. As a result, one colloquial meaning of *transistor* now is "a compact or miniature radio receiver, operating on batteries, small enough to be carried easily in the hand." Even in the relatively short lifetime of this word, the process of transfer by phrase-shortening has created for it a new and quite unpredictable meaning.

Other examples of this kind of transfer are abundant. In England, *motor* is often used with the meaning "automobile," as a result of shortening the phrase *motor car*. More commonly this phrase has been shortened to *car*, whose primary meaning for most English speakers today is "automobile." In American railroading the term *steam engine* was first extended to apply to the steam locomotive; then the phrase was shortened to *engine*, so that the meaning "locomotive" was transferred to that word. When steam as a source of power was replaced by Diesel motors, the new locomotives were quite naturally called *Diesel engines*. Finally another shortening transferred the meaning of the whole phrase to *Diesel*.

Other examples of this type of transfer are the special meanings of *capital* (from *capital city*), *principal* (from *principal sum* or *principal teacher*), *vacuum* (from *vacuum cleaner*), and *freight* (from *freight train*).

## 5. Sources of New Words: Borrowing

We have seen that the demands for new meanings which are made by changes in the physical and cultural environment are frequently met by extension or transfer of the meanings of already existing words. But new words are often needed as well. They come from many sources, the principal ones being **borrowing, derivation, compounding, back formation, clipping, blends, acronyms, proper names, sound imitation,** and outright **coinage.** In English, borrowing has been the most important source of new words. So extensive has it been that by far the greater part of the present-day English vocabulary is made up of borrowed rather than native words. It is true that the *core* of the vocabulary—most of the function words and the words dealing with fundamental and relatively unchanging realities—is still mostly native. Since these words are of frequent occurrence, they make up a larger proportion of any sample of discourse than they do of the total vocabulary. But even such apparently basic words as the verbs *take* and *die*, the nouns *wall* and *place*, the adjectives *second* and *blue*, the pronoun *they*, and the preposition-conjunction *till* have come into English by borrowing. Few languages in history have made so much use of words from other languages to fill out their lexicons.

One reason for this extensive borrowing is the fact that the particular circumstances favoring it have existed frequently in the history of English. The chief of these is **language contact,** that is, the presence in close geographical, political, and economic proximity of communities making use of different languages.[3] An almost inevitable concomitant of language contact is a certain amount of **bilingualism**—the knowledge and use of two languages by the same speaker. Bilingualism is of various kinds, ranging from the complete and approximately equal use of two languages for both speaking and writing on all levels to the restricted use of a second language for some special purpose, such as scholarship, diplomacy, or religion. In most cases of bilingualism, both individual and cultural, one language is dominant—usually the first one learned, and the one used for most common daily purposes. Under these circumstances, the larger amount of borrowing is from the dominant language into the second language. But the bilingual speaker may use a word from his second language to fill what may be a gap in the lexicon of his dominant or native language or a gap in his own knowledge of it. The borrowed word, if it is taken up by other speakers, becomes in the first case an addition to the total semology of the native language, and in the second case a synonym for an existing word. English borrowings have been of both kinds. Words like *boomerang* and *raccoon* name things which had no English names; words like *perish* and *incline* exist beside their older synonyms *die* (itself a replacement for *starve*, as we have seen) and *lean*. Extensive borrowing of the latter sort has furnished English with a large stock of synonyms, often differentiated in usage by style. In one style of speaking we can say rather bluntly *He got a job*; in another, somewhat fancier style *He obtained a position*. It is usually, though not always, the borrowed words that mark the more elaborate style. But we should not forget that the person who *praises plain language* is using three borrowed words to do it.

As long as only bilingual speakers use a borrowed word, they retain some awareness of the fact that it is a newcomer to the language. The bilingual speaker tends to preserve the foreign quality of the loan-word, especially in pronunciation. We can see this in the use today of such French words as *esprit* and *élan*, which are seldom used except by those with some knowledge of French, and are pronounced with at least an attempt at the proper French sounds. But as soon as borrowed words get taken up by monolinguals, their sounds are adapted to the sound-system of the host lan-

3. Uriel Weinreich, in his important study *Languages in Contact* (New York: Linguistic Circle of New York, 1953) restricts the use of the term *language contact* to the alternate use of two or more languages by the same person.

guage, as in our pronunciation of less recent borrowings from French such as *medicine* and *surgeon*. Within a generation or two of its first use the fact that a word is borrowed usually is forgotten by monolingual speakers; it has become naturalized. From then on, its history of change—in pronunciation as well as meaning—will be no different from that of native words.

In fact, the regular sound changes that affect the whole vocabulary indiscriminately may so reshape borrowed words that only the trained etymologist can perceive their original source. The modern form *cheese* bears little resemblance in pronunciation or spelling to its Latin source, *caseus*. Every difference can, however, be accounted for in terms of the sound changes that have taken place over the fifteen hundred years or more since the word was first taken into Germanic as *kasi*. Another word from the same source, *casein*, shows by its form that it is of much more recent adoption in English. Since sound changes can be approximately dated, it is possible to estimate roughly the dates at which borrowed words became naturalized. Thus any words taken directly from Latin (not via French) that begin with *ch-* like *cheese*, are very early indeed—earlier than the change of Old English /k/ to /č/ before front vowels, which happened about the sixth century, soon after the Angles, Saxons, and Jutes crossed to England. A few other words belonging to this group and still used in English are *cheap*, *chalk*, *chest-* (in *chestnut*), and *chester* (as in *Winchester*). On the other hand, words like *cap* and *caster* (as in *Lancaster*) show that they were borrowed later. But the ordinary speaker of the language uses words like *choose*, *cheap*, and *chase* without any awareness of the fact that *choose* is a "native" word while the other two were borrowed from Latin and French respectively. They are all good English now.

## 6. *Sources of Borrowed Words: Latin*

Before the Angles, Saxons, and Jutes crossed to Britain—even before their speech had deviated from that of their Germanic neighbors enough to be called a separate language—words from Latin were being borrowed. It will be remembered that the Romans conquered and colonized Gaul during the first century B.C. Their conquest was so complete and their colonizing so thorough that Latin became the dominant language in Gaul, and ultimately the Celtic language of the Gauls became extinct. North of the Gauls lived the various tribes which the Romans lumped together under the name *Germani*. From the Rhine north to the North Sea and the Baltic and into southern Scandinavia was their territory, and their Germanic tongue already showed the dialectal variety which was ultimately to result in its separation into the various Germanic languages (see pp. 73, 92).

The Romans never succeeded in conquering and colonizing this territory. If they had, we might today be speakers of a Romance language, and Germanic might have gone the way of Gallic. Instead, the Romans and the Germans preserved an uneasy peace along the borders of the empire, which allowed some trade and other intercourse between periods of friction and warfare. There even were German cohorts in some of the Roman legions—men who had to learn some Latin to get along with their fellow soldiers and superiors. Thus Latin and Germanic were in contact for several centuries before the Anglo-Saxon migration to England. During these centuries, Germanic—especially the western branch of it along the Rhine and the eastern, Gothic branch—and the colloquial (or Vulgar) Latin of Roman soldiers and merchants borrowed many words from each other.

The Latin borrowings into Germanic of this period were mostly nouns, especially those naming concrete objects such as utensils, buildings, articles of clothing, and plants. As might be expected, there were military terms as well. Many of the words borrowed during this period spread through the whole Germanic area and became part of the vocabulary of all the subsequently differentiated Germanic languages. Others had more limited distribution. The majority of those that lasted long enough in English to be recorded —i.e., into the seventh century—have since become obsolete, often superseded by later reborrowings from Latin or its descendant French. But some have survived into our own day. In the list of examples below,[4] notice how sound-changes in English since the time of borrowing have reshaped the words, often to such a degree that one could scarcely guess the Latin source without special knowledge of the great changes that have taken place in English phonology since Germanic times.

4. For the examples here, as well as for most of the illustrations of borrowed words given in this chapter, I am indebted to Mary S. Serjeantson, *A History of Foreign Words in English* (London: Routledge and Kegan Paul, 1935), an admirably complete and compendious treatment of word-borrowing in English.

| Latin word and meaning | | Old English | Modern English |
|---|---|---|---|
| pondō | "weight" | pund | pound |
| moneta | "coin, money" | mynet | mint |
| discus | "disc, plate" | disc | dish |
| coquīna | "kitchen" | cycene | kitchen |
| strāta (via) | "paved road" | stræt | street |
| scriptum | "writing, decree" | scrift | shrift |
| vīnum | "wine, vine" | wīn | wine |
| cāseus | "cheese" | cese | cheese |

When the people who were to become the English invaded the island of Great Britain, they took over what had been for several centuries a province of the Roman Empire. In Britain Latin had not completely superseded the native Celtic of the conquered, as it had in Gaul, but it had become the language of the ruling class. Latin words had been borrowed into British, and many place names were Latin or Latinized Celtic in form. On the whole the invading English had little of the kind of contact with the British that produces bilinguals and extensive borrowing. Instead they killed them off or drove them into the mountainous areas of Wales and across the English Channel to Brittany. For this reason, there was no extensive borrowing into English of Latin words during the first centuries after the invasion. But many place names, including that of London itself, as well as all the -*chester* and -*caster* towns whose names recall their origin as military posts, were preserved and Anglicized. Some other Latin words—most of them now obsolete— also were borrowed at this time. The following are a few that have survived:

| Latin word and meaning | | Old English | Modern English |
|---|---|---|---|
| cista>cesta | "container" | cest | chest |
| tripedem | "tripod" | trefet | trivet |
| furca | "fork" | forca | fork |
| monachus | "monk" | munuc | monk |

The last of these examples reminds us that the Romanized Britons were Christians, since Christianity had become the official religion of the Empire. But it was more than a century before the pagan Anglo-Saxons themselves began to be Christianized. Hence the third period of Latin borrowing dates from about the year 600, when missionaries from Rome and from Ireland began to make

effective progress in converting the English. With them they
brought Latin, the official language of the Church and of the Bible.
For the next thousand years, Latin was to be the language not only
of religion and theology, but of learning and scholarship in most
other fields as well. It was also a source from which words were
borrowed to expand the English vocabulary.

The Germanic traders and soldiers and the Anglo-Saxon conquerors and settlers had drawn chiefly upon the colloquial vocabulary of everyday spoken Latin, often called Vulgar Latin by linguists because it was the Latin of the *vulgus*, or common people.
This was the tongue which through normal processes of change and
dialectal divergence ultimately became the various "Romance" (or
Roman) languages—French, Spanish, Portuguese, Italian, Ruma-
nian, and the rest. The language of the Church, on the other hand,
was an artificially preserved and bookish language. It is true that
many churchmen wrote and spoke it fluently; in that sense it was—
and still is—a living language. But it was never their native tongue;
it was always a second, learned language.

As a result, the Latin borrowings after A.D. 600 tend to be
**learned words**—words more often encountered in books and
formal educated discourse than in daily conversation. At first, a
considerable vocabulary of religion and the church had to be supplied. Some of these words, such as *abbod*(*abbot*), *ælmesse*(*alms*),
and *mæsse*(*mass*) seem indeed to have come from colloquial Latin.
But the larger number—the originals of our *creed*, *deacon*, *bishop*,
*martyr*, *disciple*, and many more—were learned words. Many of
them (including all the examples above except *creed*) had already
been borrowed into Church Latin from Greek, the original language of the New Testament. Most of the formal vocabulary of
religion and the church consisted of these newly borrowed Latin
or Latinized Greek words. Sometimes, however, native words were
used with a new meaning. Some words of this sort are still very
much alive: among them are *Easter*, *Lent*, *heaven*, *hell*, *God*, *Holy
Ghost* and *sin*. Others—such as *inwit*("conscience"), *bead*("prayer"), *hallow* ("saint"), *houseling* ("confession") and *ghostly*
("spiritual")—have been replaced by words subsequently borrowed from Latin or, after the Norman Conquest, from French.
Unlike German, which has clung much more tenaciously to its
Germanic vocabulary, English has preferred borrowed words for
new, specialized vocabularies like that of the Church, especially
from the Middle English period to our own time.

Latin continued to be the language not only of the Church but of all scholarship and learning throughout the Middle Ages and the Renaissance and well into the Modern English period. For about a thousand years, educated men kept using Latin words in their written English, and to a lesser extent in their speech. After the Norman Conquest, this tendency was strengthened by the extensive borrowings from French. Old French, the direct descendant of the spoken Latin of the later Empire, preserved many Latin words with little change either in pronunciation or in spelling. Educated Frenchmen, thoroughly familiar with Latin, were in the habit of adopting—or reviving—Latin words in their writing. For this reason it is often hard to tell whether a particular English word of Latin derivation was taken directly from Latin or came in via French. The English scholar who used a word like *possession* was usually familiar with both the French word *possession* and the Latin *possessio* (accusative *possessionem*) which was its ultimate source. It is thus inaccurate to attribute words of this sort exclusively to either language. They came to form a kind of common vocabulary of the three languages widely used by educated Englishmen.

Because of the influence of French, certain conventions arose concerning the form which Latin loan-words took in English. In general, the forms of French nouns which survived were those developed from the oblique case forms of Latin, but with loss of the inflectional endings. Thus the Latin accusative *possessionem* became French *possession*, the Latin accusative *florem* (nominative *flos*) became French *flour* (later *fleur*), Latin *auctoritatem* became *auctorité*, and so on. As a result, certain endings such as *-ity* (Latin *-itatem*), *-tion*, *-cion* (Latin *-tionem*), and *-ment* (Latin *-mentum*) passed through French to become English morphemes which could be applied to native or borrowed stems to produce new words like *jollity*, *starvation*, and *acknowledgment*. Similarly Latin adjective endings like *-osus* and *-abilis* gave rise both directly and through French to adjective-forming suffixes like *-ose* (*verbose*), *-ous* (*famous*), and *-able* (*lovable*). A verb-forming suffix *-ate* derives from the Latin past participle ending *-atus*, but now appears as part of many words that would not have had this suffix in Latin, though they may be made up of Latin elements (*substantiate*, *vaccinate*, *assassinate*, etc.).

Latin borrowings of the Renaissance were even more on the learned side than those of the Middle Ages. With the revival of interest in classical literary Latin and the cultivation of Ciceronian

# 138    THE VOCABULARY OF ENGLISH

style by the humanists of the sixteenth and seventeenth centuries, many writers succumbed to the temptation to import large numbers of Latin words into English. The naturalized word-endings established regular patterns for converting Latin words to English, which, together with the large number of Latin words already present in the language, gave the new borrowings an English look and an English sound on their first appearance. Their meanings, also, were readily deducible by an audience which was itself thoroughly familiar with Latin—though some writers, like Sir Thomas Elyot, often paired the new Latinisms with synonyms of longer standing.[5] But he also used many words like *odible* ("hateful"—which had already been used occasionally since 1412), *jurate*("one who has sworn an oath"), and *timorosity* (used previously by Caxton), fully expecting his readers to see through the Anglicised form to the Latin source. These words have not survived into modern English, but many other of the humanistic borrowings have. In one sentence of forty-seven words, Elyot uses the following Latin-based words, here given with the date of their first citation in the Oxford Dictionary: *dependeth* (1413), *contractes* (1386), *convencions* (1490), *commutations* (1509), *mutuall* (1477), *intelligence* (1390), *benevolence* (1384), *societie* (1531), *obseruinge* (1390), *malefactours* (1440), *iniuries* (1382), and *propretie* (*c.* 1300). As the dates show, many of these words had appeared in English as long as 150 years before Elyot wrote, though some are quite new and one, *societie*, makes its first appearance in written English in Elyot's book. What is remarkable is the large number of them in a single sentence, and the fact that all of them are in common use today.

By the middle of the seventeenth century the proportion of Latin borrowings and Latin-based words in the English vocabulary had attained about the level it has today. In a sense, the vocabulary of Latin had been so extensively mined that there was not a great deal left to exploit except the rarer and more unusual words. Nevertheless a diminished stream of Latinate words has continued to come

5. His book *The Gouernour* (1531) is full of phrases like "contumelyouse or reprocheable versis," "thynges of great importaunce or estimation," "subuercion and ruyne," "vaine and superfluous appetite," "society or felowship of mankinde." Speaking of the Aristotelian virtue of Magnanimity, he says, "But now I remembre me, this worde Magnanimitie, being yet straunge, as late borrowed out of the latyne, . . . I will adventure to put for Magnanimitie a worde more familiar, callynge it good courage." (Everyman's Library Edition, p. 239.) Elyot published a Latin-English dictionary in 1538.

into English down to our own time. Some of these are legal words (*alibi, deficit*), some scientific (*nebula, nucleus, cirrus*), some political (*propaganda, ultimatum*), some mechanical (*pendulum, fulcrum*), and some medical (*serum, lumbago, insomnia*). But many of them, although their first uses may have been learned, have since become part of the common working vocabulary. Such words as *complex* (adj.), *minimum, lens,* and *extra,* all of which are new in English since 1650, carry no special aura of erudition about them, in spite of the fact that they are pure Latin in origin, without even the modifications of spelling which often were given to earlier Latin borrowings.

## 7. *Sources of Borrowed Words: French*

After the Norman conquest of 1066–69, French words began to be borrowed into English in increasing numbers. Albert C. Baugh has estimated that during the four hundred years or so of the Middle English period, something like ten thousand French words were adopted into English.[6] The effect on the vocabulary of English—not only the total vocabulary, but the common stock of words by which the ordinary work of the language is carried on—has been tremendous. One indication of the pervasiveness of the French element in our vocabulary is the fact that most English speakers find it easier to acquire a reading knowledge of French than of German—even though, genetically speaking, English and German are closely related, deriving from a common ancestor not much more than 2000 years ago, while English and French are genetically related only by common descent from Proto-Indo-European.

Chronologically, the borrowing of French words divides naturally into three periods: (1) the Norman period, *c.* 1150–1250; (2) the later Middle English period, *c.* 1250–1500; and (3) the Modern English period, since 1500. Both the number and the nature of the words borrowed are different in each of these periods.

**The Norman Period.** The Normans who invaded and subjugated England in the later eleventh century were themselves descendants of Vikings who had settled in the area in northwestern France still called Normandy. Their language was a dialect of French

6. Albert C. Baugh, *A History of English Language,* 2d ed. (New York: Appleton-Century-Crofts, 1957), p. 215.

differing in some respects from the Central French of the Ile de France—the area around Paris—which is the ancestor of modern standard French. It had, for instance, an initial /w/ sound, where Central French had /gw/ later simplified to plain /g/. Words descended from Latin words beginning with *ca-* had *ca-* in Norman French but *cha-* or *chie-* in Central French. Norman French had an *ei*-diphthong from Latin *eg*, where Central French had *oi* (at first pronounced /oy/, later /wa/). As a result it is often possible to identify words which were borrowed during the period when the ruling class in England spoke the Norman variety of French (called Anglo-Norman), rather than the Central French which became popular later on. Sometimes, indeed, we have pairs of words, one from Anglo-Norman and one from Central French:

| ANGLO-NORMAN SOURCE | ENGLISH DERIVATIVE | CENTRAL FRENCH SOURCE | ENGLISH DERIVATIVE |
|---|---|---|---|
| cacher | catch | chacier | chase |
| léal | leal | loyal | loyal |
| wardein | warden | guardein | guardian |

Other pairs are *cattle : chattel, reward : regard, real : royal.*

French words did not begin to appear in written English until seventy-five to a hundred years after the Conquest. The *Poema Morale*, a sincere but rather dull moral ode written about 1150, has no French words at all. But about the same date—in the Laud manuscript of the Old English Chronicle, which breaks off in 1154—some French words make their appearance: *castel* (Norman—cp. Central French *chateau*), *prisun, tur* (*tower*), *justice, pais* (*peace*), all appear here for the first time in English, as do *countess, emperice* (*empress*), and *court*. These are exactly the kind of words which we would expect the feudal Norman society to supply to English.

The reasons for the delay in making such borrowings are soon apparent. In the first place, it took at least a generation to develop the kind of language contact, including considerable bilingualism, that facilitates extensive borrowing. Secondly, the written language is usually more conservative than speech: it is likely that many of these words were used widely in speech before they were written down. In the third place, the amount of written English surviving from this period is sparse. Not a great deal of English was written, and much of what was has not survived. So if we want probable dates of the actual first use in English of French loan-words, it is probably safe to push back by thirty to forty years the dates of the first citations given in the Oxford Dictionary, which are, of course, the dates of the earliest surviving written examples.

By the time of the writing of the *Ancrene Riwle* (1185-1200), a brief sample of which we examined in Chapter Three (pp. 100-101), many French words had become English. Much of the vocabulary of the church and religion, as well as of warfare, feudalism, hunting, law, and government, came in during the Norman period. If we had no other historical evidence of the fact, the vocabulary alone would make it apparent that the ruling classes in church, state and countryside were French-speaking. But they were a minority, and they did not attempt to impose their language on the whole populace. Instead some of them, at least, learned enough English to communicate with the English-speaking people, which encouraged the word-borrowing that is a consequence of bilingualism.

**The Later Middle English Period.** But it was during the later Middle English period, especially the fourteenth century, that the great flood of French words entered the language. By this time, the Central French of Paris and its environs had come to be preferred over the Norman and Anglo-Norman dialects. Many of the borrowed words now entered by way of literature, since French romances and other literary works had wide circulation among educated Englishmen. Poets like Chaucer and Gower read and wrote French as readily and naturally as they did English, and they and the courtly audiences for whom they wrote found it easy and natural to transfer numbers of words from one vocabulary to the other. It is not that these writers were often the first to make these borrowings—in most cases others had used the words before them. But they found the French words natural and understandable, and gave them wider circulation in their work. Mary Serjeantson has estimated that on the average about 13 per cent of the words in Chaucer's poetry are of French origin[7]—a large shift in vocabulary to have taken place within two centuries.

All sorts of words were borrowed during this period. Some continue to reflect the upper-class milieu in which French continued to be spoken: such are the extensive vocabularies of cookery, of dress, of polite accomplishments like music, hunting, dancing, and courtly love. But French contributed a great deal of the working

7. *A History of Foreign Words in English*, pp. 151-52.

vocabulary of business men and merchants, lawyers, doctors, architects, and builders—words like *contract, import, debt; felony, criminal, judge; ointment, medicine, surgeon; chamber, lodge, chapel, buttress, portal,* and *vault* indicate how much of the vocabulary of these various professions came in at this time. Finally many words of wide general use, especially verbs and adjectives, came in to supplement or replace older English words. Just a few examples, cited fom the much longer lists given by Baugh,[8] are: (verbs) *allow, arrange, change, declare, endure, furnish, increase, move, pass, quit, reply, save, travel, wait;* (adjectives) *active, brief, calm, double, easy, faint, gentle, honest, large, natural, poor, safe,* and *usual.* It is hard to imagine our language without these words and the hundreds like them which were brought in during the Middle English period. English would, of course, have met the need for new words by some other means, since it is a universal quality of languages to develop the vocabulary needed by the culture of the people who speak them. But the fact that French, which had already developed an extensive vocabulary of feudal society, was available and known to virtually all educated men made it the natural source for new words and has given a strong French cast to the modern English vocabulary.

**The Modern English Period.** Although direct political and feudal ties between England and France ceased at the end of the Middle Ages, the two nations have continued to have a close political and cultural relationship ever since. They have fought against each other, as in the wars of the eighteenth century which culminated in the Napoleonic wars of the early nineteenth century, and they have fought together against a common enemy, as in the World Wars of 1914-18 and 1939-45. In the intervals of peace, travel in France has been part of the education of every English gentleman, and knowledge of French has been a requirement in polite society. French is still the most commonly taught modern language in many parts of the English-speaking world (it runs just second to Spanish in the United States), and French literature has been and continues to be widely read, both in the original and in translation. The result has been continued borrowing of French words.

Words of more recent French origin often reveal that fact by their pronunciation. As we noted above (p. 132), borrowed words

8. *A History of the English Language*, pp. 207-09.

once they have been accepted in a language cease to be treated as foreign, and follow the same changes that native words do. French words borrowed during the Middle English period have undergone the same sound changes that have affected older English words. Thus when older English long *i*, pronounced much like modern *ee* in *meet*, changed to /əy/ and then to /ay/ during the period from about 1450 to 1700, this change affected not only native words like *find* but French borrowings like *fine*.

Another difference between older and more recent French borrowings is in stress. French has never had a marked or significant contrast between stressed and unstressed syllables. Such significance as stress may have is part of the phrase and sentence patterns, not of the individual words. English, on the other hand, uses stress as a distinctive and contrastive feature of words. Such words as *contract*, *imprint*, and *suspect* are noun or verb depending on where the stress falls. Since in most English words of two syllables, the stress is on the first syllable, the evenly stressed two-syllable words of French sound to English speakers as if they were stressed on the last syllable. Therefore when French words of this sort are borrowed into English, they are usually given final stress, as in *prestige*, *café*, *chauffeur*. This was true in Middle English as well; words like *honour*, *corage*, and *nacioun* were given final stress when they were first borrowed. But in the later Middle English period the stress was shifted forward to the first syllable. The transitional state is represented by many words in Chaucer's poetry, which have what is sometimes called **hovering stress**: they can be stressed on either syllable, to suit the rhythm or meter of the sentence. It is therefore usually true that words borrowed from French that still have the stress on the last syllable are post-medieval borrowings.

There have been pronunciation changes in French, too, since the medieval period. One that has already been alluded to is the change of the diphthong /oy/ to /wa/. Another is the change of the consonant spelled *ch* from a sound like the initial sound of *cheat* to one like the initial sound of *sheet* (from /č/ to /š/, that is). Yet another is the disappearance of *s* between a vowel and *t*, whereby Old French *feste* became modern *fête*. In this last case, English has borrowed the word twice: once as *feast* /fi:st/, preserving the Old French /s/ and showing the later English change in pronunciation of the vowel, and again as *fête*, usually pronounced /fe:t/ like *fate*, which is the nearest English can come to the French pronunciation.

In the light of these various changes, it is easy to see that words like *point, engine, native,* and *cherish* are Middle English borrowings, while words like *soirée, machine,* and *prestige* are more recent. But even some of the recent borrowings, especially if they are in fairly common use, are undergoing changes that adapt them more closely to English patterns. This is especially true in England, where such words as *garage, café,* and *croquet* are usually stressed on the first syllable, with consequent reduction or change in the pronunciation of the final syllable. British pronunciations of these words sound to Americans as though they should be spelled *garridge, caffy,* and *crokey.*

The words borrowed from French since 1500 are of great variety, reflecting the diversity of French culture and the complexity of the relationships between the two countries. Mary Serjeantson[9] gives extensive lists; a few of her examples, with their categories and dates of first citation, are the following:

**Military and naval:** *colonel* (1548), *dragoon* (a doublet of *dragon,* 1622), *reveille* (1644), *corps* (1711 in the military sense; *corpse* "body" is from 1325), *sortie* (1795), *barrage* (1859 "dam"; 1917 in sense of "bombardment").

**People:** *viceroy* (1524), *bourgeois* (1564), *coquette* (1611), *chaperon* (1720, used earlier to mean "hood"), *habitué* (1818), *chauffeur* (1899).

**Buildings and furniture:** *scene* (1540), *parterre* (1639), *attic* (1696), *salon* (1715), *chiffonier* (1806), *hangar* (1902).

**Literature, art, music:** *rondeau* (1525), *hautboy* (1575; later spelled *oboe*), *burlesque* (1656), *tableau* (1699), *connoisseur* (1714), *brochure* (1765), *carillon* (1803), *renaissance* (1840), *matinee* (1880).

**Dress, fashion, and materials:** *grogram* (1562, borrowed again as *grosgrain,* 1869), *cravat* (1656), *denim* (1695), *chenille* (1738), *corduroy* (1787), *blouse* (1840), *cretonne* (1870), *suede* (1884).

**Food and cooking:** *fricassee* (1568), *table d'hôte* (1617), *soup* (1653), *croquette* (1706), *aspic* (1789), *restaurant* (1827), *chef* (1842), *mousse* (1892).

Many more categories could be named and many more examples cited. But these should be sufficient to indicate that French continues to be an abundant source of new loan-words in English.

9. *A History of Foreign Words in English,* pp. 160-69.

## 8. Sources of Borrowed Words: Other Languages

No other languages have approached Latin and French as sources for loan-words in the English vocabulary. But during the 1500 years of its independent history, English has come into contact more or less intimately with many other languages. The result has been continuous borrowing and adaptation of foreign words and their frequent naturalization into English. It would be unusual if not impossible to open an ordinary desk dictionary at random and not find, on the facing pages, at least one word of a source other than Anglo-Saxon, Latin, or French.

1. **Celtic.** After Latin, the earliest language with which English came into contact was the Celtic spoken by the pre-Anglo-Saxon inhabitants of Great Britain. But as we noted above, the Anglo-Saxons did not establish with the British the close and more or less harmonious kind of relationship which leads to bilingualism and consequent borrowing. So except for geographical names like *Avon* and *Carlisle* and topographical terms like *down* (n. "low hill") and *tor*, few Celtic words came into English at this time. Even these seem often to have come via Latin, since the Roman occupants also took over Celtic place-names, as in Exeter (earlier *Execestre*) and *Winchester*, which combine a Celtic first element with the Latin *castra* (see above, p. 135). Sometimes the Anglo-Saxons made the same kind of hybrids with Celtic and English elements, as in *Salisbury*, *Edinburgh*, and *Lichfield*.

Except for the Irish missionaries, who helped introduce some of the Graeco-Latin vocabulary of Christianity into English (pp. 135-36 above), there was little intimate contact between the English and the Celtic-speaking inhabitants of Ireland, Wales, Cornwall, the Highlands of Scotland, and the Isle of Man. But beginning in the fourteenth century, Irish, Welsh, and Scottish words began to be borrowed in moderate numbers. Most of them still refer to characteristic aspects of the land or culture of the people from whom they were borrowed: no one has any doubt of the origin of such words as *shamrock* (1521), *leprechaun* (1604), *banshee* (1771), and *colleen* (1828) from Irish; *loch* (1375), *plaid* (1512), *cairn* (1535), *pibroch* (1719), and *sporran* (1818) from Scotch Gaelic; or *cromlech* (1603) and *eisteddfod* ("a congress of bards" 1822) from Welsh. A few of these Celtic loan-words have attained wider circulation and lost their exclusively Celtic flavor. Perhaps the best-known is *whiskey* (1715)—a shortening of Gaelic *uisge beatha*, literally "water of life" and hence a **doublet** of the Latin *aqua vitae* and French *eau de vie*. Others are *bard, clan, bog, slogan*, and *penguin* (this last possibly from Welsh *pen* "head" and *gwyn* "white").

2. **Scandinavian.** The English, themselves descendants of sea-raiders and colonizers, were harassed by Norwegian and Danish pirates and marauders during the eighth, ninth, and early eleventh centuries. These people spoke variant dialects of Old Norse, the antecedent of modern Swedish, Danish, Norwegian, and Icelandic. The Norwegians went around the north of Scotland and down the west coast of Great Britain, establishing settlements in the Orkney Islands, the northwestern part of England, and Ireland (Dublin was at one time a Norse city). The Danes went across the North Sea to the northeast part of England and southeastern Scotland. After Alfred's treaties with Guthlac (p. 79 above), the Scandinavian invaders settled in the Danelaw in peaceful relationship with the English. The result was the kind of language contact which is productive of much word-borrowing.

Since the Old Norse of the Norwegian and Danish settlers was also a Germanic language, it was quite close in vocabulary, grammar, and phonology to Old English. It was thus easy to transfer words from Norse into English. Many words, in fact, were the same in the two languages, and it is even possible that Norse speakers and English speakers could understand one another albeit with some difficulty. The Scandinavians, who were the minority, apparently soon gave up their native tongue, but they carried into their English many Norse words which English speakers also took up.

The result was a rather large infiltration of Norse words into the English of the Danelaw region. These were homely words of everyday use. Large numbers of them are used to this day as regional and local dialectal forms. What is a *brook* in southern England is a *beck* in the north, and a *shirt* is in Scottish a *sark*. The following is a short sampling of words of Old Norse origin still used locally in the north of England, as reported in the recently published first volumes of the *Survey of English Dialects*:[10]

---

10. Harold Orton and Wilfrid J. Halliday, eds., *The Six Northern Counties and the Isle of Man*, being Vol. I, parts 1 and 2 of *Survey of English Dialects* (Leeds: E. J. Arnold & Son, Ltd., for the University of Leeds, 1962).

| | | |
|---|---|---|
| *bracken* | — | coarse fern |
| *breck* | — | sheepfold or section of field |
| *garth* | — | yard |
| *gate* | — | path |
| *gimmer* | — | young ewe-lamb |
| *grain* | — | fork or branch |
| *kist* | — | chest (ultimately from Latin; see p. 135) |
| *loup* | — | jump (cognate with English *leap*) |
| *skep* | — | basket |
| *stee* | — | ladder or stile |
| *thack* | — | thatch |

Many Norse words were also taken up into the general vocabulary of English, where they supplemented or in some cases supplanted the native English words. We have already discussed the relationship of OE *steorfan* (*starve*) and ON *deyja* (*die*). Other common words of Norse origin are the verbs *take*, *call*, and *hit*, the nouns *law*, *skill*, *egg*, and *sky*, the adjectives *ugly*, *wrong*, *meek*, the preposition-conjunction *till*, and the pronoun and predeterminer *both*. The most remarkable of the Norse borrowings is the replacement of the OE third person plural pronoun *hie* by the Norse *þai*. This occurred in the North in the thirteenth century and the *th*-forms gradually worked their way south. Chaucer, writing in the late fourteenth century, used the Norse nominative form *thei* but the English possessive *here* and objective *hem*. By the time of Caxton, the forms with *th-* were standard everywhere. It is possible that the objective form usually written *'em* is a survival of the English *hem*, or it might also be a clipping of *them* similar to *'at* for *that*, as in the colloquial "Attaboy!"

Sometimes Norse words and their English cognates have persisted side by side, often with differentiation of meaning. In Old Norse, the /sk/ combination did not become /š/ as it did in English, and /k/ in the vicinity of front vowels did not change to /č/. Hence many English words with /sk/ and /k/, especially in initial position, betray their Norse origin. We have already mentioned *skill* and *sky*; others are *scowl*, *scrape*, *skin*, and *scant*. Scottish *kirk* is a doublet of English *church*; *skirt* and *shirt* are doublets in spite of the difference of meaning. Caxton comments on the difficulties of some Northern merchants in Kent; when they asked for *eggs* the landlady of their inn was at a loss until someone explained that they meant *eyren*. In this case the Northern word of Norse origin has become the standard one.

The Scandinavian languages have been negligible as a source of English words since the end of the Middle English period. Some Scottish words of Norse origin such as *gley* ("quick, clever") and *blether* ("talk nonsense") have attained some circulation as a result of being used by Robert Burns. New borrowings have been few and many of them relate to Scandinavian geography and culture. Among these are, *troll*, *rune*, *floe*, *saga*, and *ski*.

3. **Other European Languages.** The various languages of the nearby continent have contributed their share of loan-words to the English vocabulary. The numbers of words borrowed and the dates of borrowing serve as rough indices of the strength of the cultural and political ties between England and the various nations of the Continent. Italian words, for example, entered in rather large numbers during the Renaissance and the eighteenth century, when travel in Italy was popular and Italian influence was strong in architecture, painting, music, and literature. From the sixteenth century, for example, date *cupola*, *cornice*, *stucco; pastel*, *fresco; madrigal*, *fugue; stanza*, *buffoon*, *sonnet*. The vocabulary of the arts was especially enriched during the seventeenth century by words like *portico*, *balcony*, *rotunda*, *opera*, *sonata*, *serenade*, *bust*, *vista*, and *burlesque*. Large numbers of musical terms were adopted in the eighteenth century; most of these are specialized and retain an Italian or quasi-Italian pronunciation, as in *soprano*, *maestro*, *arpeggio*, and *cantabile*. Italian contributions in other areas have brought their names along with them, such as *spaghetti*, *pizza*, *umbrella*, and *vendetta*. A few words have Anglicized their pronunciation completely and attained a wider use: *gusto*, *ditto*, *studio*, and *inferno* are examples.

English borrowed considerably from Spanish in the sixteenth century, when England and Spain were imperial rivals in North and Central America, and again in the eighteenth and especially the nineteenth century, when contact between English and Spanish speakers in Texas, California, and the Mexican border areas was extensive. From the former of these periods come *galleon*, *armada*, *negro*, *punctilio*, and *bravado;* from the latter *cigar*, *mustang*, *lasso*, *rodeo*, and *pueblo*. Some Spanish loan-words are largely restricted to discussion of Spanish or Spanish-American culture and history (*toreador*, *hacienda*, *mantilla*, *bolero*); others (*siesta*, *stampede*, *albino*) have attained wider distribution.

The nearness of the Low Countries to England, and the relations both friendly and warlike between the two areas since the earliest times, have ensured a steady flow of Low German and Dutch words into English. Some, such as *snatch* and *tackle*, go back to early Middle English. In the fifteenth century, nautical terms like *buoy*, *deck*, *splice*, *sloop*, and *skipper* began to come in. Later came art terms like *easel* and *sketch*, as well as miscellaneous words like *hanker* and *hustle*. Some Dutch words entered English because of contact in the New World or in South Africa: *stoop* ("porch"), *spook*, *waffle*, *boss*, and *trek*. One interesting Rhineland German dialect, the Pennsylvania Dutch, which has been spoken for two hundred years in eastern Pennsylvania, has contributed a few words, like *smear case* and *loafer*, to the American English vocabulary. People who live in the region, even though they do not speak Pennsylvania Dutch, make use of other words like *spritz* ("to sprinkle") and *toot* ("paper bag").

Standard, or High, German has been drawn upon since the eighteenth century principally for words in certain specialized fields. Much of the vocabulary of mineralogy and petrology, for example, is of German origin: *quartz*, *gneiss*, *shale*, and *nickel*. Large numbers of German emigrants during the nineteenth century, especially to the United States, introduced various aspects of German culture and the vocabulary that goes with them into the English-speaking world. Food and drink are represented by *sauerkraut*, *pumpernickel*, *frankfurter*, and *lager*; social life by *rathskeller*, *turnverein*, and *waltz*; education by *kindergarten*, *seminar*, and *semester*; dogbreeding by *dachshund*, *schnauzer*, and *pinscher*. World War II added military terms which may prove to be short-lived as the techniques of warfare change; even today terms like *panzer-division*, *blitzkrieg*, and *Stuka* seem to be of historical interest only, as do **loan-translations** like *storm-trooper*.

Loan-words from other European languages are relatively few, and even fewer of them have been extended very far beyond immediate reference to the countries or cultures using the same languages. Simply to illustrate the diversity of sources, we may list the following examples:

Russian: *tsar, ruble, vodka, samovar, sputnik*
Czech: *robot*
Polish: *polka, mazurka*
Hungarian: *goulash, paprika*
Finnish: *sauna*
Portuguese: *veranda, tank*

F

**4. Languages of the Middle and Far East.** We sometimes forget that the highest civilization of the so-called Dark Ages in the west was the Arabic culture of the Mediterranean. Especially as mathematicians, astronomers, and physicians, but also as transmitters of much of classical culture (including the works of Aristotle), the Arabic-speaking peoples of Spain, North Africa, and the Near East made invaluable contributions to western civilization. Little direct contact between Arabic and English speakers occurred until much later, when English travelers, followed often by merchants and sometimes armies, moved into the Near and Middle East. The early loan-words from Arabic reached English through one or more intermediate languages, usually French or Spanish, sometimes Italian. Words like *alchemy*, *algebra*, *alembic*, *elixir*, *zenith*, and *azimuth* belong to the common vocabulary of Europe and testify to the early influence of Arabic science. It is not always possible to be sure what route they followed into English, but those which came in before the sixteenth century were most commonly part of the great influx from French. In the sixteenth century Spanish and Italian became more common intermediate sources, and by the eighteenth century many words were being borrowed directly from Arabic. The following examples, with their dates of first occurrence, will illustrate various types of Arabic loan-words: *admiral*(c. 1200), *algorisme*(*Ancrene Riwle*, c. 1200), *alchemy*(1362), *alkali* (Chaucer, c. 1385), *lemon* (c. 1400), *algebra* (1541, 1551 in mathematical sense), *alcohol* (1543), *fakir* (1609), *harem* (1634), *albatross* (1681), *houri* (Dr. Johnson, 1737), *ghoul* (1786), *alfalfa* (1845), *safari* (through Swahili, 1907).

Contact between English and the languages of India, especially Hindi, began in the seventeenth century, increased greatly in the eighteenth with the expanding activity of the East India Company, and continued through the nineteenth with the establishment of imperial rule in India. Many Englishmen—soldiers, civil officials, and merchants—spent large parts of their lives in India, returning to England to retire. Although many of the words they borrowed were used principally in India and related to local matters, a number of them attained wider circulation and passed into the general vocabulary. Some of these are *nabob* (1612—often used facetiously in the eighteenth century to refer to returned Englishmen who had made their fortune in India), *chintz* (1614), *punch* (the drink, 1632), *juggernaut* (1638), *dungaree* (1696), *bandana* (1752), *shampoo* (1762), *thug* (1810), *polo* (1872).

Persian, an Indo-European language of the same large family as Hindi and other languages of India, has added to the English vocabulary mostly through intermediate languages. The oldest route was through Greek and Latin; in this way were borrowed words like *tiger* and *paradise*. Later, in the Middle English period, French was the immediate source; at this time English borrowed much of the vocabulary of chess (*rook, check, check mate*). Beginning in the sixteenth century, Persian words reached English through Turkish and Hindi, and some began to be borrowed directly as a result of contact between English travelers and merchants and the people of Persia. From this period date *shah* (1564), *divan* (1586), *jackal* (1603), *shawl* (1662), *seersucker* (1757), *khaki* (1857).

The languages of the Far East—the various "dialects" of Chinese (really separate languages), Japanese, the Malayo-Polynesian languages of southeast Asia and the Pacific—have contributed relatively few words to the general vocabulary of English, though locally many more are used—even to the point of creating **pidgin** languages, using simplified English grammar and a polyglot vocabulary. Some more widely known words are *silk* and *tea* from Chinese; *kimono, hara-kiri,* and *tycoon* from Japanese; *gingham* and *bantam* from Malayan; *taboo, tattoo,* and *luau* from Polynesian. World War II and the subsequent occupation of Japan brought large numbers of Americans into contact with speakers of Japanese, but there was very little effect on the general vocabulary. The traffic in words has mostly gone the other way: as a result of the rapid Westernization of Japanese society and the more recent American influence, the Japanese language has borrowed extensively from English.

5. **Languages of the New World.** Except for brief and linguistically negligible Scandinavian settlements in North America, the first extensive contact between Europeans and the indigenous peoples of the New World was in the Caribbean area and South America, where Spaniards and Portuguese conquerors and traders became established. The English did not become seriously interested in the Americas until the middle of the sixteenth century, and they did not establish settlements of the kind that would lead to bilingualism and word-borrowing until the seventeenth. Meanwhile words from various Indian languages of the Caribbean, Mexico, and Central and South America were being borrowed into Spanish, whence many of them found their way into English—such words

as *canoe, hurricane, hammock, potato*, and *tobacco*. But even after
the English had established their own colonies, continuing contact
between Spanish and English speakers—still strong in the southwest of our country—kept open this channel for the borrowing of
words ultimately American Indian in origin. Some of these words
are used only in the region of contact, but many others—partly
owing to the wide popularity of "Western" fiction, movies, and
television dramas throughout the English-speaking world—have
become part of the general vocabulary of English: *tomato* (1604),
*chili* (1662), *pampas* (1704), *poncho* (1748), *cougar* (via French,
1775), *mescal* (1828), *coyote* (1850).

Beginning with the early seventeenth-century settlements in
Virginia and New England and continuing through the exploration
and ultimate settlement of the West, English speakers were in
frequent contact with speakers of various North American Indian
languages. The result has been a steady, though never very extensive, borrowing of words from these languages into English.
Most of these words relate either to indigenous American animals
and plants or to objects and aspects of American Indian culture. To
the first group belong *moose* (1606), *raccoon* (1608), *opossum*
(1610), often shortened to *possum*; *terrapin* (1613); *musquash*
(1624), later altered by popular etymology to *muskrat*; *skunk*
(1634); *hickory* (1676); *woodchuck* (1689); *tamarack* (1841),
and *catawba* (1857). Examples of the second group are *moccasin*
(1612); *sachem* (1622); *pow-wow* (1624); *squaw, tomahawk*, and
*papoose* (1634); *totem* (1760); and *tepee* (1872).

But the greatest contribution of the languages of North America
has been in place-names. From Aroostook County in Maine to Tal-
lahassee in Florida, and from the Potomac to the Yosemite, the
towns, rivers, lakes, and mountains of the United States and Canada
bear names more or less accurately reflecting Indian sources. Not
vocabulary items in the usual sense, these names serve to remind us,
as do the Celtic and Roman place-names of Britain, that speakers of
other tongues were there before the speakers of English.

## 9. Other Sources of New Words

Though borrowing has been the most prolific source of
additions to the vocabulary of English, we acquire or create new
words in several other ways. Those which will be discussed here, in
descending order of importance, are **derivation, compounding,**

**functional shift, back formation** and **clipping, proper names, imitation, blending,** and **original coinage.**

1. **Derivation.** The derivational process (already discussed in Chapter Two, pp. 33-36) consists of using an existing word—or in some cases a bound morpheme or morphemic structure—as a stem to which affixes are attached. Thus our imaginary word *pandle* might become the stem for such derivatives as *pandler, pandlette, depandle,* and *repandlize.* Affixes like these are called **productive;** all native speakers know their meanings and feel free to add them to various kinds of stems in accordance with analogy or the rules of English derivation. By this process any new word, whatever its source, may almost immediately become the nucleus of a cluster of derivatives. Thus *plane,* formed by clipping from *airplane,* has produced *emplane* and *deplane,* presumably by analogy with *entrain* and *detrain,* themselves formed by analogy with *embark* and *debark,* which were borrowed from French. When *telegraph* was formed by compounding of two Greek elements, it soon gave rise to *telegrapher, telegraphy, telegraphic,* and *telegraphist,* all of which were self-explaining derivatives.

So obvious is the process of forming derivatives with productive affixes that all of us probably do it much more frequently than we realize. The words we thus "create" in most cases have been frequently used before and are listed in the dictionary, but we may not know that. This process allows us to expand our vocabulary without specifically memorizing new words. But this reliance on analogical derivation may sometimes trap us into creating new words that are unnecessary because other derivatives already exist and have become standard. The student who wrote about Hamlet's *unableness to overcome his mental undecidedness* undoubtedly was familiar with *inability* and *indecision,* but under the pressure of an examination he forgot them and created his own derivatives instead.

2. **Compounding.** In a sense, compounding is a special form of derivation in which, instead of adding affixes (bound forms) to a stem, two or more words (or in some cases bound bases) are put together to make a new lexical unit. Compounding has been a source of new words in English since earliest times, and is particularly common in present-day English. Perusal of any daily paper will turn up countless examples of compounds that are new within

the last few years or months: *launching pad, blast-off, jet-port, freeway, ski-tow, free loader, feather-bedding, sit-in.* Our writing system does not indicate whether items like *weather satellite* are compounds or constructions. Many of them begin as constructions but then assume the characteristic stress patterns of compounds: some people still pronounce *ice cream* with the stress pattern of a construction (as in *iced tea*), but most treat it as a compound (as in *iceboat*). Some of the older compounds have gone through sound (and spelling) changes that have completely obscured their compound origin. Typical of these is *lord*, which began in early Old English as *hlāf-weard*, a compound of the ancestors of our *loaf* and *ward*, and passed through the stages of OE *hlāford* and ME *loverd* to its present monosyllabic form. Other examples are *woman*, originally a compound of the ancestors of *wife* and *man*, and *hussy*, from *house* and *wife*, hence etymologically a doublet of *housewife*.

The semantic relationships between the parts of compounds is very varied. If compounds are thought of as the product of a transformation process, this variety can be revealed by reconstructing the phrase from which the compound might have been created.[11] This may range from a simple modification, in which the transformation involves only a change in stress pattern (*hot dog, blackboard, bluebird*), to complete predication, where the transformation involves complicated reordering and deletion (as in *salesman* from *man who makes sales* or *movie camera* from *camera that takes movies*). Compounds may themselves enter into compounds to produce elaborate structures like *aircraft carrier* and *real estate salesman*. These must be considered compounds, since they have the characteristic stress-pattern with the strongest stress on the first element (*áircràft càrrier, réal estàte sàlesman*), in contrast to the stress pattern of modification constructions (as in *àircràft desígner* or *rèal estàte invéstment*).

One special group of compounds, most of them of quite recent origin, includes those words—mostly technical and scientific terms—which are made up of morphemes borrowed from Greek. Many

<hr/>

11. Full discussions of the types and meanings of compounds from differing grammatical points of view may be found in Otto Jespersen, *A Modern English Grammar on Historical Principles,* Part VI (Copenhagen: Ejnar Munksgaard, 1942), chapter IX, and Robert B. Lees, *The Grammar of English Nominalizations* (Bloomington, Indiana: Indiana University Research Center in Anthropology, Folklore, and Linguistics, 1960), chapter IV.

of the elements so used were free forms—words—in Greek, but must be considered bound bases in English. The practice of compounding them began in Greek: *philosophia* is compounded from *philos* "fond of" and *sophia* "wisdom." Words of this sort were borrowed into Latin in ancient times, and ultimately reached English by way of French. Renaissance scholars, who knew Greek and recognized the combining elements, began to make new combinations which did not exist in the original Greek. With the growth of scientific knowledge from the seventeenth century on, new technical and scientific terms were commonly invented this way.

Words created can be roughly divided into two groups. The first includes those which have wide circulation in the general vocabulary—like *telephone, photograph,* and *thermometer.* These are constructed out of a relatively small number of morphemes, whose meanings are well known:

| | |
|---|---|
| *tele* | "far, distant" |
| *phone* | "sound" |
| *photo* | "light" |
| *graph* | "write, mark" |
| *thermo* | "heat" |
| *meter* | "measure" |
| *dyna* | "power" |
| *hydro* | "water, moisture" |
| *bio* | "life" |
| *morph* | "shape, form" |

Inventors and manufacturers of new products often create names for their inventions from elements of this sort. Sometimes the Greek elements are combined with Latin ones, as in *automobile* (Greek *autos* "self," Latin *mobilis* "movable") and *television,* or even with native English elements, as in *dynaflow.* Recent creations in this group are *astronaut* and *cosmonaut,* from Greek *aster* "star," *kosmos* "universe," and *nautes* "sailor." Actually *cosmonaut* was first used in Russian, whence it was borrowed, but since both of its bases were already in use in English (as in *cosmology* and *aeronaut*), it might just as well have originated in English.

The second group of Greek-based compounds comprises the large number of technical and scientific terms whose use is almost wholly restricted to specialists. As in the case of *cosmonaut,* most of these words are readily interchangeable among the languages in which scientific publication is extensive. Since it is often difficult if not impossible to determine the language in which they were first used, the Merriam-Webster editors have recently made use of the term *International Scientific Vocabulary* (abbreviated ISV) to describe them. A few examples of wide enough circulation to be included in an abridged dictionary are the following:

> *hypsography:* "recording (*graphy*) of elevation (*hypso*)"
> *telethermoscope:* "instrument that perceives (*scope*) heat (*thermo*) at a distance (*tele*)"
> *electroencephalograph:* "instrument that records (*graph*) electric current (*electro*) within (*en*) the head (*cephalo*)"
> *schizogenesis:* "reproduction (*genesis*) by division (*schizo*)"

In all cases, since at least two of the combining elements are bases, these words must be considered compounds. They may also give rise to derivatives formed by the addition of affixes in regular patterns, such as *electroencephalography* and *schizogenetic*. It is in this way, rather than by direct borrowing, that Greek has made its great contribution to the English vocabulary.

3. **Functional Shift.** Since the late Middle English period, when most of the inflections surviving from Old English finally disappeared, it has been easy to shift a word from one part of speech to another without altering its form, at least in the unmarked base form. A verb like *walk* can be turned into a noun simply by using it in a syntactic position reserved for nouns, as in *he took a walk*, where the determiner *a* marks *walk* as a noun, direct object of *took*. This process, called **functional shift,** is an important concomitant of the historical change of English from a synthetic to an analytic language, and has greatly enlarged the vocabulary in a very economical way. Since the words so created belong to a different part of speech and hence have a different grammatical distribution from that of the original, they must be considered new words, homonymous in the base form with the words from which they were derived, rather than merely extensions of meaning. From another point of view, they may be thought of as derivatives with zero affixes. In some cases they may take a different stress pattern in their new use: the noun *implement*, with weak stress and the weak central vowel /ə/ in the last syllable, when shifted to a verb took secondary stress on the last syllable, whose vowel was changed to /e/. Since there is overt

change in pronunciation, this is true derivation rather than functional shift. But the two processes are obviously closely related.

Older instances of functional shift commonly produced nouns from verbs: in addition to *walk*, already cited, we might mention *run*, *steal*, *laugh*, *touch*, *buy*, *break*, and many others. In present-day English the shift from noun to verb is much in favor. In the past, short words like *brush* and *perch* were sometimes shifted from noun to verb, but today, longer nouns like *implement*, *position*, *process*, *contact* are often used as verbs. Even compound nouns get shifted to verbs; the secretary who said "I didn't back-file the letter, I waste-basketed it" was speaking twentieth-century English, however inelegant.

4. **Back Formation** and **Clipping** are two modes of word creation which can be classed together as different types of **reduction**. In each case, a shorter word is made from a longer one, so that the effect is the opposite of derivation and compounding. **Back formation** makes use of analogy to produce a sort of reverse derivation. The existence of *creation*, *create*, and *donation* readily suggests that if there is not a verb *donate* there should be. This seems so natural to us that it is hard to believe that less than a century ago *donate* was considered an American barbarism by many puristically inclined British speakers of English.[12] Other words that have come into English by back formation are *edit* (from *editor*), *burgle* (from *burglar*), *enthuse* (from *enthusiasm*), *televise* (from *television*, by analogy with pairs like *supervise*: *supervision*), *automate* (from *automation*), *laze* (from *lazy*), and many more. Once pairs of words like these have become established, only the historical record proving prior use of the longer forms serves to distinguish them from normal derivational pairs.

**Clippings**, on the other hand, are shortenings without regard to derivational analogy. They are frequent in informal language, especially spoken, as in the school and university use of *exam*, *lab*, and *maths*. They are possible because often a single syllable, usually the one bearing the main stress, is sufficient to identify a word, especially in a rather closely restricted context, so that the remaining syllables are redundant and can be dropped. Most of them preserve a colloquial flavor and are limited to the special

12. See H. L. Mencken, *The American Language*, Fourth Edition (New York: Alfred A. Knopf, 1936), pp. 121, 165.

vocabularies of occupational groups. Others, however—often over the objections of purists—attain wide circulation and may ultimately replace the longer forms on most or all levels of usage. Some that have done so are *van* (from *caravan*), *bus* (from *omnibus*), *cello* (from *violoncello*), *mob* (from Latin *mobile vulgus* "unstable crowd"), *piano* (from *pianoforte*), and *fan* (in sense "ardent devotee," from *fanatic*). Others which are in acceptable, though perhaps characteristically informal, use alongside the longer unclipped words are *phone* (for *telephone*), *taxi* and *cab* (from *taxicab*), and *plane* (for *airplane* or older *aeroplane*). A rather special form of clipping is that which reduces long compounds or idiomatic fixed phrases to one of their elements—often the modifying element rather than the head—as in *express* from *express train*, *car* from *motor car*, and *outboard* from *outboard motor* (*boat*). This process often accounts for what otherwise seem strange transfers of meaning (see above, p. 130).

An extreme form of clipping is that which reduces words to their abbreviations and longer phrases to their initials. Abbreviation is, of course, a standard device of the writing system to save space by reducing the length of common or often repeated words. Usually it is confined to writing, and to rather informal writing at that. But some common abbreviations have been adopted in speech and ways have been found to pronounce them. The common abbreviations for the two halves of the day—A.M. and P.M.—which stand for the Latin phrases *ante meridiem* ("before noon") and *post meridiem* ("after noon") are frequently used in speech, where they are pronounced /é:+èm/ and /pí:èm/. These must indeed be considered words, though their spelling is that of abbreviations. The same is true of B.C. and A.D. in dates, O.K. (which has become an international word), U.S., G.I., L.P., TNT, TV, and DDT. In all these cases the pronunciation is simply the syllabic names of the letters, usually with the strongest stress on the last: /yù:+és/, /dì:+dì:+tí:/, and so on.

If the initial letters of a phrase, used as an abbreviation, happen to make a combination that is pronounceable, what results is an acronym—a word whose spelling represents the initial letters of a phrase. Though very popular in recent times, acronyms are by no means an innovation of the twentieth century. The early Christians made a famous one when they took the initials of the Greek phrase Ἰησοῦς Χριστὸς θεοῦ υἱὸς σωτήρ ("Jesus Christ, son of God, Savior") to make the Greek word ἰχθύς ("fish") and adopted the fish as a symbol of Christ. Acronyms have become more frequent in English since World War II. Everyone talks about NATO, UNESCO, and NASA, often without being able to supply the longer title whose initials created the acronym. In fact, acronyms have become so popular that some longer titles have been created by a kind of back formation from the desired initials. It was certainly more than a happy accident that led the American Navy in World War II to call its feminine branch "Women Assigned to Volunteer Emergency Service," or WAVES. More recently an organization devoted to finding foster parents for orphan children from foreign lands has called itself "World Adoption International Fund" so its initials would spell WAIF.

5. **Proper Names.** The giving of individual names to persons, places, geographic features, deities, and sometimes to animals is a universal human practice, apparently as old as language itself. A proper name, since it is closely restricted to a single specific referent, does not have the general and varied distribution and reference that characterize ordinary nouns. But there is frequent interchange across the line separating proper names from other words. Many proper names, such as *Taylor*, *Smith*, *Clark*, and *Wright* are derived from common nouns describing occupations; others like *Brown*, *Strong*, and *Wild* derive from adjectives that may once have described the person so named. Place-names also frequently show their derivation from common nouns, as in *Northfield*, *Portsmouth*, and *Fairmount*.

There has also been interchange in the other direction, by which the proper name of a person or place becomes generalized in meaning, usually to refer to a product or activity connected with the referent of the proper name. One famous example is the name *Caesar*, originally a nickname coined from the Latin verb *caedo* "to cut" to describe Julius Caesar, who was cut from his mother's womb by the operation still called *Caesarian section*. The name was assumed by Julius's nephew Octavius, the first Roman emperor, and then by the subsequent emperors, so that it became virtually a synonym for *imperator* "emperor." In its later history it was borrowed into Germanic, ultimately becoming German *Kaiser* (there was also a Middle English word *kayser*, now obsolete), and into Slavonic, whence came *tsar*. Another interesting set of words derived from names are the adjectives *mercurial*, *saturnine*, and *jovial*, referring to temperaments supposed to be characteristic of people under the dominance of the planets Mercury, Saturn, and Jupiter. The corresponding *venereal* (from *Venus*) has been restricted in meaning almost entirely to medical use, but *venery* is still a rather high-flown word for love-making. Those supposed to derive instability from the changeable moon used to be called *lunatic* (from Latin *luna*, the moon). The punishment visited upon Tantalus, forever doomed to be within sight of food and water that receded when he reached for it, has given us the verb *tantalize*, formed by adding the productive suffix *-ize* (itself ultimately derived from Greek) to his name. Also ultimately Greek in origin are *hector* ("a bully, to bully") from the Trojan hero in the *Iliad* and *mentor* ("teacher"—now often used in the sports pages for "athletic coach") from the adviser of Telemachus in the *Odyssey*.

During the history of English since the beginning of the Middle English period, various words have been derived from proper names. Some earlier ones are *dunce* (from the scholastic philosopher Duns Scotus—used in ridicule of scholastic philosophy in the later sixteenth century), *pander* (from the character Pandarus in Chaucer's *Troilus and Criseyde*, c. 1385), *mawmet* (from Mahomet; at first it meant "idol," later "puppet, doll"). The Bible, widely read from Reformation times on and frequently discussed for its symbolic as well as its literal or historical meaning, has contributed many words of this sort, such as *jeremiad* ("a denunciatory tirade"), *babel, lazar* (from Lazarus; common for *leper* in Middle English), *maudlin* (from Mary Magdalen and her noted tears), and *simony* ("taking or giving money for church offices," from Simon Magus). On the border between proper and common nouns are names of Biblical and other personages taken in figurative meanings, though usually capitalized in writing, indicating that the transfer to common noun is not complete: *the old Adam, raising Cain, a doubting Thomas, a Daniel come to judgment*.

Some proper names that have assumed general meanings have undergone pronunciation changes that obscure their origins. The adjective *tawdry* ("cheap and flashy") comes from a clipping of *Saint Audrey*, and presumably was first used to describe a kind of cheap lace sold at St. Audrey's Fair. *Bedlam*, which to us means "uproar, total confusion," was a proper name as late as the eighteenth century, when it was used as a short name for *St. Mary of Bethlehem*, a London insane asylum. The word *mawkin*, used dialectally in England for "scarecrow," comes from *Malkyn*, a girl's name, ultimately a nickname from *Mary*. The parallel nickname

*Moll* gave rise to an American slang word for a criminal's girl. The history of *doll* is similar but more complicated; it passed from a clipped form of *Dorothy* to describe a miniature (usually female) figure, then to describe a small and pretty girl.

The names of historical characters—often those of unsavory reputation—have given us some rather common words. One of the most interesting of these is *guy*, from *Guy Fawkes*, used in England to describe the effigies of that notable traitor which are customarily carried in procession and burned on November 5, the anniversary of the discovery of his "Gunpowder Plot." The term came to mean "a figure of fun, a butt of scorn," and as a verb "to poke fun at, tease." In America it has become a universal colloquial term for any male not held in high respect. In phrases like *a nice guy* (when not used ironically) it has lost all of its original pejorative flavor.

Names of products derived from the names of their places of origin are rather plentiful in English. Textiles like *calico* (from *Calicut*, or *Calcutta*), *denim* (*serge de Nîmes*), *cashmere* (*Kashmir*), and *worsted* (from the name of a town in Norfolk, England) are well known. So are products like *china* (clipped from *chinaware* from *China ware*), *gin* (clipped from *Geneva*), *cognac*, and *cayenne*. Specialized and technical vocabularies are especially fond of words adapted from proper names. Skiing has its *telemark* and *christiania* (usually clipped to *christy*); librarians speak of *Dewey decimal classification* and *Cutter numbers;* horticulturalists of *fuchsia, dahlia,* and *wistaria;* physicists of *roentgen rays, curies,* and *angstrom units;* electricians of *ohms, watts,* and *amperes;* doctors of *rickettsia* and *Bright's disease.*

6. **Imitation.** A relatively small number of words in English apparently owe their origin to attempts to imitate natural sounds. *Bow-wow, meow, baa, moo,* and other words for animal cries are supposed to remind us of the noises made by dogs, cats, sheep, and cows. They are not accurate imitations, since they are pronounced with sounds characteristic of the sound-system of English, which these animals, not being native speakers of English, do not use. Other languages have other, often quite different imitative words. Both *cock-a-doodle-doo* and *kikiriki* are supposedly imitative of a rooster's crow; unless we assume that English and Greek roosters make quite different sounds, we must attribute the difference between these words to the differing sound-systems of the two languages.

Related to imitation is the phenomenon sometimes called **sound symbolism**: the habit of associating a certain type or class of meanings with a certain sound or cluster of sounds. There seems to be in English an association between the initial consonant cluster *sn-* and the nose (*snarl, sneer, sneeze, sniff, snivel, snore, snort, snout,* and *snuffle*). When slang words referring to or involving the nose are coined they may begin with this cluster, as in *snook* and *snoop*. English speakers associate the sound-combination spelled *-ash* (/æš/) with a sudden loud sound or rapid, turbulent, or destructive motion, as in *crash, dash, flash, smash,* and *splash*; and a final *-er* on verbs suggests rapidly repeated, often rhythmic motion, as in *flicker, flutter, hover, quiver, shimmer, waver*. This last example is perhaps a morpheme in its own right, though to call it one would give us a large number of bound bases that occur nowhere else. But it is well on the way to the morphemic status which certainly must be accorded to the *-le* or *-dle* of *handle, treadle,* and *spindle*.

Imitation was once considered so important as to be made the basis for a theory of the origin of language—the so-called "bow-wow theory." This theory is commonly discounted nowadays.

7. **Blending** is a combination of clipping and compounding, which makes new words by putting together fragments of existing words in new combinations. It differs from derivation in that the elements thus combined are not morphemes at the time the blends are made, though they may become so afterward as a result of the blending process, especially if several blends are made with the same element and the phenomenon of **false etymology** is present.

The poem "Jabberwocky" in Lewis Carroll's *Through the Looking Glass* contains many ingenious blends, though only a few of them (called **portmanteau words** by Humpty Dumpty in the book) have passed into the general vocabulary. Thus *slithy* (from *lithe* and *slimy*) and *mimsy* (from *miserable* and *flimsy*) are not used outside the poem, but *chortle* (*chuckle* and *snort*) and *galumphing* (*galloping* and *triumphing*) are not uncommon words, though they are usually restricted to colloquial or facetious use.

The history of *-burger* illustrates the way in which blending can give rise to a new morpheme. The name *Hamburger steak* (varying with *Hamburg steak*) was given to a kind of ground beef in America in the 1880's. It was soon shortened by phrase-clipping to *hamburger*, losing its proper-name quality in the process. The *-er* here is simply the normal German suffix for making an adjective from a proper noun (as in *Brandenburger Tor* "Brandenburg Gate"). But to those who did not know German, the word looked (and sounded) like a compound of *ham* and *burger*. So the *-burger* part was clipped and combined with various other words or parts of words to make *cheeseburger*, *deerburger*, *buffaloburger*, and many more. These have the form of compounds made up of one free base and a bound base *-burger*. Meanwhile by further clipping, *hamburger*, already short for *hamburger steak sandwich*, was cut down to *burger*, which now became a free form—a word. Thus what began as the last two syllables of a German proper adjective has become first a bound morpheme and then a full word in English.

Other morphemes which owe their origin to blending are *-rama*, *-orium*, *-teria*, and *-omat*. The first of these began with words of Greek origin like *panorama* and *cyclorama*.[13] The combining elements in Greek were *pan* "all," *kyklos* "circle, wheel," and *horama* "view," a noun derived from the verb *horan* "see." But the *-rama* part of these words was blended with *cine* (from *cinema*) to make *cinerama*, describing a type of wide-screen motion picture. Subsequently *-rama* was blended with various other elements to make new words like *colorama* and *vistarama*, as well as many trade and commercial names. It certainly must now be considered a separate morpheme, conveying a vague notion of grandeur and sweep (or so its users hope) to the words in which it is used. Similarly *-orium*, split off from *emporium* (a rather fancy Latin loan-word for "shop"), *-teria*, split off from the Spanish loan-word *cafeteria*, and *-omat*, split off from the trade name *Automat*, itself a clipping from *automatic*, have become separate morphemes, as in *lubritorium*, *valeteria*, and *laundromat*. The process of blending has thus produced not only new words but new morphemes capable of entering with some freedom into new compounds and derivatives. Many of the words thus coined never get any farther than their first application by an enterprising advertiser or proprietor, and those that do usually have a brief life. But a few seem to fill a real need and remain as part of the general vocabulary of English.

8. **Coinage.** Very few words are simply made up out of unrelated, meaningless elements. The other resources for making new

13. See John Lotz, "The Suffix '-rama,'" *American Speech*, 39:156-58, 1954.

words and the abundant vocabularies of other languages available for borrowing supply so many easy ways of producing new words that outright coinage seldom suggests itself. The outright coinage—unlike the compound, clipping, derivative, and blend—is also hard to remember because it has no familiar elements to aid the memory. So wholly new coinages are both harder to make and less likely to be remembered and used. It is no wonder that they are relatively rare. Some words, however, are indubitable coinages, and others for which etymologists have found no source may be tentatively assumed to be. Words like *quiz, pun, slang,* and *fun* have no cognates in other Germanic languages, cannot be traced to other languages as loan-words, and, since they are monosyllabic, are not compounds or derivatives, though they might be blends to which we have lost the key. One can imagine that *slang*—an eighteenth-century creation—combined elements from *slovenly* and *language*, but this is pure guesswork. These, together with more recent words, most of them facetious or slangy, like *hooch* and *pooch, snob* and *gob* ("sailor"), most probably originated as free coinages, sometimes involving sound symbolism.

More elaborate coinages, having more than one syllable, are likely to combine original elements with various other processes of word formation, especially derivation. Thus the stems of *segashuate, sockdologer,* and *spifflicated* seem to be coinages, but the suffixes are recognizable morphemes. In fact, it would be exceedingly unlikely for a native speaker to coin a word of more than one syllable without making use of one or more of the word-forming devices we have been discussing.

## 10. Conclusion

As even this brief chapter must have made obvious, the vocabulary of English is large, complex, highly diversified in origin, and constantly changing. No dictionary, however large, can contain it all. Or, if such a dictionary should be prepared, it would be out of date by the time it was printed, since new meanings, new borrowings, and new creations are being added every day. Nor can any single individual know it all. Speakers of English share a large vocabulary in common, it is true, but every individual speaker has his own unique inventory of the less commonly used words and meanings, reflecting his unique experience with language.

Many people—perhaps most people—go through life with a vocabulary adequate only to their daily needs, picking up new words when some new facet of life makes it necessary, but never indulging in curiosity and speculation about words. Others are word-lovers—collectors and connoisseurs. They like to measure one word against another, trace their etymologies and shifts of meaning, use them in new and exciting or amusing combinations. They play word-games like *Scrabble* and *Anagrams*, they do cross-word puzzles, they make puns and rhymes and nonsense jingles. Some make poems, which are the highest form of word-game. But even those who aspire no further than to the writing of good clear expository prose must become at least amateur connoisseurs of words. Only this way—not by formal exercises or courses in vocabulary-building—will they learn to make the best possible use of the vast and remarkable lexicon of English.

## Exercises

*I. What kind of linguistic unit is each of the following? List and classify all the units of which each is made up.*

1. hymnal
2. geese
3. write up (vb.)
4. chicken feed
5. halve
6. alcohol
7. perfection
8. parataxis
9. island
10. threepence-halfpenny ticket

*II. In how many different kinds of construction can you use the word* iron? *Give an example of each. In a foreign language which you know, would the same word be used to translate* iron *in each example? (If you don't know a foreign language well enough to answer this, find someone who does.)*

*III. Find an illustration of the spectrum, as in* Webster's Third New International Dictionary, *facing page 448. Put a piece of transparent tracing paper over the illustration and ask a speaker (preferably a native speaker) of some foreign language to draw lines between the colors and write their names. Repeat the experiment with speakers of as many different languages as you can find. Do it yourself for English. Then compare the results with one another and with the Japanese and Thai example on page 119.*

*IV. List as many meanings as you can think of for* book. *Then go to the* Oxford English Dictionary *(if available) and to the largest other dictionary you can find and list all the meanings not marked as obsolete. How many did you miss? How many are totally new to you?*

*V. Make a list of ten words which you consider slang and write your definitions of them. Then check* Webster's Third New International Dictionary *or the latest abridged dictionary available to you to see if the words are accurately defined there.*

*VI. The last volume of the* Oxford English Dictionary *was published in 1928 and the Supplement in 1933. List five words which you would expect to have undergone changes of meaning since those dates. Describe the processes of meaning change involved. Check your guesses by looking up the words in the* Oxford English Dictionary *and in* Webster's Third New International Dictionary *or the latest abridged dictionary available to you.*

*VII. List all the words on pages 38-39 of* Webster's New World Dictionary *(excluding proper names) that have been borrowed into English from other languages. In each case give both the immediate and the ultimate source language. Select ten of these words and for each make an informed guess as to when it was borrowed into English. If you have access to the* Oxford English Dictionary, *verify your guesses.*

*Exercises VIII–X are on entries from the* Oxford English Dictionary; *the entries are reproduced by permission of the Clarendon Press, Oxford.*

| | | | |
|---|---|---|---|
| *a* (as *a*1300) | = *ante*, before | OHG. | = Old High German |
| app. | = apparently | ON. | = Old Norse (Old Icelandic) |
| *arch.* | = archaic | | |
| Da. | = Danish | OSl. | = Old Slavonic |
| Du. | = Dutch | OTeut. | = Original Teutonic |
| Fris. | = Frisian | | |
| G. | = German | | |
| Goth. | = Gothic | pa. pple. | = passive or past participle |
| Gr. | = Greek | | |
| *intr.* | = intransitive | pa. t. | = past tense |
| L. | = Latin | pl., *pl.* | = plural |
| MHG. | = Middle High German | pple. | = participle |
| | | sb., *sb.* | = substantive |
| *obs.* | = obsolete | Sp. | = Spanish |
| OE. | = Old English (= Anglo-Saxon) | Sw. | = Swedish |
| | | *v.,* vb. | = verb |
| OFris. | = Old Frisian | | |

Before a Word or Sense
† = obsolete.
‖ = not naturalized.

In the Quotations
* sometimes points out the word illustrated.

In the List of Forms
1 = before 1100.
2 = 12th c. (1100 to 1200).

3 = 13th c. (1200 to 1300).
5-7 = 15th to 17th century.

In the Etymologies
* indicates a word or form not actually found, but of which the existence is inferred.
:— = extant representative, or regular phonetic descendant of.

The printing of a word in SMALL CAPITALS indicates that further information will be found under the word so referred to.

**Die** (dəi), *v.*[1] Pa. t. and pple. **died** (dəid):
pr. pple. **dying** (dəi·iŋ). Forms· *a.* 2–4 deȝ-en,
dei-e(n, 3 deiȝ·en, deaiȝ-e, 4 day-e, 4–5 deghe,
4–6 dei(e, dey(e. (5 deyn), 4–6 (*north.*) de, 4–
dee. *β.* 4–5 diȝ-en, dyȝ-en, digh-e, dygh-e,
dy-en, di-en, 4–7 diy, (5 dyi), 4–8 dye, 4– die.
l'a. t. *a.* 3 deiȝede, dæide, deaide, 3–5 deid(e,
4 daide, dayed, deȝed, deied(e ; *north.* deyt,
ded, 4–5 deyd(e, deyed, 5 deghit, -et, -t, 5–
*north.* deed, deit, deet. *β.* 4 dyede, 4–5 dyde,
4–6 dide, (5 dyet), 4–8 dyed, 4– died. [Early
ME. *dēȝen, dēghen.* corresp. to ON. *deyja* (orig.
*dőyja*, OSw. and ODa. *döia*, Da. *döe*, Sw. *dö*),
OFris. *deia, deja*, OS. *dóian*, OHG. *touwan*, MHG.
*töuwen* ; these represent an OTeut. strong verb of
the 6th ablaut class \**daw-j-an*, pa. t. *dőw*, pa. pple.
*dawan*-, the strong inflexions being retained in
ON. (*dó*-:–\**dőw, dáinn* :–\**dawans*). In the other
langs. and in Eng. a regular weak verb. No instance of the word is known in OE. literature (its
sense being expressed by *steorfan, swelten*, or the
periphrastic *wesan dēad*, pa. t. *wæs dēad* : see DEAD
1 d) hence it is generally held to have been early
lost in OE. (as in Gothic, and as subsequently in
all the continental WGer. langs.), and re-adopted·
in late OE. or early ME. from Norse; but some
think that the facts point rather to the preservation
of an OE. *dīegan, dȳgan*, in some dialect ; the word
appears to have been in general use from the 12th
c., even in the s.w. dialects (see Napier in *Hist.
Holy Rood*, E.E.T.S., 1894). The ME. *dēȝen,
dēghen* came regularly down to 1500 as *deye*, which
was retained in the North as *dey, dē, dee* (still current from Lancashire to Scotland) ; but in standard
English *dēghe* was in 14th c. (in conformity with
the common phonetic history of OE. *eh, eah, eoh*,
as in *dye, eye, fly, high, lie, nigh, thigh*, etc.) narrowed to *dīȝe, dighe*, whence the later *dye, die*.

The oldest text of Cursor M. (Cotton) has only *dey* ; in
the later texts this is frequently altered to *dighe, dye*, when
not in rime, in the late Trinity MS. sometimes even in rime,
with change of text. Chaucer used both *dey* and *dye*, the
C. T. (Ellesm. MS.) contains in the rimes 22 examples of
*deye* and 50 of *dye*. Both forms are also used in the Wy-
clifite version, and both occur in Caxton's works.

The stem *dau*- appears also in Gothic in the ppl. *a. dauþs*,
OE. *dēad* (:–*daud-oz*) DEAD, and the sb. *daupus*, OE. *dēaþ*,
DEATH ; also in *afdôjan* (:–*afdôwjan*), pa. pple. *afdauid*-
(:–*afdôwid*-) vexed, worried. (The relationship of Gothic
*diwanô, undiwanei*, etc. is uncertain.) The simple verb has
shown a notable tendency to die out, and leave its place to
be taken by derivatives : thus in Gothic *dauþnan* to die.]

---

**VIII. On Die *v.*[1]**

1. *During which period does the spelling seem to have been least
standardized? Can you give some reasons for the lack of standardization? (If necessary, return to Chapter Three.)*

2. *According to the spellings, in which part of England did the past
first show monosyllabic forms?*

3. *On what basis do the dictionary editors consider themselves justi-*
   *fied in implying that the word was "early lost in OE"? Why not*
   *assume instead that it never existed in OE?*

4. *The word occurs today as Scottish* dee *and standard English* die.
   *Which of these is the direct descendant of the recorded ME*
   *form? How is the other accounted for?*

> **Swine** (swəin). Pl. swine. Forms: *Singular*
> and *Plural.* 1–4 swin, 1–6 swyn, 4–5 suyn,
> 4–7 swyne, (4 suine, swiyn, squine, *Ayenb.*
> zuyn, 4–5 squyne, 5 swyyn, swyyne, sweyne,
> sqwyne, 6 suyne, swyin, swyen, 7 sweyn,
> shwine), 5– swine. *Plural* in -*s.* 5 swynes, 6,
> 8–9 swines. [Common Teutonic: OE. *swín*
> str. n. = OFris., OS., MLG. *swín*, MDu. *swijn*,
> (NFris. *swinn*, EFris. *swin*, WFris. *swyn*, LG.
> ʒwien, Du. *zwijn*), OHG., MHG. *swîn*, (G.
> *schwein*), ON. *svín*, (Sw., Da. *svin*), Goth.
> *swein* :— OTeut. *\*swīnom*, neut. of adj. formation
> with suffix -*īno*- (cf. L. *suínus*, OSl. *svinъ* swinish,
> and see -INE *suffix*[1]) on the root of L. *sūs*, Gr. *ûs*,
> and Sow *sb.*[1]
> The orig. use may have been either generic or
> restricted to the young of the swine; for the latter
> cf. Goth. *gaitein*, OHG. *geiʒʒín* young goat, kid,
> cogn. w. OE. *gǽten* of goats, L. *hǽdínus* of kids
> :— Indo-eur. *\*ghaidíno-*, f. *ghaid*- GOAT.]

## IX. *On* SWINE.

1. *Put the various cognate Germanic forms onto a chart like that on*
   *page 75. (Note that Original Teutonic, abbreviated OTeut., is*
   *the same as Proto-Germanic.) Why is there an asterisk in front of*
   *the form* \*swinom?

2. *What is the relationship of the Old Slavonic, Latin, and Greek*
   *words cited to the Germanic word?*

3. *If the* Oxford English Dictionary *is available to you, look up* Sow
   *sb.*[1] *and explain its relationship to* SWINE.

> **Shock** (ʃɒk), *v.*[2] Forms: α. 6 shok, 6–7
> shocke, 6– shock; β. 6 chock, 7 chocke,
> chocque, 8 choak. [app. a. F. *choquer* (13th c.)
> = Sp. *chocar*, of obscure origin.
> Some regard the vb. as an adoption from Germanic, com-
> paring OHG. *scoc* swing, MHG. *schocken* to swing. But
> an early OF. *ch* can hardly represent G. *sch*, and the affinity
> of sense is not close. Others suppose that the original sense
> is 'to stumble, knock against', the vb. being f. OF. *choque*
> tree-stump; cf. OF. *choper* to stumble, f. *chope* tree-stump.
> The senses below are all from Fr. *choquer*, and were intro-
> duced at different periods: see note to sense 4. The older
> SHOCK *v.*[1] appears to be unconnected.
> ꝓ The form *chock* (prob. to be regarded as a distinct word)
> occurs (in the 16–17th c.) in various senses of Fr. *choquer*.
> *trans.* **a.** To knock about, buffet.  **b.** To give a blow to;
> to 'chuck' under the chin.  **c.** To knock one against the
> other, to jingle (coins).
> **a.** 1567 TURBERV. *Epit.*, etc. 128 Now, now the churlish
> chanell me doth chock, Now surging Seas conspire to breede
> my carke.

**b.** 1583 [see CHUCK *v.*²]. 1607 MARKHAM *Caval.* IV. vi. 29 The verie manner of bringing a horse vnto it, which is by chocking him in the mouth. *Ibid.* viii. 38 You shal neither chock him in the mouth, nor [etc.]. 1658 [see CHUCK *v.*³ 1].

**c.** 1627 DRAYTON *Agincourt* 63 In the Tauerne, in his Cups doth rore, Chocking his Crownes.]

**1.** *intr.* To come into violent contact, to collide, clash *together*; esp. to encounter in the shock of battle. Now only *arch.* or as a Gallicism.

1576 TURBERV. *Venerie* xvii. 45 They beginne then both of them to vault, and to scrape the grounde,with their feete, shocking and butting one against another. 1584 HUDSON *Du Bartas' Judith* III. (1608) 46 Together soone they shock with hatefull yre. 1640 tr. *Verdere's Rom. of Rom.* I. xxv. 116 One would have said, that four towres torn from their foundations, by so many whirlwinds, had shocked together. 1742 HUME *Ess., Parties* (1817) I. 54 Two men, travelling on the highway, the one east, the other west, can easily pass each other, if the way be broad enough: but two men, reasoning upon opposite principles of religion, cannot so easily pass, without shocking. 1774 GOLDSM. *Nat. Hist.* (1862) I. 49 Two mountains shocked against each other, approaching and retiring with the most dreadful noise. 1832 TENNYSON *Love thou thy Land* 78 If New and Old, disastrous feud, Must ever shock, like armed foes. 1872 — *Gareth* 939 All at fiery speed the two Shock'd on the central bridge. 1888 *Chamb. Jrnl.* 6 Oct. 626/2 Carriage after carriage shocked fiercely against the engine and the compartments in front of it.

† **b.** *trans.* To collide with, jostle. *Obs.*

1783 JUSTAMOND tr. *Raynal's Hist. Indies* V. 151 It is necessary to fix them with several anchors, to prevent their shocking each other. 1794 *Rigging & Seamanship* II. 268 The rudder is shocked by the water.

† **c.** To run counter to, to oppose. *Obs. rare.*

1667 DRYDEN *Ind. Emp.* I. ii, That Monarch sits not safely on his Throne, Who bears, within, a power that shocks his own. 1676 — *Aurengz.* II. i, Advise him not to shock a Father's Will.

† **2.** To assail with a sudden and violent attack, to charge (an enemy) with troops, etc. *Obs.*

1614 GORGES *Lucan* III. 110 But whosoever of the foes Did shocke their sides, or changed blowes With Brutus shippe, him grappling fast, He boords. 1699 *Relat. Sir. T. Morgan's Progr. France* 7 Major-General Morgan demanded of his Excellency, whether he would Shock the whole Army at one dash, or try one Wing first? 1767 *Ann. Reg., Acc. Bks.* 276/1 The Christians rowed forwards..and shocked the enemy's gallies with the spurs or beaks of theirs.

† **3.** To throw (troops) into confusion by an onset or charge; to damage or weaken by impact or collision; to destroy the stability of. Also *fig.*

1568 GRAFTON *Chron.* II. 1364 The Countie Egmond..recharged vpon them with all his forces together so terribly that he shokt all their battayle. 1674–5 STILLINGFL. *Serm.* 24 Feb., Wks. 1710 I. 215 They who could not be shocked by persecution were in danger of being overcome by flattery. 1726 G. ROBERTS *Four Yrs. Voy.* 351 That Sea that shock'd the Vessel, was a Forerunner of a greater. 1770 LANGHORNE *Plutarch* (1879) II. 770/1 It carried down trunks of trees.., which much shocked and weakened the pillars of his bridge.

† **b.** To shake (a building, etc.) with an earthquake shock. *Obs.*

1731 [see RAISE *v.* 4 a]. 1742 PLANT *Earthquakes* in *Phil. Trans.* XLII. 34 It continued roaring, bursting, and shocking our Houses all that Night.

**4.** In early use, to wound the feelings of, offend, displease. In later use, with stronger sense: To affect with a painful feeling of intense aversion or disapproval ; to scandalize, horrify ; to outrage (a person's sentiments, prejudices, etc.). Often in passive, to be scandalized or horrified *at*.

The prevalent 17th c. spelling (see β) shows that the sense was then regarded as a use of the F. *choquer*.

α. **1694** CONGREVE *Double Dealer* v. xvii, Thy stubborn temper shocks me, and you knew it would. **1711** STEELE *Spect.* No. 6 P 2 They are no more shocked at Vice and Folly, than Men of slower Capacities. **1767** LADY S. BUNBURY in Jesse *Selwyn & Contemp.* (1843) II. 178 I am shocked to death to see you must be back by the end of September. **1815** SCOTT *Guy M.* iv, They durst not at once shock the universal prejudices of their age. **1849** MACAULAY *Hist. Eng.* ii. I. 188 Every moderate man was shocked by the insolence, cruelty, and perfidy with which the nonconformists were treated. **1867** SMILES *Huguenots Eng.* x. (1880) 164 The priests who visited the slaves at the galleys were horribly shocked at the cruelties practised on them. **1880** L. STEPHEN *Pope* vii. 175 Pope.. was terribly shocked when he found himself accused of heterodoxy.

β. **1656** COWLEY *Odes, 2nd Olympique* Introd., The Reader must not be chocqued to hear him speak so often of his own Muse. **1663** SIR G. MACKENZIE *Relig. Stoici* x. (1685) 97 To abrogate, by our practice, whatever chocks our present humor. **1708** SWIFT *Abol. Christianity* Misc. (1711) 174 The Gentlemen of Wit and Pleasure are apt to murmur, and be choqued at the sight of so many daggled-tail Parsons.

**b.** *absol.*

**1820** BELZONI *Egypt & Nubia* I. 109 Those [customs] which shock at first sight, lose their effect on him.

**5.** To impart a physical shock to, to cause (a person or a part of the body) to suffer a nervous shock.

**1733** BELLOSTE *Hosp. Surg.* ii. 17 Mercury produces its effect .. by its shocking and disengaging the fibres. **1747** tr. *Astruc's Fevers* 213 The corresponding parts of the medullary substance are so shocked, that the animal spirits there contained are more vigorously protruded into the nerves. **1841** J. T. HEWLETT *Parish Clerk* I. 271 The nervous system was so much shocked. **1900** *Brit. Med. Jrnl.* 3 Feb. 257/2 The state of the patients, as to collapse, when first seen varied enormously .. : some were absolutely ' shocked ', others not at all so.

**b.** To give (a person) an electric shock.

**1746** WATSON in *Phil. Trans.* XLIV. 741 It remains now, that I endeavour to lay before you a Solution why our Bodies are so shocked in the Experiments with the electrified Water. **1769** E. BANCROFT *Guiana* 196 The Torporific Eel, caught by a hook, violently shocks the person holding the line. **1882** *Nature* XXVI. 260, I got severely shocked [by lightning] when sending my report.

X. *On* SHOCK *v.*[2]

1. *Do you agree that the form* chock *is "probably to be regarded as a distinct word"? Why?*

2. *What is the major difference between sense 1 and sense 2? Is this primarily a semantic or a grammatical difference?*

3. *Under sense 3 appears the notation "Also* fig[urative]." *What does this mean? Which of the quotations under sense 3 illustrates a figurative use?*

4. *The verb* shake (OE scacan) *is etymologically unrelated to* SHOCK. *What influence might the accidental similarity of these two verbs have had on the semantic development of* SHOCK? *(See especially sense 3b.)*

5. *Which of the three main types of meaning change is illustrated by sense 4? By sense 5? Explain.*

6. *Look up* SHOCK vb *in* Webster's Third New International Dictionary. *Are there any senses there which are not covered in the* Oxford English Dictionary? *If so, describe the semantic changes involved.*

# For Further Reading

Although not exactly designed for continuous reading, the indispensable tools for study of the English vocabulary are the great dictionaries, especially the *Oxford English Dictionary*, the *Century Dictionary*, and *Webster's New International Dictionary*. The Oxford is especially valuable for the history of words, since it includes words from the beginnings on, unless they became obsolete before 1100, and gives many dated citations. *Webster's Third New International* (1962), is notable not only for the fact that it is the most recent unabridged dictionary, but also for its thorough treatment of meanings and synonymies. It is of less value for historical study, however, since it does not date its citations and includes only words in circulation since 1755.

Among the many books about the vocabulary of English, the following may be cited for reliable and accurate scholarship combined with readable and untechnical style.

Greenough, James B., and George L. Kittredge, *Words and Their Ways in English Speech*. London: Macmillan & Co., Ltd., 1902.

Marckwardt, Albert H., *American English*. New York: Oxford University Press, 1958 (also in paperback).

McKnight, George H., *English Words and Their Backgrounds*. London: Appleton, 1923.

Pyles, Thomas, *Words and Ways of American English*. New York: Random House, 1952 (also in paperback).

Robertson, Stuart, and Frederic G. Cassidy, *The Development of Modern English*. 2d ed. Englewood Cliffs, N.J.: Prentice-Hall, 1954. Chs. 7-9, pp. 146-278.

Sheard, J. A., *The Words of English*. New York: W. W. Norton

& Company, Inc., 1966. (Originally published as *The Words We Use*. London: André Deutsch, 1954.)

Vallins, G. H., *The Making and Meaning of Words: A Companion to the Dictionary*. London: A. & C. Black, Ltd., 1949.

## Five

# ENGLISH SPEECH
# AND WRITING

### *1. The Two Channels of Communication*

A language consists of a lexicon—a set of words—and a grammar—a set of rules by which words are combined into meaningful constructions. But for a language to carry out its main function, communication, there must be a channel through which these meaningful constructions can be passed from one person to another. All living languages have one such channel, **speech**. In addition, fewer than half the languages of the world, including English, have a second channel, **writing**. All the other modes by which language can be communicated derive from one or the other of these.

Within each of these channels, communication is controlled by a system whose structure consists of a relatively small set of units and a set of rules governing their use. The system controlling the speech channel is the **phonological system**; the system controlling the writing channel is the **graphological system**. Every language has its own phonological system, and every language which uses the writing channel has its own graphological system. Although the actual speech sounds or the letter shapes used by two languages may be quite similar, the systems behind them are different.[1] English and Dutch, for example, use the same alphabet,

---

1. The Chinese system, whose graphic units are based on morphemes rather than phonemes, is actually used by a variety of "dialects" which are really separate, mutually unintelligible languages.

but any literate English speaker knows that *lijk* is an impossible structure according to the graphological system of English, just as any literate Dutchman knows that *night* cannot be Dutch.

In this chapter we will examine the phonological and graphological systems of English, with regard to their internal structure, the ways in which they represent language, and the relationship between them. Since everyone learns to understand and produce speech before he learns to read and write,[2] the phonological system has first claim on our attention.

## 2. *Phonemes*

The units of the phonological system are **phonemes.** Phonemes, not themselves sounds, are manifested as sounds when people speak. This is not a trivial or hairsplitting distinction. The sounds people make are almost infinitely varied, but the phonemes represented by these sounds belong to a limited and sharply defined set. As an analogy, consider the positions on a football team. A great many boys and men play football. But on any given team playing according to the standard rules, there are only eleven positions, each distinct from the others in formal and systematic ways. At any given time, the position of outside right is filled by a certain player. But the player is not the position; he simply represents or manifests it at that time. If a substitution is made, the individual player changes but the position remains. It is the same way with phonemes. In any specific instance of speech, or **utterance,** a particular phoneme may be represented by a certain specific sound; in another utterance by the same or a different speaker, the same phoneme may be represented by a somewhat different sound. The different sounds that may represent a phoneme in the speech of a given individual are the **allophones** of that phoneme.

To change the analogy to another sport, the allophones of a phoneme are like the bowlers of a cricket team. On each side there may be five or six different individuals designated as bowlers. But whenever the team is playing, only one of these players is *the* bowler at any given moment. The position of bowler is manifested

2. This applies, of course, only to normal people learning their first or native language. The deaf may learn to write and read before learning to speak, and many people learn to read and write a second language without ever being able to speak it.

in that person at that moment. In the same way, at a particular point in an utterance where a given phoneme is called for, it is manifested by a sound which is one of its allophones.

As compared with the number of morphemes or words in a language, both of which run into tens or hundreds of thousands, the number of phonemes is quite small. Some languages have as few as fifteen; others have as many as sixty. English has thirty-two.[3] All utterances in English can be thought of as manifesting patterns built out of these thirty-two fundamental units, arranged according to the phonological rules of English. Spoken English can be compared to chess, in which hundreds of thousands of games, all different, result from the manipulation of thirty-two pieces in accordance with stringent rules of position and movement. Both speech and chess are strikingly and characteristically human inventions. In both, a great, virtually infinite range of structures can be built out of a small set of distinct units and a finite set of explicit rules for putting them together.

The phonemes of English can be classified in several ways. The most important basic distinction is that between syllabic and nonsyllabic phonemes. This division derives from the concept of the **phonemic syllable** as the lowest level of construction into which phonemes are combined. The phonemic syllable consists of three parts, a **peak** preceded by an **onset** and followed by a **coda**. The peak must always be present; the onset or the coda, or both, may be missing. A **syllabic** is a phoneme which constitutes the peak of a syllable; a **non-syllabic** is a phoneme which occurs as all or part of the onset or coda. Since a few of the thirty-two English phonemes may sometimes be syllabics and sometimes non-syllabics, this actually gives us a threefold division: syllabics, non-syllabics, and **semi-syllabics.**

Another classification, based on the phonetic nature of the sounds which represent the phonemes, is the familiar division into **consonants** and **vowels.**[4] In general the syllabics are called vowels and the non- and semi-syllabics are called consonants, though different analyses of English phonology differ on this point. A third classification, also phonetically based, puts the syllabics and semi-

3. According to the dialect and system being presented here. Other treatments of English recognize as many as forty-seven.
4. The terms **consonant** and **vowel** are commonly used to refer to letters as well as to phonemes. In this chapter, however, the terms **consonantal (grapheme)** and **vocalic (grapheme)** will be used to refer to letters.

syllabics into a class of **resonants** and the non-syllabics into a class of **non-resonants** or **obstruents**. These different classifications, with the symbols commonly used to designate their members, may be brought together into a single table:

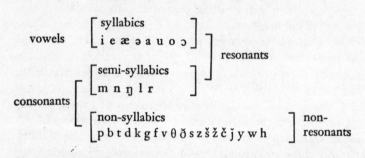

As this table shows, vowels are always syllabic; non-resonant consonants are never syllabic; and resonant consonants can be either syllabic or non-syllabic.

## 3. The Consonants of English

Further classification of phonemes is based on the way in which their allophones are produced. Thus /p b t d k g/ are called **stops,** because the breath stream is completely stopped for a brief period during the articulation of their allophones. A stop can be demonstrated by holding the central consonant of *rabbit* for an artificially long time. The stops divide into three pairs, depending on what part of the mouth is used in forming them. Since the stop for /p/ and /b/ is produced by the lips, these are **labial stops.** The stop for /t/ and /d/ is usually made by placing the tip or **apex** of the tongue against either the upper front teeth or the hard ridge of gum (the **alveolar ridge**) behind them; they are thus conveniently called **apical stops.** The third set, /k/ and /g/, are produced by placing the back, or dorsum, of the tongue against the soft palate; they are thus called **dorsal stops.**

Another type of contrast accounts for the difference between /p/ and /b/, /t/ and /d/, /k/ and /g/. When the first consonant of each of these pairs is spoken, the vocal cords, whose vibration produces **voice,** are relaxed and inoperative, when the second consonant in these pairs is spoken, the vocal cords are tense and vibrating. You can test the difference by putting your hands over your ears and saying pairs of words like *pip* and *bib, tut* and *dud,* *kick* and *gig*. It is easy to perceive that the allophones of /p t k/ are **voiceless,** while those of /b d g/ are **voiced.**

The next set of non-resonant consonants includes /f v θ ð s z š ž/. When the allophones of these phonemes are produced, the air passage through the mouth is narrowed to so small an aperture that the air passing through makes a rushing frictional noise; for this reason they are called **fricatives.** These phonemes divide into four pairs on the basis of the position in the mouth where the narrowest aperture occurs. For /f/ and /v/ this is usually between the lower lip and the upper teeth, though it may be between the two lips. Since at least one lip is always involved, these consonants are most simply called **labial fricatives.** The pair /θ/ and /ð/ can be illustrated by the first sounds in *thin* and *then*, in which the narrowest aperture is between the tongue and the upper teeth. They are **dental fricatives.** Since /s/ and /z/ are commonly produced in a narrow aperture between the tongue and the alveolar ridge behind the upper front teeth, they are **alveolar fricatives.** Finally /š/ and /ž/, as in *Asher* and *azure*, are produced farther back on the hard palate and are thus called **palatal fricatives.** As in the pairs of stop consonants, the first consonant in each of the fricative pairs is voiceless and the second voiced. You can test the difference by covering your ears and saying *luffing* and *loving*, *ether* and *either*, *facing* and *fazing*, *fission* and *vision*.

The next pair of non-resonant consonants, /č/ and /ǰ/, occur at the beginning of *cheap* and *jeep*. Like the other pairs we have been examining, the first consonant, /č/, is voiceless and the second, /ǰ/, is voiced. They resemble both stops and fricatives in the way that their allophones are made: in effect they begin like stops and end like fricatives. Thus /č/ starts like /t/ and ends like /š/, while /ǰ/ starts like /d/ and ends like /ž/.[5] The technical name for them is **affricates.** Since they are the only affricates there are in English, it is not necessary to name the position of their articulation in the mouth. They may, however, be called **alveolar affricates.**

The next two non-resonant phonemes, /y/ and /w/, have in common the fact that their allophones are characterized by movement rather than fixed position in the mouth. For this reason they are called **glides.** For /y/ at the beginning of *yet* and *use*, the tip of the tongue starts close to the alveolar ridge and moves down and

5. In some discussions of English phonology these are treated as clusters, /tš/ and /dž/, instead of as unit phonemes.

away, while for /y/ at the end of *try* and *boy* it moves up and forward, closer to the alveolar ridge. It is thus an **apical glide**. For /w/, as in *wan* and *now*, the glide position involves both the back of the tongue and rounding of the lips; we can call it simply a **dorsal glide**, though **labiovelar** is a more precise term.

The allophones of /h/, the last of the non-resonant consonants, are produced by a generalized friction noise in the vocal tract, chiefly the mouth, while it is in position for a following vowel or glide; /h/ is thus an **oral fricative**. Since there is no voiced-voiceless contrast for the glides (whose allophones are usually, though not always, voiced) or for /h/ (whose allophones are usually, though not always, voiceless), it is not necessary to specify this feature in describing them.

### Non-resonant Consonants

| Type | Position | Voiceless | | Voiced |
|------|----------|-----------|--|--------|
| stops | labial | /p/ | | /b/ |
| | apical | /t/ | | /d/ |
| | dorsal | /k/ | | /g/ |
| fricatives | labial | /f/ | | /v/ |
| | dental | /θ/ | | /ð/ |
| | alveolar | /s/ | | /z/ |
| | palatal | /š/ | | /ž/ |
| | oral | | /h/ | |
| affricates | (alveolar) | /č/ | | /ǰ/ |
| glides | apical | | /y/ | |
| | dorsal | | /w/ | |

The resonant consonants /m n ŋ/ are called **nasals** because their allophones are produced by closing the mouth passage and allowing the sound to come through the nose. They contrast with one another in the position of the mouth closure. For /m/, the mouth is closed by the lips as for /p/ and /b/; /m/ is called a **labial nasal**. The position of closure for /n/ is about the same as for /t/ and /d/; /n is an **apical nasal**. The closure for the allophones of /ŋ/, as in *sing* and *song*, is made with the back of the tongue; hence /ŋ/ is a **dorsal nasal**. Most of the allophones of /m n ŋ/ are voiced, but voiceless ones occur in some pronunciations of such words as *smith* and *sniff*. Since these voiceless pronunciations do not contrast with pronunciations of these words using voiced allophones, the voiced-voiceless distinction is not significant for the nasals.

The resonant consonants /l/ and /r/ are commonly called **liquids.** The allophones of /l/ are formed by closing off the center of the mouth with the tongue while leaving one or both sides open for the passage of the sound. For this reason /l/ is called a **lateral.** Most allophones of English /l/ are voiced, but voiceless ones may occur in some pronunciations of words like *clean* and *please.* As with the nasals, the difference between voiced and voiceless laterals is not a significant contrast in English (though it is in some other languages, such as Welsh). Nor is the position of articulation significant: any lateral is an allophone of /l/. In practice the articulation is usually apical, but it may be dorsal or both apical and dorsal at the same time.

The allophones of /r/ vary considerably from one dialect to another and from one speaker to another. The forms most common in American English are **retroflex,** when the tip of the tongue is turned up toward the roof of the mouth, and **constricted,** when the whole tongue is drawn back and somewhat humped in the middle. There may also be an accompanying rounding of the lips. In standard British English a **flap,** formed by rapidly tapping the tip of the tongue against the alveolar ridge, is used in words like *sorry.* To Americans this sounds like an allophone of /d/ or /t/. Scottish English makes use of a **trill,** in which the tip of the tongue is vibrated against the alveolar ridge. Most allophones of /r/ are voiced, but voiceless ones may be used in words like *prince* and *truck.* In any case the voiced-voiceless difference is not a significant contrast, nor is the difference between one or another type of articulation; all varieties of English have only one /r/ phoneme.

In words like *mum, nun, long,* and *wrong,* the resonant consonants belong to either the onset or the coda of the phonemic syllable; they are non-syllabic. But resonant consonants may also be syllabic, as in the final syllables of one kind of pronunciation of *happen, button, bottle,* and *butter.* The difference is due partly to the phonemic environment and partly to a prolonging of the resonant to give it extra length. Some pairs of words illustrating the contrast between non-syllabic and syllabic resonants are *prayed: parade; cress:caress; claps:collapse.* The first word of each of these pairs has only one syllable; their resonants are non-syllabic. The second word of each pair has two syllables, one of which has a resonant consonant as its syllabic. The same kind of contrast can be heard in a pair like *hymnal* and *liminal,* the second of which has three syllables because (in one pronunciation, at least) there is a syllabic /n/ for the middle syllable.

## 4. *The Vowels and Diphthongs*

The most common syllabics in English, as in other languages, are **vowels**. These are phonemes whose allophones are **central oral resonants** (sometimes called **vocoids**), produced without narrowing the central mouth passage sufficiently to produce local friction noise. They are always voiced. Sometimes the nasal passage is partly open, in which case **nasalized** allophones are produced.[6] The vowels are distinguished from one another by their **timbre**. Variations are made by changing the shape of the mouth cavity to change the harmonics or overtones of the voice which are reinforced and those which are suppressed. The vowels thus differ from one another somewhat as a note on a violin differs from a note of the same pitch on a flute.

We change the shape of the mouth cavity in three principal ways: (1) by moving the tongue and the lower jaw up or down, (2) by moving the highest part of the tongue forward or back, and (3) by pursing or rounding the lips or spreading them. We can thus speak of vowels as **high, mid,** or **low;** as **front, central,** or **back,** and as **round** or **unround** (or in some cases **spread**). The allophones of a specific vowel phoneme usually are alike in all three of these dimensions. The allophones of /i/, for instance, are high, front, and unround, so that /i/ can be called a high front unround vowel.

Speakers of English vary in the number of vowel phonemes they use, the number ranging from six to ten. This is one of the major ways in which regional varieties or dialects of English differ. To present even a selection of the great variety of vowel patterns in different dialects of English would carry us far beyond the scope of this discussion. Instead, let us here examine one type of English, a variety of the English of Philadelphia, the principal city in the East Midland (Middle Atlantic) dialect area of the United States. Readers from other regions of the United States and from

6. In many languages, French for example, nasalized vowels are separate phonemes.

other English-speaking countries should compare their own vowel systems with the one presented here.

In this variety of English there are eight short vowel phonemes: three front, three back, and two central. The allophones of the three front and two central vowels are all unround; the allophones of the three back vowels are rounded, though the amount of rounding varies a good deal. In general the two higher back vowels are more rounded than the lower one. The three front vowels are high front /i/ as in *bit*, mid front /e/ as in *bet*, and low front /æ/ as in *bat*. The three back vowels are high back round /u/ as in *wool*, mid back round /o/ as in *whole* (which contrasts with *hole*), and low back round /ɔ/ as in *Poll*. The two central vowels are high central /ə/ as in *but* and *hull* and low central /a/ as in *father* (contrasting with *bother*, which has /ɔ/). These eight vowels may be arranged in a scheme which shows their relative positions:

|  | front | central | back |
|---|---|---|---|
| high | i |  | u |
|  |  | ə |  |
| mid | e |  | o |
| low | æ | a | ɔ |

In addition to the eight simple vowels, contrast among syllabics is attained in two other ways: **length** and **diphthongs**. Length has three components, which usually appear in combination. The first of these is **duration**: the vowel is held for a longer time. The second is **raising**: the allophone of the vowel either is somewhat higher than the short allophones or starts at the same height but glides to a slightly higher position. The third is **tension**: the muscles of the throat and mouth are more tightly contracted than they are in the production of the short vowel allophones.

In the dialect under consideration, length may affect the three front and three back vowels, but not the two central ones. Contrast between words having long and short vowels will illustrate these differences. The syllabic of *beet* (or *beat*) /biːt/[7] compared with that of *bit* /bit/ shows all three components of length; it is higher, tenser, and somewhat longer. It may be slightly higher and fronter at the end than at the beginning, especially in stressed final position,

7. The phonetic and phonemic symbol for length is /ː/.

G

as in "Who, *me*?" This effect is somewhat more pronounced in *bait* /beːt/ contrasted with *bet* /bet/. The syllabic of /beːt/ begins very much like that of /bet/ but rises quickly until at the end it is as high as a low allophone of /i/.

The contrasts in length of the two higher back vowels closely parallel those of the two higher front vowels. The syllabic of *fool* /fuːl/ is higher, tenser, and somewhat longer than that of *full* /ful/. It is also somewhat more rounded and may move upward and backward toward the end. The syllabic of *hole* /hoːl/ contrasts with that of *whole* /hol/ principally in its upward glide almost to the position of /u/ at the end. It is also tenser and somewhat longer.

The low front and low back vowels, when long, are higher, tenser, and longer than the corresponding short vowels but do not show any upward glide. When compared to that of *pad* /pæd/, the syllabic of *bad* /bæːd/ is higher (nearer to the position of /e/), considerably more tense, and somewhat longer. The same is true of the syllabic of *caught* /kɔːt/ contrasted with that of *cot* /kɔt/; in this case there is somewhat more rounding as well.

**Diphthongs** are syllabics exhibiting a marked glide from one vowel position to another. We have seen that /iː eː uː oː/ may have some of this glide movement; they may be diphthongs phonetically, though it is more convenient to treat them as long vowels phonemically. But there are four phonemic diphthongs widely used in this dialect. They are analyzed as a sequence of two phonemes: a short vowel followed by one of the two glides /y/ or /w/. The glide cannot be in the same position in the front-to-back dimension as the vowel; therefore front vowels combine with /w/, back vowels with /y/, and central vowels with either. The syllabic of *tide* (or *tied*) /tayd/ begins in the low central position of /a/ and ends in the lower high front area of /i/. The syllabic of *noise* /noyz/ begins in the mid back position of /o/ and moves to the same final position as /ay/. The syllabic of *loud* /lawd/ begins in the low central position of /a/ and moves to the high back round position of /u/. The syllabic of *news* /niwz/ begins in the high front position of /i/ and moves to the high back round position of /u/. Phonetically these diphthongs may vary considerably, depending on the consonant phonemes with which they appear, but phonemically they are always /ay/, /oy/, /aw/, and /iw/.

There are, then, eighteen contrasting kinds of syllabics involving vowels or diphthongs in the dialect here dealt with: eight short vowels, six long vowels, and four diphthongs. Some examples of

## Vowels and Diphthongs

/i/   bit, bid, myth, minute, lily, mirror
      /bit, bid, miθ, mínit, líli:, mírr/

/i:/   beet, bead, field, machine, dearer
      /bi:t, bi:d, fi:ld, məší:n, dí:rr/

/e/   bet, bed, breath, length, effect, merry
      /bet, bed, breθ, lenkθ, əfékt, méri:/

/e:/   bait, made, day, obeyed
      /be:t, me:d, de:, obé:d/

/æ/   hat, had, math, contract, marry
      /hæt, hæd, mæθ, kəntrǽkt, mǽri:/

/æ:/   pass, mad, path, man, candy, Mary
      /pæ:s, mæ:d, pæ:θ, mæ:n, kǽ:ndi:, mǽ:ri:/

/ə/   but, bud, muss, above, hurry
      /bət, bəd, məs, əbə́v, hə́ri:/

/a/   balm, cart, father, lager, starry
      /bam, kart, fáðr, lágr, stári:/

/u/   put, full, puss, good, value, unite, jury
      /put, ful, pus, gud, vǽlyu, yunáyt, júri:/

/u:/   loot, fool, loose, unit, Jewry
      /lu:t, fu:l, lu:s, yú:nit, jú:ri:/

/o/   whole, home, only, wont
      /hol, hom, ónli:, wont/

/o:/   boat, hole, hoe, owner, lonely, won't
      /bo:t, ho:l, ho:, ó:nr, ló:nli:, wo:nt/

/ɔ/   cot, bomb, fog, gloss, hostage, bother, logger, sorry
      /kɔt, bɔm, fɔg, glɔs, hɔ́stij, bɔ́ðr, lɔ́gr, sɔ́ri:/

/ɔ:/   caught, dog, law, loss, sausage, soaring
      /kɔ:t, dɔ:g, lɔ:, lɔ:s, sɔ́:sij, sɔ́:riŋ/

/ay/   tide, tight, nice, try, admire, idyllic
      /tayd, tayt, nays, tray, ədmáyr, aydílik/

/oy/   noise, Freud, boy, loyal, spoil
      /noyz, froyd, boy, lóyəl, spoyl/

/aw/   loud, out, coward, flowery, cow
      /lawd, awt, káwrd, fláwrri:, kaw/

/iw/   tune, dude, dew, news, chew, Judy
      /tiwn, diwd, diw, niwz, čiw, jíwdi:/

these eighteen syllabics are presented above. It is to be emphasized that these represent a "correct" or "standard" pronunciation of these words not for all speakers of English but only for those who speak the same dialect as the author. Other regions have their standards, which differ from this and from one another both in the number and type of their syllabics and in the distribution of syllabics in words.

## 5. Syllables and Phonological Words

When phonemes are put together in accordance with orderly rules of combination, the results are **phonological constructions.** Just as each language has its own set or inventory of phonemes, so each language has its own set of combining or **tactical** rules, which are different from those of other languages. It is not permitted in English, for example, to begin a syllable with combinations like /mb nd ŋg/, but initial combinations like these are quite possible in many languages. The reason for their absence in English is not that they are "hard to pronounce," though speakers of English who have had no occasion to practice them may consider them so. It is simply a rule of the English phonological system, which can be stated very simply: no initial consonant clusters in English begin with nasals.

The smallest kind of phonological constructions are **syllables.** As we have already seen, the indispensable part of a syllable is a syllabic —a vowel, diphthong, or resonant consonant appearing as the peak. Some syllables, such as the first syllable of *omit*, consist of nothing more than a syllabic. Others may have an onset as well, consisting of from one to three consonants, as in *the* /ðə/, *tree* /tri:/, and *straw* /strɔ:/. Syllables may also have a coda, consisting of from one to four consonants following the syllabic, as in *at* /æt/, *ax* /æks/, *inched* /inčt/, and *Ernst's* /r̩nsts/ (the first /r/ is the syllabic). Finally, syllables may have both onset and coda, as in *bat* /bæt/, *clapped* /klæpt/, and *strength* /streŋkθ/.

There are strong restrictions on the combinations or **clusters** of consonants that may appear in the onsets and codas of syllables. In other words, both **selection** and **order** are important tactical features of syllable construction. For example, if the onset contains three consonants, the first must be /s/, the second must be one of the voiceless stops /p t k/, and the third must be either a glide or a non-nasal resonant /w y r l/. Even some of the combinations permitted by these restrictions are missing: /stl/ and /spw/ for example. Similar but more complicated rules govern the selection and ordering of consonants in two-consonant clusters: /šr/ is permitted but not /sr/, /kl/ but not /tl/, /sp/ but not /šp/(except in a few German words), and so on. The selection and ordering of consonants in the codas of syllables are also subject to rigorous restrictive rules. For example, sequences of fricative and stop or fricative and fricative must be either voiced or voiceless throughout: /sk/ as in /æːsk/ and /θs/ as in /smiθs/ are permitted, but not /zk sg ðs θz/.

The rules for the construction of English syllables are too complicated to be given in full here, though it is possible to state them explicitly and rigorously. But it is an interesting fact that, like the rules for grammatical constructions, they are subconsciously known to every native speaker of the language. If you ask a native speaker of English to make up a one-syllable nonsense word, it is almost certain that he will not violate the syllable-construction rules (unless, of course, he consciously tries to do so). He will produce combinations like /glæp/, /skrɔːnč/, and /grəŋk/, but never ones like /zmroːk/ or /gdžeː/. Faced with these last, he may well say that they are impossible to pronounce. They aren't; speakers of Polish use them all the time. They simply do not conform to the tactical rules of English syllable construction.

The next larger unit we encounter as we move up the scale of phonological constructions is the **phonological word**. It is important to realize that the phonological word is a construction of the phonological system alone; it does not necessarily represent a word in the lexical system of the language (which we defined in Chapter Four, pp. 113–16) nor yet a graphic word, which is simply what we write with space on either side. It may correspond to one or both of these, or it may not. When we say *Why don't you come?* in a manner quite normal in easy conversation, the middle part comes out as /dóːnču/. This is a single phonological word, for reasons which we shall shortly explain. But as we wrote it above, the phrase corresponds to two graphic words, ⟨don't⟩ and ⟨you⟩,[8] since the occurrence of space in the line of letters (or absence of hyphen at the end of the line) is what marks the division between graphic words. And when we analyze the phrase grammatically, we find that it consists of three lexical words, {*do*}, {*not*}, and {*you*}. It is important to remember that each of the subsystems making up the over-all system of a language has its own units and its own constructions.

A **phonological word** can be defined as a construction of one or more syllables, bounded by open transition and characterized

---

8. To distinguish graphemes from other linguistic units, they are enclosed in angle brackets ⟨ ⟩.

by the presence or absence of stress. In order to understand this definition, we must understand two important concepts, **open transition** and **stress.**

When the sounds that represent phonemes—the allophones—are strung together in speech, they normally merge into one another in a way that blurs the boundaries between them and causes their phonetic qualities to overlap and run together. Two words like *ant* and *apt*, which phonemically differ only in their second phoneme (/ænt/ contrasted with /æpt/), are phonetically different all the way through. In *ant*, the quality of the syllabic /æ/ is much influenced by the fact that the next sound is a nasal; in *apt* the /t/ following the /p/ is different from that following the /n/ of *ant*. This blurred and smeared fashion of going from one sound to another is **normal transition.** But phonemes also have allophones that are not influenced by preceding or by following sounds; they are the ones that come at the beginnings or ends of utterances. If I say *get out* as a complete utterance, the /g/ of *get* is **initial**; it follows silence, rather than another sound, and appears in a characteristic initial allophone. Similarly the /t/ of *out* is a **final allophone** and may be different from the /t/ of *get*. All phonemes which may be initial—which means all except /ŋ/ and, for most speakers, /ž/— have initial allophones, and all phonemes which may be final—all except /h/—have final allophones.

Every so often in the stream of speech two successive phonemes, instead of being in normal transition, appear in their final and initial allophones respectively. When this happens, there is an **open transition** or **disjuncture.** It gives the effect of a very short pause in the stream of speech, though the pause is actually an illusion. What happens is that the hearer, unconsciously very sensitive to the differences among allophones, identifies the final allophone of one phoneme and the initial allophone of the next one as making a break or joint in the phonological structure of what is being said. These breaks are the divisions between phonological words.

For example, the usual way of pronouncing *a name* in the stream of speech is with normal transition between the /ə/ and the /n/, making /əné:m/, a single phonological word. But the sequence *an aim* is usually said with disjuncture between the article and noun. If we use /+/ to mark this disjuncture, *an aim* appears as /ən+é:m/, or two phonological words. By this means we indicate a contrast between the two otherwise identical utterances: *he hasn't a name* /hi:+hæznt+əne:m/ and *he hasn't an aim*/hi:+hæznt+ən+e:m/.

Other examples: *not a tall man* /nɔtə+tɔ:l+mæn/ and *not at all, man* /nɔtət+ɔ:l+mæ:n/; *it's a tome* /itsə+to:m/ and *it's at home* /itsət+ho:m/.

Phonological words also exhibit the phonemic feature of **stress**, which is prominence added to a syllable primarily by pronouncing it more loudly and energetically than other syllables in the environment. Some short phonological words have no stress, such as the /ən/ in *he hasn't an aim*. Others may have **major** or **minor stress**, or, if they consist of more than one syllable, both of these. Thus *permit*, when it is a noun, has major stress (marked /'/) on the first syllable /pŕmit/ and, when it is a verb, on the second syllable /prmít/. Phonological words of several syllables, such as *corroboration*, are likely to have one major stress and one minor stress (marked /`/): /krrɔ̀brré:šn/. In any case, a phonological word never has more than one major stress.

Now that we have identified the tactical feature of disjuncture, we can state the rule determining whether or not a resonant consonant is syllabic. The general rule is relatively simple: a resonant consonant (/r l m n ŋ/) is syllabic when it occurs with a consonant or a disjuncture on each side. Diagrammatically, where *C* is any consonant, *R* is any resonant consonant, and + is disjuncture:

$$\left.\begin{matrix} C \\ + \end{matrix}\right\} R \left\{\begin{matrix} C \\ + \end{matrix}\right.$$

A few examples will show how the rule works:

| | | |
|---|---|---|
| 1. *environment CRC* | burnoose | /brnú:s/ |
| | catapult | /kǽtəplt/ (or /kǽtəpɔ̀lt/ with a vowel) |
| | content | /kntént/ |
| | compose | /kmpó:z/ |
| 2. *environment CR+* | banner | /bǽnr+/ |
| | bottle | /bɔ́tl/ (or /bɔ́təl/ with a vowel) |
| | button | /bɔ́tn/ |
| 3. *environment +RC* | earth | /rθ/ |
| | ulterior | /ltíri:yr/ (or /əltíri:yr/ with a vowel) |
| | entire | /ntáyr/ (or /intáyr/ with a vowel) |
| 4. *environment +R+* | man or beast | /mǽ:n+r+bí:st/ |
| | they'll go | /ðé:+l+gó:/ |
| | cat and dog | /kǽt+n+dɔ́:g/ |

As the table indicates, many of these words have an alternative pronunciation, vowel followed by a non-syllabic resonant consonant. The only syllabic resonant consonant that can have stress is /r/; hence words like *ultimate, enter,* and *comfort* always have a vowel before the resonant consonant in the stressed syllable: /ɔ́ltimit/, /éntr/, /kɔ́mfrt/.

A second rule is needed to determine which resonant consonants are syllabic when two or more of them appear in sequence. First we must rank the resonants in order of increasing constriction:

1. all vowels and diphthongs     no oral constriction at all
2. /r/     some constriction, medial opening
3. /l/     medial oral constriction, lateral opening
4. /m n ŋ/     complete oral constriction, nasal opening
5. all other consonants

The second rule may now be stated as follows: a resonant is syllabic if it is of rank equal to or higher than the rank of the phonemes on both sides of it. Note that this rule automatically makes all vowels syllabic; since it is of the highest rank, a vowel is at least equal to any possible contiguous phoneme. Some examples:

Hitler
/hítlr/
51532+

The /i/, a 1 between two 5's, is naturally syllabic; the /l/ is of lower rank than the following /r/, so it is not syllabic; the /r/, between the lower-ranking /l/ and the following +, is syllabic. Two syllables.

littler
/lítllr/
315332+

The second /l/, between the lower ranking /t/ and the following equal /l/, is syllabic; the next /l/, of lower rank than the following /r/, is not; the final /r/ is. Three syllables.

corroborate
/krrɔ́brrè:t/
52215221 5

The first and third /r/'s are syllabic; the second and fourth are not. Four syllables.

mountainous
/máwntnnəs/
41  454415

Only the second /n/, between lower-ranking /t/ and equal following /n/, is syllabic. (The /w/, as part of the first syllabic, does not count as a consonant.) Three syllables.

## 6. Phonological Phrases

The next type of phonological construction we encounter as we move up the scale of complexity is the **phonological**

**phrase.** This is the smallest kind of phonological construction that appears as a free, independent, and complete element. Every utterance, then (unless it is artificially interrupted or cut off), must consist of at least one phonological phrase. The phonological phrase can be defined as a sequence of one or more phonological words, bounded by terminals and characterized by a pitch contour. This definition involves two more tactical features, **terminal** and **pitch contour,** which combine with the already described features of selection, order, open transition, and stress to govern the combining of phonemes into organized phonological constructions.

Any musical tone has a pitch, which is determined by the fundamental frequency of vibration of the string, reed, column of air, metal or glass plate, or bell, or whatever it is that produces the tone. The greater the number of vibrations per second, the higher the pitch. The human voice, produced by the vibrating vocal cords, also has pitch. Since we can change the rate of vibration of the vocal cords by varying the amount of tension with which they are contracted, we are capable of varying the pitch of the voice. In singing this is done in order to produce the musical effect of a melody. In speech it is done to produce the **pitch contours** which are a characteristic feature of phonological phrases.

The pitches used in speech are relative, not absolute. Unlike the singer, who must closely control the exact level of pitch to produce the desired melody without singing "off key," the speaker need vary his pitches up and down only in relation to one another. Speech pitch is therefore relative, since the natural ranges of men's, women's, and children's voices are too different to permit them all to use the same set of absolute pitches.

Normal pitch contours make use of three relative levels of pitch: **normal,** marked /2/; **low,** marked /1/; and **high,** marked /3/. A fourth level, **extra-high,** marked /4/, is used for certain special pitch contours. Some variation of pitch occurs within each level. Not all syllables spoken on normal pitch, even within the same phonological phrase, are on exactly the same musical note, but they never vary so much as to become confused with the neighboring levels. Pitch levels, in other words, are contrastive and exhibit the same kind of non-significant variation we call allophonic when it concerns phonemes.

Transitions from one pitch to another are made in two ways, by abrupt **shifts** and by gradual **glides.** Shifts occur at the boundaries of syllables—often, though not always, at disjunctures. Glides occur over a span of phonemes in normal transition; they are so gradual that it is not possible to mark the point of transition from one pitch level to another but only to distinguish the starting and ending points. A commonly used glide, in fact, descends from high to low pitch, sometimes within the span of a single syllable, without pausing on normal pitch anywhere in its course.

The boundaries of phonological phrases are set by **terminals.** These occur at disjunctures and are marked by a slowing up of the tempo, sometimes a slight pause, and a characteristic feature of pitch extending over the last resonant phoneme preceding the position of disjuncture. In a **level terminal**, marked /→/, the pitch remains level; in a **rising terminal**, marked /↗/, it turns slightly upward; in a **falling terminal**, marked /↘/, it drops slightly and then fades perceptibly. A rising terminal may be heard at the end of a question like *Are you going away?* A falling terminal is the most usual way of ending statement sentences like *I'm going tomorrow.* Level terminals are relatively rare at the ends of utterances; they more commonly appear between two phonological phrases in the same sentence or utterance. One may appear after *it* in a sentence like *I'd do it if I dared*, though this may also be spoken as a single phonological phrase, with only the falling terminal at the end.

A pitch contour, then, consists of a series of pitch levels—at least two and seldom more than three—and a terminal. Pitch contours of three pitches begin on normal pitch and at some point shift up or down to high or low pitch. The shift usually occurs at the beginning of a syllable that has major stress and places the **accent** of the phonological phrase on that syllable. The syllable that has the accent is made more prominent than any other syllable in its phonological phrase by this combination of pitch-shift and major stress. The accent is most commonly on the last major-stressed syllable in the phrase, but it may fall elsewhere. When the accent falls on the first syllable of a phrase, there is no actual occurrence of normal pitch before it, but the fact that the phrase begins on high or low rather than normal pitch gives the effect of a shift from a zero occurrence of normal pitch. If there is only one syllable with major stress in a phrase, the normal position of the accent is determined.

The most common pitch contour in American English, used for most statement sentences, many questions, and some exclamations, begins on normal pitch, shifts to high pitch at the last major-stressed syllable, glides to low pitch, and ends in a falling terminal. It can be

indicated by the formula /2 3̑ 1 ↘ / (the joining 3 and 1 indicates that this is a glide, not a shift). Some examples, with positions
of pitch beginnings and endings marked (accent is marked ×):

No.    /³nó:¹ ↘/

Hello.    /²he³ló:¹ ↘/

How are you?    /²háw+r+³yú:¹ ↘ /

He's reading a book.    /²hì:z+rí:diŋ+ə+³búk¹ ↘/

The examination will be held tomorrow.

/²ði:+igzæminé:šn+wìlbi:+héld+tə³mɔ́ro¹ ↘/

As these examples show, the number of syllables or phonological
words on normal pitch before the accented syllable may vary from
none, in *No*, to a rather large number, as in the last example. But if
the number gets very large, there is always a tendency, especially
in deliberate speech, to break the long phonological phrase into
two by inserting a terminal, usually level or rising, and another
accent. Our final example, for instance, might be spoken:

/²ði:+igzæmi³né:šn²→²wìlbi:+héld+tə³mɔ́ro¹↘/

or even, very deliberately:

/²ði:+igzæmi³né:šn²→²wìlbi:+héld²→²tə³mɔ́ro¹↘/

The first phonological phrase in each of these exhibits another
pitch contour, /2 3̑ 2 →/, commonly used to mark a phonological
phase as closely connected to another one immediately following.
If we end an utterance with this contour, the effect is of uncertainty or tentativeness, as in ²*I may go to*³*morrow*² → [*but then again
I may not*].

A pitch contour commonly used in questions is /2 3 3 ↗/.
This may cover the whole question, as in *Would you like some
coffee?*

/²wùjə+láyk+sm+³kɔ́:fi:³↗/,

or it may present alternatives, as in *Will you have coffee, tea, or
milk?*

/²wìlyə+hǽv+³kɔ́:fi:³ ↗³tí:³ ↗²ɔr+³mílk¹ ↘/.

Note that the last phonological phrase of this sentence has the
/2 3̑ 1 ↘/ contour, indicating that the question means "which of

the three would you like?" If this phrase had also had the /2 3 3 ↗/ contour, the over-all meaning of the question would be "will you have any of the three (or perhaps nothing)?" It is obvious that pitch contours not only serve to organize phonological phrases but also correlate with or manifest grammatical features of the sentences which these phrases represent.

Further prominence can be given to the accented syllable of a phonological phrase by raising the pitch another level, to extra-high /4/. Thus extra-high pitch can be considered as a reinforced or extra-accented high pitch. It is commonly used for extra emphasis, exclamation, or contrast. Thus a statement such as *It's raining*

/²íts+³ré:niŋ¹↘/

becomes an exclamation (*It's raining!*) when extra-high pitch is used:

/²íts+⁴ré:niŋ¹↘/.

In emphatic or contrastive sentences, when the accent falls on what in a normal statement would be an unstressed or minor-stressed syllable, this reinforced high pitch often calls attention to the unusual position of the accent. Thus the normal contour for a sentence like *He can do it* is /2 3 1 ↘/ with the accent on *do*:

/²hì:+kn+³dú:wit¹↘/

But if we wish to emphasize *can*, it receives the accent, often reinforced by extra high pitch:

/²hì:+⁴kǽn¹+dú:wit¹↘/

The word *can*, which was totally unstressed in the normal statement, here is given very special prominence by receiving major stress, accent, and reinforced accent and by containing the whole downward glide from extra high to low pitch. It also has a vowel /kæn/ rather than a syllabic /n/ — /kn/. The last phonological word, which contained the accent and the down-glide in the normal statement, is reduced to a weak appendage between the accent and the terminal.

## 7. *Summary of Phonology*

The phonological system is one of the channels through which a linguistic construction—a string of words in grammatical arrangement—can be communicated from one person to another.

The phonological system is not itself speech, but it is manifested as speech for purposes of communication. It is thus an intermediate strand of language structure between the lexico-grammatical system and articulate, audible speech.

The units of the phonological system are phonemes. These are a set of forms which are minimal (they cannot be subdivided) and contrastive (each is recognized as different from all the others). In speech, the phonemes are manifested by sounds or phones, which may be of great variety. All the phones which can manifest a single phoneme are the allophones of that phoneme. The allophones of a phoneme differ somewhat in sound (*i.e.*, phonetically), but they are equivalent phonemically. A phoneme thus may be thought of as manifested by a **set** of non-contrastive sounds.

The phonemes of English may be classified according to the phonetic nature of their allophones as vowels and consonants, the consonants being further subdivided into resonants and non-resonants. They may also be classified according to their position in phonological constructions as syllabics, semi-syllabics, and non-syllabics. Diphthongs, combining a vowel and a following glide consonant (/y/ or /w/), are classed with the syllabics.

The phonological system also has a set of tactical rules which govern the way in which the phonemes are combined into phonological structures. These rules introduce tactical features, which are of two kinds: boundary markers (disjuncture and terminals) and internal features (selection, order, stress, pitch, and accent).

The smallest phonological construction is the syllable, which has a syllabic—a vowel, diphthong, or resonant consonant—at its center and may have an onset of one to three consonants, a coda of one to four consonants, or both. When two or more syllables are combined into a larger construction, some of the consonants forming the coda of the first syllable may also be part of the onset of the second; there may thus be syllable overlap. Another way of putting it is that there are not always boundary markers to indicate the limits of syllables.

A syllable or group of syllables set off by disjuncture on both sides constitutes a phonological word. A phonological word is a structure of the phonological system that may or may not coincide with a lexical or graphological word. It also exhibits the feature of stress, a type of added prominence given to a syllable, which is manifested in speech as louder, more energetic articulation. Stress may be major, minor, or lacking altogether. No more than one syllable of any phonemic word may have major stress.

One or more phonological words may constitute a phonological phrase, which is bounded on either side by terminals. Terminals, which occur only at positions of disjuncture, are manifested in speech as a slowing of tempo and a characteristic treatment of pitch at the very end of the phonological word. There are three kinds of terminals: level, rising, and falling. A phonological phrase also has a pitch contour, consisting of two or three pitch levels. Movement from one pitch level to another is by means of either an abrupt shift or a gradual glide. The first major-stressed syllable following a pitch shift is the usual location of the accent. Only one syllable in a phonological phrase—usually the last major-stressed one—may be accented.

The phonological phrase is the smallest phonological unit that can occur as an independent utterance. Thus every normal uninterrupted utterance consists of one or more phonological phrases. Since the boundaries of utterances (silence) coincide with the boundaries of phonological phrases (terminals), terminals with the boundaries of words (disjunctures), and disjunctures with the boundaries of syllables (onsets and codas), every utterance consists of a specific and finite number of phrases, words, syllables, and phonemes. An utterance such as *Oh!* /'ṓː¹ ↘/ is thus not only a phoneme but also a syllable, a word, and a phrase. At the other extreme, a long speech may contain many thousands of each. Theoretically there is no limit to the length of an utterance, although various practical and social considerations usually keep utterances within relatively short compass.

## 8. The Writing System

The other channel through which a linguistic message may be communicated from one person to another is writing. As we have already suggested, this system is secondary to speech in three respects. (1) Historically it was invented much later than speech. (2) The structure of the writing system of English was originally derived in large part from the structure of the phonological system. (3) Normally people learn the phonological system of their native language several years before they learn the writing system; in fact, some never learn the writing system at all. Before we proceed to look at the writing system as it is today, it would not be amiss to examine some of the implications of these facts.

Since speech, made up of sounds in the air, is as perishable as a passing breeze, there is no way that we can know directly when or how it originated. Until the invention of the phonograph and later the tape recorder, machines which could only be devised by an advanced civilization with a long tradition of knowledge accumulated in writing, there was no way to preserve an accurate and reproducible record of speech. We can only surmise, on the indirect evidence of prehistoric archaeology, that man has had language, manifested in speech, for half a million years or even longer. There has been much speculation as to how language was invented, but none of it is more than guesswork. The most primitive peoples now on earth—the bushmen of central Africa and the aborigines of Australia—possess well-developed languages, completely adequate to their needs and exhibiting the same general features of structure that characterize the languages of the most elaborate civilizations. Presumably the languages of Stone Age men were equally well developed. The origin and early history of language and speech are lost beyond recall.

Not so with writing. The earliest true writing systems were invented not much more than 6000 years ago, a mere moment of time compared to the great age of speech. They were developed to meet the needs of growing civilizations whose cultures had become too complicated to be kept running and passed on from one generation to another by word of mouth. The decrees of rulers, the sacred records of religion, the commercial transactions of a complex business community all needed to be transmitted and preserved in some form more durable than the memories of men. So the Egyptians and the Babylonians seem to have independently contrived quite different ways of recording language in tangible, visible, and preservable form.

The very earliest forms of visual message—they can hardly be called writing—aimed at representing not the linguistic message itself but the facts behind the message. They were **pictographic.** A picture of two men walking, with a river in front of them and three suns in the sky, might convey some such message as "after we two had walked for three days, we came to a river." But the limitations of a pictographic method are obvious. Many of the ideas that men want to communicate are too complicated and abstract to be put into pictorial form. Writing proper began when men got the idea of representing in visual form not the facts themselves but *a linguistic statement of the facts.* Therefore means had to be found for manifesting linguistic constructions not as speech that can be heard but as writing that can be seen, preserved, and carried about.

The earliest true writing systems worked directly from the lexico-grammatical core of language, without reference to the phonological system. Since the smallest unit of the lexico-grammatical system is the morpheme, and since languages have large numbers of morphemes and even larger numbers of words, a writing system of this sort needs large numbers of visual signs. The only surviving writing system of importance that has continued to make use of this method is the Chinese, which has a large number of **characters**, each representing a morpheme or a construction of two or three morphemes. In spite of certain great advantages, such a system is cumbersome and difficult to learn.

The Egyptians and other peoples of the ancient Middle East discovered that the phonological system of a language furnishes a ready-made structure on which writing can be based. This seems such an obvious idea to us, who have inherited their tradition, that we wonder why it took ancient civilizations so long to think of it. But like many other great inventions, the simplicity of the idea is an illusion. It is by no means obvious to preliterate peoples that the structure underlying speech can be given visual form. Speech goes by very rapidly; it is a continuous, blurred stream of sound, and the segmented structure underlying it is by no means obvious to the listener, though subconsciously he has trained himself to perceive it. So the first writing systems based on phonology used not the phonemes but the smallest phonological constructions, the syllables, as basic units. The syllabic writing system (**syllabary**) still required a large number of signs but nowhere near as many as morphographic systems like the Chinese do. And since all languages make use of order as a structural device and have some kind of phonological border markers, it was possible to string syllabic signs together in linear sequence parallel to the time sequence of phonological syllables and divide the string up into words by inserting a marker or leaving a space at the points where word-bounding phonological phenomena occurred. The oldest Greek writing, the recently deciphered Minoan Linear B, was a syllabic writing system of this sort.

A further step toward reducing the number of graphic units and more closely matching the tactical features of the phonological system was taken by the peoples of the Eastern Mediterranean who developed the alphabet. **Alphabetic writing** depends on the perception of the phoneme as the basic unit of phonology, and the realization that with one character for each phoneme it is possible to reproduce any phonological construction, at least in its selection of phonemes and their ordering and grouping into larger constructions. Many tactical features, such as intonation and stress, are harder to represent and are usually omitted. These early alphabetical systems, like most modern ones, relied on the fact that the phonological structure of languages is **redundant**—that is, contains more information than is absolutely needed. Thus the omission of many phonological features from the representation very seldom made the message unintelligible, though it certainly increased the amount of actual or potential ambiguity in writing as compared to speech.

The earliest alphabets, used by Semitic peoples of the Middle East, were consonantal; the characters represented only the consonants. Readers had to rely on the context to fill in the vowels as well as to supply the tactical features not represented in the writing. Modern Hebrew and Arabic writing is still basically consonantal, though indicators to show the vowels have been developed for use when needed. When the Greeks borrowed a Semitic alphabet to replace their earlier syllabic system, there were some consonantal characters left over, which they used to represent vowels. All modern alphabets used in the West and wherever Western influence has spread are developments from the Greek tradition. It established the basic **alphabetic principle,** which can be succinctly stated as a one-to-one relationship between graphemes of the writing system and phonemes of the phonological system. The Czech linguist Vachek has called it "acrophony."

## 9. The Relation of Writing and Speech

The degree of accuracy with which one linguistic system, such as a writing system, represents a related system, such as a phonological system, is known as **fit.** If the fit is perfect—if every significant feature of each system has its counterpart in the other —the two systems are **isomorphic.** The great advantage of isomorphic systems is that once you have learned one of them, you need only learn a relatively simple set of equivalence rules to learn the other. Simple substitution cyphers are an example. So is Morse code. Its structure is isomorphic with that of the writing system; in order to use it one simply learns a set of dot-and-dash patterns for each grapheme and strings them together in the same order.

One need not learn a wholly new structure, with its own inventory of units and its own tactical rules.

It is almost as simple to devise a writing system that is isomorphic with the phonological system of a language. Some differences— such as the fact that phonemes are ordered in one-dimensional time while written symbols are ordered in two-dimensional space—have to be taken care of by arbitrary conventions; such as that horizontal left-to-right or vertical top-to-bottom direction in writing is the equivalent of the past-to-future movement of time in speech. The system of phonemic transcription we used earlier in this chapter is an example of a writing system that is isomorphic with a phonological system. There is one unit, a **grapheme,** in the writing system for each phoneme in the phonological system and a set of conventions for representing the tactical features of order, disjuncture, terminal, stress, pitch, and accent. Anyone who knows these relatively simple equivalence rules can convert a phonological structure into a transcription, or the reverse, without difficulty. The very fact that we have to have such a transcription for representing phonology accurately indicates that our standard writing system is not isomorphic with the phonological system. Let us explore the reasons for this state of affairs and some of its consequences.

In the first place, the situation is complicated by the fact that more than just the two systems are involved. The ultimate purpose of both the speech and the writing systems is not to represent or reproduce each other but to act as different channels through which structures in the central lexico-grammatical system of language can be communicated. The situation may be schematically represented this way:

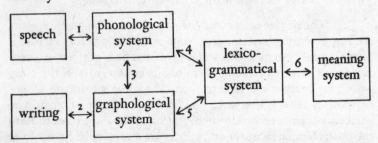

To the left are speech and writing as physical events—sounds made with the mouth and shapes made with the fingers. The double-headed arrows indicate **manifestation** or **representation**. Arrow

1 means that a spoken utterance **represents** a structure in the phonological system, and, conversely, a phonological structure **manifests itself** as a spoken utterance. Arrow 2 indicates that the same
relationship exists between a graphological structure and its physical manifestation as some form of writing. Arrows 4 and 5 indicate
that phonological and graphological structures are separate representations of structures in the lexico-grammatical system, structures which are built out of morphemes according to the rules of
grammar. Arrow 6, in turn, reminds us that when we speak or
write, we do not simply translate meaning into speech or writing.
Instead the message must go through three stages of manifestation:
first into a grammatical structure, then into either a phonological
or graphological one, and finally into speech or writing. In understanding speech that we hear or writing that we read, we reverse
the process and interpret them in terms of the intervening systems
until we reach (we hope) a structure of meaning. The process seems
complex, and indeed it is. But it is this very complexity that makes
it possible to communicate an infinite variety of messages by means
of speech or writing.

Arrow 3 indicates that there is a direct relationship between the
phonological and graphological systems, in addition to their indirect relationship as parallel manifestations of the lexico-grammatical system. The fit between them is by no means isomorphic.
In fact, it is quite complicated and often inconsistent. If it were less
so, learning to read and to spell in English would not be as difficult
as they are. The inexactness of fit between writing and speech is
attributable principally to the fact that the two systems have had
divergent histories. Gradual and unobserved changes in the phonological system have not always been matched by parallel adjustments in the graphological system. There have even been conscious
changes in the writing system that have reduced rather than increased the closeness of the fit between the two. A brief look at
these changes will help make clear why our writing system is so far
removed from being an isomorphic representation of our speech.

## 10. *The History of English Writing: Old English*

The writing system which we use today is descended from
one originally devised at the time of the conversion of the Anglo-
Saxons early in the seventh century. It was not a newly invented
system but was borrowed, with necessary adaptation, from the

system used by Latin. An earlier system, the runic alphabet (see p. 73), also based on the Roman, had been used in limited ways for English as well as for the Scandinavian languages, but it had never been used extensively for written documents. We do not know who the scribes were who first used the Roman alphabet to write English, but presumably they were speakers of English who had acquired literacy in Latin and wished to transfer this knowledge to their native tongue. In any case, their attempt seems to have been to develop a writing system that would have a close fit to the sound system of Old English, at least as regards the segmental phonemes. Since we cannot be sure of all the details of the phonological system of Old English, we cannot judge exactly how well they succeeded. But in general they seem to have done quite well.

Since the number and types of phonemes in Old English were different from those of Latin, the Latin alphabet could not be simply transferred in its entirety to Old English. The Latin alphabet was lifted, however, for those phonemes in Old English whose allophones were roughly similar to those of Latin. For those Old English phonemes which had no close counterparts in Latin, the scribes used three different expedients: (1) they adapted otherwise unused Latin graphemes, (2) they used graphemes from the older runic alphabet, and (3) they made up new graphemes. The result was the following repertory of graphemes with their probable phonemic equivalents in Old English.

### Old English Graphemes

| | | | | |
|---|---|---|---|---|
| p = /p/ | t = /t/ | c = /k/ | | |
| b = /b/ | d = /d/ | g = /g/ | | |
| m = /m/ | n = /n/ | | | |
| f = /f/ | þ, ð = /θ/ | s = /s/ | | |
| l = /l/ | r = /r/ | h = /h/ | ᵽ = /w/ | |
| i = /i/ | e = /e/ | æ = /æ/ | | |
| a = /a/ | o = /o/ | u = /u/ | y = /ü/ | |
| x = /ks/ | | | | |

In the usual alphabetic order this alphabet then used twenty-four signs: ⟨a, æ, b, c, d, e, f, g, h, i, l, m, n, o, p, r, s, t, þ, ð, u, ᵽ, x, y⟩. Two of these, ⟨æ⟩ and ⟨ð⟩, were made up by combining or altering other letters. Two others, ⟨þ⟩ (called *thorn*) and ⟨ᵽ⟩ (called *wyn*), were taken from the runic alphabet. The scribes also made occasional use of ⟨k⟩ and ⟨z⟩, which were Greek letters used infrequently in Latin writing. They did not use ⟨q⟩ at all, and our modern j and v were at that time simply variants (**allographs**) of ⟨i⟩ and ⟨u⟩. Modern ⟨w⟩, which replaced the runic ⟨ƿ⟩ during the early Middle English period, developed, as its English name indicates, from uu.

To point out the fine details of the fit of this system to Old English phonology would necessitate going into the phonemic system of Old English, which is beyond our present concern. A few important matters, however, should be observed, since they affected the later history of the system we use today. In the first place, the list of consonant graphemes is isomorphic with the list of consonant phonemes, except in two places. (1) ⟨x⟩ is used to represent not a single phoneme but a cluster of two, /ks/, each of which also has its own representation. This cluster is also represented by ⟨cs⟩. (2) The phoneme /θ/ is represented by two letters of quite different shape and origin, ⟨þ⟩ and ⟨ð⟩. Since this phoneme had two allophones, voiceless [θ] and voiced [ð], it is possible that the scribes originally intended the two letters to represent each of these individually—though writing systems seldom do indicate allophonic differences, which may go unperceived by native speakers. In any case, no surviving texts show this clear-cut separation. In late Old English writing the practice grew up of using þ in initial position and ð medially and finally, so that they came to be in complementary distribution instead of free variation.

Some further complications arise in the representation of vowels. For one thing, Old English had a phonemic distinction between long and short vowels which is not regularly represented in the writing system. Furthermore, the scribes made use of certain pairs of vowel characters, ⟨eo io ea ie⟩, to represent what may have been diphthongs or, in some cases, simple vowels; scholars are uncertain about their exact reference. Finally, the various dialects of Old English differed from one another in their phonological systems, especially the vowels. In spite of these complications, however, we can conclude that on the whole the Old English alphabet did a fair job of representing the segmental phonemes. But as in virtually all alphabets in the Latin tradition, there was no attempt to indicate such tactical features as open transition, terminals, stress, and pitch. Word spacing and some punctuation were used, but these, like their counterparts in our present-day writing system, were representations of features of the lexico-grammatical rather than the phonological system.

Very soon after the adoption of this writing system things began to happen which affected the closeness of its fit to Old English phonology. The earliest of these were changes in the phonemic system, especially of the consonants. Since Old English scribes were not as firmly committed to an orthodox and set spelling system as we are today, it was possible for them to change the writing system to accommodate it to these phonological changes, and they usually did so sooner or later. The changes they made, though often ingenious, were usually departures from the one-to-one correspondence of graphemes to phonemes which characterized the original system. They began the series of patchwork adjustments which was to result, after a thousand years, in the complicated and inconsistent fit between the writing and sound systems of present-day English. Let us observe a few of the most important of these phonological and graphological changes.

1. In early Old English, the voiceless dorsal stop /k/ had allophones farther front in the mouth—formed in the region of the palate—before front vowels. This is also the case in modern English: if you pronounce *kick* and *cook* in rapid succession, you will observe that the tongue touches the roof of the mouth much farther forward at the beginning and ending of *kick* than it does in *cook*. This is not a phonemic difference in modern English; these sounds are not in contrast. But in Old English they came to be contrastive in certain environments, and hence separate phonemes. The palatal /k/ came to be pronounced like the modern English affricate /č/. The scribes continued to use the grapheme ⟨c⟩ to spell this new phoneme. But in some cases they indicated the different pronunciation by putting an ⟨e⟩ or an ⟨i⟩ after the consonant symbol, thus creating **digraphs**—a digraph being a pair of letters which, taken together, represents a single phoneme. Thus the verb which gives us the *-seech* part of *beseech* was pronounced /séːčan/ and spelled ⟨secean⟩, with ⟨ce⟩ for the medial /č/. In much the same way today, in words like *noticeable* and *manageable*, we use the digraphs ⟨ce⟩ and ⟨ge⟩ to represent /s/ and /j/.

2. Two other important Old English digraphs which developed quite early were ⟨sc⟩ for /š/ and ⟨cg⟩ for /j/. These also resulted from changes in the phonological system. Early Old English had a consonant cluster /sk/, spelled quite normally as ⟨sc⟩. But a process of palatalization and fusion occurred, resulting in a new phoneme, /š/. Since all examples of the /sk/ cluster underwent the same change, there was no contrast between /sk/ and /š/, so

that the ⟨sc⟩ spelling continued to be used. Since it had come to represent a single phoneme, however, ⟨sc⟩ was now a digraph and therefore one more departure from the original isomorphic fit. Later, when words were borrowed from Norse, in which the palatalization and fusion of /sk/ to /š/ had not occurred, the /sk/ cluster was reintroduced, now usually spelled ⟨sk⟩, as in *sky* and *skirt*.

In some cases in Old English when the ⟨sc⟩ digraph was followed by a grapheme standing for a back vowel, an ⟨e⟩ was introduced, thus forming a **trigraph** ⟨sce⟩ to spell the single phoneme /š/, as in *sceolde*, the ancestor of modern *should*. Later on, under the influence of French scribes in the Middle English period, an ⟨h⟩ was used instead of the ⟨e⟩, giving the trigraph ⟨sch⟩ as the common spelling for /š/. Still later the ⟨c⟩ was dropped, giving the modern digraph ⟨sh⟩, parallel to ⟨ch⟩, which had replaced the older ⟨c⟩ or ⟨ce⟩ spellings for /č/.

3. In certain positions Old English had developed a long or **geminated** /g/, which the scribes quite properly represented by a double ⟨g⟩, as in *dogga*, our modern *dog*. But under certain conditions geminated /g/ also became palatalized and ultimately developed into a new phoneme, the voiced affricate /ǰ/. Perhaps because of their awareness of the ⟨c⟩ spelling for the voiceless counterpart of this phoneme, the scribes came to use the digraph ⟨cg⟩ to spell /ǰ/, as in *brycg* (modern *bridge*). This digraph also underwent change, to ⟨dg⟩, in the Middle English period. Middle English scribes also took to adding an ⟨e⟩ to this combination when it was not already followed by an ⟨e⟩ or ⟨i⟩, so that most modern English words descended from Old English words that had ⟨cg⟩ for /ǰ/ now have the trigraph ⟨dge⟩, as in *bridge*, *sedge*, *ridge*. Meanwhile words were being borrowed from French, which also had a /ǰ/ phoneme, usually spelled with ⟨i⟩ initially and ⟨g⟩ or ⟨ge⟩ elsewhere. Finally, as late as the seventeenth century, j, up to then simply an allograph of ⟨i⟩, came to be used as a distinct consonantal grapheme ⟨j⟩. The result of this complicated history is that today we have five common ways of representing the single phoneme /ǰ/: ⟨j⟩ as in *just*, ⟨dg⟩ as in *budget*, ⟨dge⟩ as in *bridge*, ⟨g⟩ as in *magic*, and ⟨ge⟩ as in *manage*.

4. Old English had a phoneme /h/ with several different allophones. Initially before vowels it seems to have been a voiceless aspirate sound such as in modern English *head*. Finally, or medially between vowels or between a vowel and a consonant, it had con-

siderable dorsal fricative quality, and thus was much like the sounds spelled with ⟨ch⟩ in German. In fact, this was probably its pronunciation in all positions in early Old English. Early Old English also had initial clusters of the /h/ phoneme with the glide and resonant consonants /r l w n/. The scribes quite properly spelled these clusters with two letters, as in *hrafn* (modern *raven*), *hlūd* (modern *loud*), *hwæt* (modern *what*), and *hnutu* (modern *nut*). Later on, the fricative element was lost and the aspiration fused with the voiceless allophones of the following consonants, so that what remained were voiceless aspirated /r l w n/. The scribes, however, continued to use the double spellings ⟨hr hl hw hn⟩, which now were digraphs. In all cases except that of /w/, the voiceless allophones were replaced by voiced ones, as in modern *raven, loud,* and *nut.* There being no phonemic contrast, the scribes dropped the ⟨h⟩, thus discarding the digraphs. But there continued to be a phonemic contrast between the voiceless aspirated initial sound of *hwæt* and the voiced unaspirated sound of *wǣt* (modern *wet*). So the scribes preserved the ⟨hw⟩ digraph to mark this distinction. During the Middle English period the digraph was inverted to ⟨wh⟩, probably by analogy with other new digraphs ⟨ch sh th⟩. Only about one half of the modern speakers of English preserve a phonemic contrast between a voiceless aspirated sound in *where, which,* and *whale* and the voiced unaspirated /w/ of *wear, witch,* and *wail.* But our modern writing system still preserves the distinction.

## 11. *The Writing Systems of Middle and Modern English*

There were other changes that affected the grapheme-phoneme fit of English during the Old English period. But the important ones we have described above are sufficient to show that, in general, the movement away from a one-to-one representation of phonemes by graphemes began quite soon after the adoption of the alphabet. This movement was greatly accelerated during the Middle English period 1100-1500. In fact, it was in that period that our writing system attained nearly its present form. As we saw in Chapter Three (p. 105), the spelling of Caxton, writing at the end of the Middle English period, is not substantially different from ours today. Printing and the spread of literacy to ever larger proportions of the population have proved to be conservative forces working against change in the writing system, in spite of the fact that there has been considerable change in the phonological system. As a result, the fit between the two has become even less perfect than it was in Caxton's day.

There is not enough space here to go into detail about changes in the writing system during and since Middle English times. But a look at the three most important general developments will help us to understand how the complications of our present system came about. Roughly in the order in which they occurred, these are: (1) the reworking of the system in terms of the writing system of French, (2) the importation of graphic conventions from Latin, Greek, and other languages, and (3) the development of a standard system independent of regional and other variations in the spoken language.

**French Spelling.** From the twelfth century until well along in the fourteenth, a large majority of the persons who wrote English were also literate in French. Many of them were native speakers of French; virtually all of them considered French a more polished and civilized language than English. It was natural for them to carry over to English writing some aspects of the French writing system, which was itself descended from that of Latin. For example, they changed the representation of /kw/ from ⟨cw⟩, which was isomorphic, to ⟨qu⟩, which is a digraph, since ⟨q⟩ does not represent /k/ anywhere else and ⟨u⟩ seldom represents /w/ in English. They adopted the French spelling ⟨ou⟩ for /u:/, which accounts for many modern spellings like *house* and *found* (OE *hūs* and *fundon*). As we have seen, they adopted the digraph ⟨ch⟩ and used it to spell not only words newly borrowed from French, like *chase* and *peach*, but also native English words like *choose* and *reach* (OE *cēosan* and *rǣcan*). They gradually dropped the Old English characters that were not in the French alphabet, replacing þ with u, uu, and finally w; þ and ð with ⟨th⟩, and dropping the ⟨æ⟩ altogether, thus creating a deficiency in vocalic graphemes from which our writing still suffers. They introduced the convention of using ⟨o⟩ to represent /u/ in the neighborhood of ⟨u n m i⟩;[9] the inconsistent application of this convention accounts for the fact

9. The reason for this was that these letters were all made with combinations of vertical strokes called **minims,** and scribes were not always careful to join ⟨m⟩ and ⟨n⟩ at the top and ⟨u⟩ at the bottom. Substituting ⟨o⟩ for ⟨u⟩ broke up some of the long "picket fences" of minims.

that in modern English *run* and *won* are a rhyme, while *shove* and *stove* are not.

Not all the changes in Middle English spelling are attributable to the influence of French. Some were the result of more or less intelligent attempts to match changes in the phonology of the language. Thus two variant shapes (allographs) of the Old English ⟨g⟩ were developed into separate graphemes. One survives as our modern ⟨g⟩. The other ⟨ȝ⟩, called *yogh* (pronounced /yɔx/ or /yɔk/) was used to spell both the high front glide /y/, which had developed from an Old English palatalized /g/ before front vowels, and the voiceless dorsal fricative /x/, which had been represented by ⟨h⟩ in Old English. The representations of the ⟨ȝ⟩ grapheme came to look more and more like ⟨z⟩, which had become more frequent in later Middle English. This is probably one reason why ⟨ȝ⟩ was dropped in favor of ⟨y⟩ to represent /y/ and ⟨gh⟩ to represent /x/. Thus we have modern *yield* from ME *ȝelde* (OE *gieldan*) and *right* from ME *riȝt* (OE *riht*). The divergent developments of the phoneme /x/ in late Middle and early Modern English account for one of the famous inconsistencies of modern English spelling: the varied significance of ⟨gh⟩ in *laugh, rough, through, though, thought, taught,* and *eight* (not to mention *doghouse*!).

**Latin and Greek Loanwords.** As we saw in Chapter Four, Latin words have been borrowed into English from the earliest times; some, indeed, were adopted by the Germanic ancestor of English before the Angles, Saxons, and Jutes came to England. These early borrowings were treated in the way that loanwords from living languages usually are: their pronunciation was adapted to the phonological system of English and went through the same history as that of native words. After English had adopted a writing system, the same thing happened to their spelling. Thus as Latin *caseus* went through various pronunciations from */kasi/ through /kese/ and /čeːzə/ to modern /čiːz/, its spelling also changed, from ⟨cese⟩ to ⟨chese⟩ and finally ⟨cheese⟩. There is little about the modern word to remind us of its Latin source.

Later on, however, in the later Middle English period and on through the Renaissance into modern times, Latin spellings were preserved virtually or wholly unchanged. After all, Latin was a second language to most scholars until well into the nineteenth century, and it seemed not only unnecessary but downright uneducated to alter the spelling of Latin loanwords to fit them to the

English writing system. As a result, a whole new set of spelling rules was grafted onto the already complex rules derived from Old English and French.

Some of the conventions of this new system derive from the fact that the form which Latin loanwords took was sometimes established by French. A number of Latin words, for example, ended in the suffix -abilis or -ibilis, which in French had became -able and -ible, the choice of vowel depending usually on the stem vowel of the underlying Latin verb. English borrowings, whether directly from Latin or through the French, use the French spelling, including the different vowel characters, even though there is no contrast in pronunciation in English. So the English writer must learn that the suffix which he pronounces /-əbl/ is spelled sometimes with ⟨a⟩ and sometimes with ⟨i⟩. A similar problem arises with the suffixes pronounced /ənt/ and /əns/, deriving ultimately from the Latin present participle ending which was -antem (in the accusative case) for first conjugation verbs and -entem for the rest, and from the ending for nouns formed from the present participle, -antia or -entia. We still have to select the spellings -ent, -ence or -ant, -ance, although the graphic contrast between ⟨a⟩ and ⟨e⟩ here corresponds to nothing in either the phonological or the lexico-grammatical system of English. Our writing system thus preserves many no longer significant vestiges of the morphological system of Latin.

The scholars of the Renaissance were so enamored of Latin that they altered the spellings of some words to make them reveal the ultimate Latin source, even though this meant making the spelling even less representative of the pronunciation. Thus our words *doubt* and *debt* came into English from French with the spellings *doute* and *dette*, which represented the pronunciation pretty accurately. But the ardent etymologists of the Renaissance, recognizing that the ultimate Latin sources were *dubitum* and *debitum* (as in the more recent Latin borrowings *indubitable* and *debit*) put the ⟨b⟩ into the spelling, in spite of the fact that there never had been a /b/ in the pronunciation in English. In the same way they changed an ⟨a⟩ to ⟨e⟩ and inserted a ⟨c⟩ into *perfect* (which was Middle English *parfit*, from French *parfait*, ultimately Latin *perfectum*) and put an ⟨l⟩ into *palm* (French *paume*, Latin *palma*). Subsequently the ⟨c⟩ of *perfect* and sometimes the ⟨l⟩ of *palm* came to be pronounced; this process is called **spelling pronunciation**. There are quite a few of these **learned restorations** in English, many of which have been followed by spelling pronunciations. Other examples are *verdict*, spelled and pronounced *verdit* as late as Milton; *victual*, French and Middle English *vitaille* and pronounced /vítl/ in Modern English; and *indict*, from Middle English *indite*, which is still pronounced /indáyt/.

The situation became even more complicated when Greek words were borrowed into English, beginning in the sixteenth century and accelerating greatly after the seventeenth century, when the practice of manufacturing scientific words from borrowed Greek morphemes became common (see pp. 154 f.). Greek, of course, had an alphabet of its own, historically related to the Latin alphabet but differing in both the number of graphemes and the shapes of their allographs. It also had many consonant clusters which were not paralleled in either Latin or English and which were consequently adapted to the phonological systems of these languages when words were borrowed. There were thus two problems to be solved in the writing of Greek loanwords in English, whether they were borrowed directly or through Latin. The first was the problem of **transliteration**–representing the Greek letters by letters of the Roman alphabet. The second was the question of whether to represent the Greek words in their original spelling as transliterated or in a spelling more accurately representing their altered pronunciation.

The transliteration problem was solved largely by the Romans, who were great admirers of Greek culture and borrowed extensively from the Greek language. For those Greek letters representing phonemes with approximate equivalents in Latin they simply substituted the more or less equivalent Roman letter. This took care of 11 of the 24 graphemes of the Greek alphabet: ⟨α⟩ became ⟨a⟩, ⟨β⟩ became ⟨b⟩, ⟨δ⟩ became ⟨d⟩, and similarly with ⟨ι λ μ ν ξ π σ τ⟩ and their equivalents ⟨i l m n x p s t⟩. Two Greek graphemes, ⟨κ⟩ and ⟨ζ⟩, were taken over and added to the Roman alphabet as ⟨k⟩ and ⟨z⟩. They were used mostly for Greek words; in native words the Romans continued to use their own ⟨c⟩ and ⟨s⟩ to represent /k/ and [z], which in Latin was an allophone of /s/. Greek ⟨γ⟩ usually was transliterated as ⟨g⟩, but when doubled it represented /ng/ and was transliterated ⟨ng⟩ in Latin fashion; thus Greek ἄγγελος ("messenger") became Latin *angelus* and ultimately English *angel*. Three Greek graphemes, ⟨θ φ χ⟩, represented aspirated stops, which contrasted phonemically with the unaspirated stops represented by ⟨τ π κ⟩. The Romans sensibly transliterated them by the digraphs ⟨th ph ch⟩. Likewise ⟨ψ⟩, representing the cluster /ps/, was written with the corresponding Latin graphic cluster ⟨ps⟩. Greek ⟨ρ⟩ had two variants, an aspirated ⟨ῥ⟩ in initial position and a plain ⟨ρ⟩ elsewhere; the Romans used ⟨rh⟩ for the aspirated form and ⟨r⟩ for the plain form. This accounts for such English spellings as *rhythm*.

In addition to ⟨α⟩ and ⟨ι⟩, the Greek alphabet had five more vocalic graphemes, all representing distinct vowel phonemes in Greek. Two of these, ⟨ε⟩ and ⟨η⟩, represented contrasting mid-front vowels; the Romans used ⟨e⟩ for both of them, since it was the only available grapheme in their alphabet. They also used their ⟨o⟩ for both the Greek ⟨o⟩(*omicron*, "little o")and the Greek ⟨ω⟩ (*omega*, "big o"). Greek ⟨υ⟩, which represented a rounded front vowel, they borrowed in its capital form Υ, which has become our ⟨y⟩. But when this letter represented the second element of a diphthong, they used their own ⟨u⟩. This practice is still reflected in English words like *psychology* (ψυχή, "soul") and *pneumatic* (πνεῦμα, "air").

As the examples quoted show, the English practice, at least from the Renaissance onward to the present, has been to use the Roman system of transliteration to represent words borrowed from Greek or made up from Greek morphemes, even though their pronunciation in English often differs both from the Greek and from the Roman adaptation. Thus ⟨ch⟩, which we have already seen as a digraph adopted under French influence in Middle English times to represent the phoneme /č/, has also come to represent /k/ in words of Greek origin like *chasm* and *monarch*. The grapheme sequence ⟨ph⟩ has come to be a digraph representing /f/, which was the later development in both Greek and Latin of the aspirated /pʰ/ of Greek.[10]

The problem of Greek consonant clusters which do not have English equivalents has been solved by the rather curious expedient of transliterating the Greek words directly and simply omitting in pronunciation one of the consonants, usually the first, in the non-English cluster. English phonology, for example, does not permit initial clusters consisting of two stops. So words based

10. In the Romance languages, initial ⟨ph⟩ was usually changed to ⟨f⟩. Therefore Greek words borrowed through French, Italian, or Spanish have ⟨f⟩, as in *fantasy* and *fancy*, contrasted with *phantasm* and *phantom*.

on Greek like *pterodactyl* and *ctenophore* are pronounced with initial /t/, although the spelling preserves a reminder of the Greek clusters /pt/ and /kt/. In medial and final position these clusters are permitted in English, so that in words like *actinic* and *crypt* we pronounce /kt/ and /pt/. The same is true of other clusters like /ps/ and /fθ/, clusters which are reduced to /s/ and /θ/ in *psychic* and *phthalic* but pronounced in full in *ellipse* and *diphthong* (though the /fθ/ cluster is often dissimilated to /pθ/ in words like *diphthong* and *naphtha*).

The result of all this has been to create a special subsystem of the English graphological system, in which special conventions of representation replace the usual grapheme-phoneme relationships. This has its conveniences; those who know Greek and those who are familiar with technical and scientific terminology come to acquire a stock of visual morphemes that are graphically distinguished from morphemes which are phonologically identical with them. Thus *psych-*, *phon-*, *phil-*, *pneum-*, and hundreds of others would lose their distinctive and self-revealing shapes if they were adjusted to the rest of the system, though I suppose we would get used to *sikopath*, *fonograff*, *fillosofy*, and *newmonia* in time. Since the great majority of words manufactured from Greek elements are technical terms that are more often seen than heard, it has seemed advantageous to preserve their distinctive graphic shapes, even at the expense of introducing many "silent letters" and conflicting grapheme-phoneme representations into the writing system of the language. Even such a magnificent construction as *pneumoultramicroscopicsilicovolcanoconiosis*, which is the longest word I remember seeing in an abridged dictionary, can be decoded by any physician, even though he might be unwilling to attempt to pronounce it.

**The Development of a Standard Writing System.** Almost from the beginning, the history of English writing reveals an alternation between periods of standardization (in older periods, often local) and periods of innovation. In a period of standardization the virtues of having a single system, in which all writers, regardless of their personal or regional phonological systems, spell the same words in the same way, are thought to outweigh its drawbacks. Usually it is an educational or political force, rather than a linguistic one, which establishes and maintains the standard. In the late ninth century, for example, the powerful influence of King

Alfred made his court the center of learning and culture in England and helped establish the West Saxon way of writing Old English as a standard which prevailed for two hundred years or more and almost totally superseded the local writing systems of other parts of England, such as Northumbria and Kent. Furthermore, the advantages of a standard system caused it to be preserved even after the phonological system had undergone considerable change.

But the political changes resulting from the Norman Conquest broke down this standard and introduced another period of innovation and variety, during which writers adapted their spelling as best they could to the changed language and the diverse local dialects. As we have seen, they also introduced innovations based on French spelling practice. Then in the late fourteenth century a new standard, based on the speech and writing practice of London, developed. There continued to be other local systems, especially in the north and west of England, but they gradually gave way to the London standard, so that by the time of Caxton a system based on London usage prevailed over most of England. Educated people, regardless of their native dialect, spelled pretty much alike.

Our present system is based on Caxton's in most of its important features. In spite of some rather extensive changes of pronunciation, there have been no major alterations in the writing system. There has, however, been change in the direction of greater consistency and virtually complete standardization. The nature of this change can be observed by noting the inconsistencies in practice in a passage from the First Folio of Shakespeare (1623):

> I have heard, that guilty Creatures sitting at a Play,
> Have by the very cunning of the Scœne,
> Bene strooke so to the soule, that presently
> They have proclaim'd their Malefactions.
> For Murther, though it have no tongue, will speake
> With most myraculous Organ. Ile have these Players
> Play something like the murder of my Father,
> Before mine Unkle. Ile observe his lookes,
> Ile tent him to the quicke: If he but blench
> I know my course. The Spirit that I have seene
> May be the Divell, and the Divel hath power
> T'assume a pleasing shape, yea and perhaps
> Out of my Weaknesse, and my Melancholly,

> As he is very potent with such Spirits,
> Abuses me to damne me. Ile have grounds
> More Relative then this: The Play's the thing,
> Wherein Ile catch the Conscience of the King.[11]

There are several things to note here:

1. Some words have more than one spelling, though there is nothing in the context or the (supposed) pronunciation to suggest a reason: *Murther~murder; Divell~Divel.*

2. The final ⟨e⟩ is used more extensively than today. Sometimes it has its modern function of indicating a preceding "long vowel," as in *these* and *shape.* At other times the quality of the preceding vowel is already indicated by doubling or digraph, as in *soule, speake, seene;* modern practice has usually dropped this redundant ⟨e⟩. The final ⟨e⟩ after a consonantal digraph, as in *quicke* and *damne,* has also been dropped.

3. Some spellings which were more accurate indications of pronunciation have been changed in modern use to indicate the morphemic structure more clearly. The only example in this passage is *Ile,* which has become our *I'll,* but elsewhere in the play occur *eene* for *even, ore* for *over, a* for unstressed *he, byrlady* for *by our Lady,* and many others.

4. Modern practice has altered the spelling of some words to alternatives already permitted by the system in 1623: *myraculous, Unkle, then* for unstressed *than* (pronounced /ðən/).

5. The use of capitals in modern practice has been regularized to two main functions: indicating sentence beginnings and marking proper names. It is hard to find a rationale for the capitalization of the Folio. There is a tendency for important nouns to be capitalized, but it is not as consistent here as it became later in the seventeenth century; thus *Murther* varies with *murder,* and certainly *soule* and *tongue* are as important as *Conscience* and *Organ.*

6. The apostrophe is used to indicate certain phonological features, such as the non-syllabic nature of the inflectional ending of *proclaim'd* and the elision of the vowels of *to* in *T'assume* and (as in modern practice) of *is* in *Play's.* There are no cases of the possessive morpheme in this passage, but at this time it was not marked by the apostrophe.

11. Quoted from the text of *Hamlet* in *The Complete Works of William Shakespeare,* the text and order of the First Folio, vol. 3 (London, Nonesuch Press, 1953), p. 604.

The idea that the writing system should be absolutely uniform, with a single correct spelling for every word, regardless of personal mannerisms and preferences and local variations in pronunciation, gradually took form and gained acceptance during the eighteenth century. By 1755, when Johnson published his famous dictionary, he could set as one of his objectives to adjust "the orthography, which has been to this time unsettled and fortuitous." This he just about succeeded in doing. With very few changes, such as the dropping of the ⟨k⟩ from final ⟨-ick⟩ at the ends of words of more than one syllable (as in *critic* contrasted with *brick*), our spelling today is that of Johnson.

It is one thing, however, to have a standard for printed material (which has been the case since the late seventeenth century) and quite another to extend that standard to all written materials, regardless of the social class or education of the writer or the purpose of his writing. This is a more recent development, coinciding roughly with the extension of free schooling to most of the populace. In the seventeenth and early eighteenth centuries it was not considered essential even for people (especially women) of some position in the world to follow a consistent standard in their spelling. A sampling of personal letters and diaries written before the middle of the eighteenth century reveals a varied and sometimes fantastically unstandard spelling. Here are two examples of family letters written by ladies of quality; the first is Lady Brilliana Harley, writing to her son at Oxford in 1639:

> My deare Ned, I beleeue you are confident that you are most deare to me, thearefore thinke it not strange, if I am stuedious and carefull that your peace should be keept with your God, whous fauor is better then life. I longe to see you, and I hope I shall doo it shortly. I hope before this, you haue reseued your hate [hat] and stockens, but Burigh is something ngligent. Your father is, I thanke God, well; he is ride abroode. In hast, I giue this ascurance that I am
>           Your most affectinat mother,     BRILLIANA HARLEY[12]

The second example from a century later—a letter from Lady Dorothy Wentworth to her brother in 1745—shows that a lady of quality could still be an individualist in spelling, even in the age of Dr. Johnson:

12. *Letters of the Lady Brilliana Harley.* Camden Society Publications, vol. 58 (London, 1854), p. 61.

H

The Rebellion makes most people chuse ather to be at their respective countreys to garde that or hear for the saifty of their persons severall that went to Bath was so frited with the reports thear that they retarned to Town directly, but they was not of the mail kind.[13]

But with the extension of free schooling to all, the teaching of spelling according to a fixed and invariable system became the rule. Noah Webster's spelling book was the foundation of his fame and fortune. That particularly American form of combined entertainment, contest, and pedagogical subterfuge, the spelling bee, was based on the assumption that there is one and only one correct spelling for every word. This idea is so prevalent today that we are strongly prejudiced against the person who misspells and inclined to consider him not only uneducated but unintelligent as well.

## 12. The Writing System Today

The modern English writing system, as a result of strong pedagogical and social pressure for standardization, has become the one part of the language which is virtually uniform wherever English is used. The exceptions to this uniformity are of four kinds. The first is a slight difference between British and American standards, most noticeable in words like *honour* and *flavour*, in which American practice uses *-or* rather than *-our*. The second is the existence of alternative spellings for a few words, either of which is accepted as standard in both Britain and America. Some examples are *medieval~mediaeval, catalog~catalogue, theatre~theater*. One area where considerable variation exists is in compounds such as *air line~airline* and *book store~bookstore*. The third deviation from standard is in the representation of spoken English, especially in fictional dialog. This usually takes the form of an attempt to indicate casual, regional, or uneducated pronunciation, as in *gonna* for *going to*, *Ah* for *I* in reporting Southern speakers, and *toid* for *third* from fictitious uneducated inhabitants of Brooklyn. Here also comes **eye dialect**, which uses incorrect spellings, such as *sez* for *says* and *wimmin* for *women*, to indicate

13. From "The Manuscripts of Mrs. Wentworth, of Woolley Park, Yorkshire." *Historical Manuscripts Commission Report on Manuscripts in Various Collections*, vol. 2 (London, 1903), p. 423.

that a speaker is uneducated. The fact is that most educated speakers also pronounce these words /sez/ and /wímin/ but the implication is that they always spell them correctly, and therefore that somebody whose dialog is misspelled would himself misspell and thereby show his ignorance.

The fourth deviation from a universal standard is the acceptance of an alternative spelling system for the literary version of Scots dialect known as Lallans. This system has a long tradition, going back to the writing of the northern dialect of Middle English in the fourteenth and fifteenth centuries. It was revived by Robert Burns and other Scots poets of the late eighteenth century and again by a group of nationalistic Scots of the twentieth century. A stanza from the modern Scots poet Hugh MacDiarmid will illustrate it:

> There was nae reek i' the laverock's hoose
> That nicht—an' nane i' mine:
> But I ha'e thocht o' that foolish licht
> Ever sin' syne;
> An' I think that mebbe at last I ken
> What your look meant then.[14]

In its frequent use of apostrophes, this stanza also is attempting to indicate speech. But spellings like *nicht*, *licht*, and *thocht* for *night*, *light*, and *thought*, and *nae* and *nane* for *no* and *none* belong to the old Scots graphic tradition.

Principally because of the two facts about the English writing system which we have discussed in the preceding sections—its complex history and its standardization—the structure of the system is very complicated. Beginning as a system to a large degree isomorphic with the phonological system, it has passed through stages of French, Latin, and Greek borrowing, in which new complexities were added to those that had already accumulated. For seven or eight hundred years it was, to some degree at least, flexible enough to be adjusted to changes in the phonological system, so that the two remained in fairly good fit until the fifteenth century. But at that point it virtually froze into the general pat-

---

14. "The Watergaw," by Hugh MacDiarmid in *The Golden Treasury of Scottish Poetry*, selected and edited by Hugh MacDiarmid (New York: The Macmillan Company, 1941), p. 132. The first line is an idiomatic expression for "It was a dark and stormy night" (literally "There was no smoke in the lark's house.")

tern it has had ever since. Therefore any change in the phonological system—and there have been many since Caxton's day—
was more likely than not to make the fit between the two less
close than it had been before. Meanwhile sub-systems, the most
important of which was the one for Greek derivatives, were inserted into the over-all pattern, thus further increasing its distance
from a one-to-one representation of the phonology.

Then, beginning in the sixteenth century and gaining acceptance and strength right on to our own time, the demand for
standardization imposed further restrictions on change. It was
difficult, though not impossible, for an individual or a small
school of scribes to change their writing habits to accord with
local variations or chronological changes in the phonological system. But when changes in the system must be accepted by the
whole English-writing world, the obstacles become virtually in-
surmountable. It is thus highly unlikely that the system will be
changed to bring about a significantly closer fit with the phonological system.

Nor is such change necessarily desirable. After all, standardization of the writing system could only be attained by giving up the
notion of a close or perfect fit with the phonological system. The
phonological system is *not* standard; it is really a collection of
largely overlapping but different systems. If writing were to be
isomorphic with speech, there would be as many different systems
of writing as there are spoken dialects. A word such as *light*
would have to be spelled in at least five different ways: perhaps
*lecht* for Scots, *lɔiʔ* for Cockney, *layt* and *leyt* for standard
British and Midland American, and *læːt* for Texans and other
South Midland speakers. The standard spelling is at least im-
partially different from all of these.

It is possible to devise a system for English which eliminates
many inconsistencies of the present system without sacrificing its
position as an interdialectal standard. It is not an easy task, and it
would require a virtually encyclopedic knowledge of dialectal
variation in English and considerable ingenuity in working out a
coordinated system that would be consistent in itself as well as
compatible with all important regional variants. Most proposals
for "simplifying" or "reforming" English spelling come from
people who lack this kind of knowledge; they are usually well-
intentioned amateurs. As a result, most of the suggestions are not
for a new system but for adjustments of individual items or sets

of items within the existing system: such things as spelling *night* and *through* as *nite* and *thru* and extending the use of the ⟨sh⟩ digraph to all the various ways of representing /š/. Such changes would no doubt make it somewhat easier to learn to read and quite a lot easier to learn to spell. But in spite of sometimes quite powerful advocacy and considerable expenditure of money, they have not caught on. It is probably safe to predict that they never will. The tremendous advantages of language-wide standardization and the vested interest in the present system represented both by the vast accumulation of material printed in it and by the pride of accomplishment of those who have mastered it will continue to protect it from reformers, amateur or professional. And as long as society continues to count mastery of the system as an indispensable attribute of educated people, we will all have to continue to learn it as part of the price we pay for the privileges of belonging to the educated class.

## For Further Reading

Gelb, I. J., *A Study of Writing*. London: Routledge & Kegan Paul, Ltd., 1952.

Gimson, A. C., *An Introduction to the Pronunciation of English*. London: Edward Arnold, Ltd., 1962.

Jones, Daniel, *The Pronunciation of English*. 4th Edition. Cambridge University Press, 1956.

Pike, Kenneth L., *Phonetics*. Ann Arbor, Mich.: University of Michigan Press, 1943.

Ward, Ida C., *The Phonetics of English*. 4th Edition. Cambridge: W. Heffer & Sons, Ltd., 1948.

Wijk, Axel, *Rules of Pronunciation for the English Language: An Account of the Relationship Between English Spelling and Pronunciation*. London: Oxford University Press, 1966.

# *Six*

# USAGE AND VARIETY IN ENGLISH

## 1. Usage

Some people pronounce *tomato* /təmé:to:/ and others /təmá:to:/. Some say *I awoke*, others *I woke up*, and still others *I got awake*. Some prefer *this data is interesting*; others *these data are interesting*. People sometimes get involved in heated arguments about matters like this. (Some would probably quarrel with my use of *get* in the preceding sentence and argue that I should have used *become*.) Since the antagonists in such an argument may both be educated and accomplished native speakers of English, they will not readily admit themselves in error. How are differences like this to be viewed? How can we tell which way of saying something is right? Or are they all right? Or none?

To answer these questions we must remind ourselves of two qualities of language (briefly discussed in Chapter One): the **arbitrariness** and the **conventionality** of language. Because language is arbitrary, we must recognize that there is no appeal to nature or to logic that will settle these questions. *Wake up* and *awake* are equally arbitrary ways of expressing the act of emerging from sleep; neither of them is more natural or logical than the other, or than *aufwachen* or *s'éveiller*, which speakers of German or French use to express this idea.

Unless people are more or less in agreement about the arbitrary expressions they use, language will fail in its communicative function. If a speaker decides to be individually arbitrary and to use *awake* where other speakers use *sing* or *wash*, he may expect not to be understood when he says *I can't awake that song* or *I didn't awake my clothes this week.* In short, the conventionality of language imposes restrictions on its arbitrariness.

The body of accepted conventions about a language or a variety of a language is called collectively **usage**. In the broad sense, then, usage is no more than the way in which a group of speakers have agreed—usually tacitly and unconsciously, though sometimes overtly—to use the language in communicating with one another. Since communication is the most important function of language, the conventions which facilitate it have great force. Their tendency is on the whole conservative, since it is simpler to retain what has already been agreed upon than to reach agreement on something new. One of the functions of formal educational systems is to preserve accepted usage by teaching it to the younger generation. Other agencies such as newspapers and magazines are usually conservative in matters of usage, both in their practice and in their columns on "correct" language. In some nations academies act as arbiters in matters of usage and legislate—or attempt to, at any rate—the new expressions that are to be admitted into the accepted body of conventions. There has never been such an academy in the English-speaking world, though many people expect dictionaries to perform a similar function.

Opposed to these conservative forces is the natural human tendency to innovate. Whether from genuine necessity, literary originality, fashion, or simple boredom with existing conventions, people are always inventing new expressions or altering old ones to fit new uses. We have discussed the changes in vocabulary which result from new technical and social innovations like the railway: no conservative forces, however powerful, could resist the development of a new vocabulary to deal with the new complex of objects and habits which the railway introduced. At most, such forces can influence the direction taken by the innovations in usage; they may help decide, for example, whether the new vocabulary should consist of new words, like *locomotive*, or new uses for old words, like *carriage* and *track*. But the innovations are chiefly controlled by the necessities of communication, which usually weed out excessive, ambiguous, or synonymous expressions. When there is relatively little communication, as between England and America during the period of the growth of railroads, usage may establish quite different terms, such as the British *goods van* and American *freight car*.

Innovations arising from other causes than the need for new expressions to match new things are likely to be much more capricious and uncontrolled. They are made by people of an experimental, original, daring, and often witty turn of mind, with a flair for metaphor and analogy and a way of infecting others with their linguistic exuberance—such as poets and the originators of slang (though not usually its users). Everyone has known people whose use of language is marked by novelty, wit, and extravagance. Most of their innovations pass by and are forgotten. But some may be taken up by others, especially within a close and self-conscious circle of people who like to emphasize their difference from the majority (teenagers, for instance, or jazz musicians). In this way, new terms get established in the slang or argot of a particular group. Finally, a few items may catch on with the public at large and become novelties in the language as a whole. This is the point at which questions of suitability, appropriateness, and "correctness" arise.

Another source of innovation and hence of problems of correctness in usage is **analogy**. People often extend the regularity of language patterning into areas where convention has established irregularity. Children who have generalized the idea of the past-tense inflection {-ed} extend the generalization to create past forms like *throwed* and *teached*. Only the strength of conservative forces keeps these regular forms from ultimately replacing the irregular forms *threw* and *taught*. In fact, over the centuries many individual items have followed this course. We say *books* rather than *beech*, which would be the normal development of the Old English plural form *bēc*. Only our familiarity with the King James Bible keeps alive *kine*, which has completely yielded to *cows* in daily speech. But we still are inclined to condemn as "illiterate" people who say *I seed it* or *hisself*, although these forms are perfectly analogous to *I paid it* and *myself*.

## 2. Types of Usage Questions

Usually there is more than one way of saying something. This may be the result of either of two quite different qualities of language. The most common reason is that language is so versatile in its structure that more than one perfectly acceptable structure in the lexico-grammatical system of the language matches a single structure in the meaning system. For example, the two sentences

in each of the following pairs are (for me) completely interchangeable so far as the vocabulary and grammar of my variety
of educated English are concerned.

1. (a) He entered the room where I was.
   (b) He came into the room where I was.
2. (a) His arrogance irritated me.
   (b) I was irritated by his arrogance.

The sentences in the first pair differ lexically; that is, 1(b)
substitutes *came into* for the synonymous *entered*.[1] The sentences
in the second pair differ grammatically; 2(a) is a kernel sentence
and 2(b) is its passive transform. In neither case is there a problem of usage; both members of each pair are completely in accord
with the conventions of the variety of English under consideration. On any particular occasion, the choice between them would
be made on rhetorical grounds—that is, on the way they would
fit into a larger context of discourse.

Other cases of two or more expressions having the same meaning result not from the versatility but from the variety of language. For example:

3. (a) I'd like a grinder and a cabinet.
   (b) I'd like a hoagie and a shake.
4. (a) Don't talk back to me!
   (b) Don't give me no lip!
5. (a) I shall solicit the opinion of the committee about this affair
       before proceeding.
   (b) I'll ask the committee for an opinion on this business before
       going ahead.

Both sentences in each of these pairs have "the same meaning,"
but they are not interchangeable in the way that those in pairs 1
and 2 were. The sentences in 3 illustrate **regional variety** in language. Both speakers are asking for a sandwich made of a long
thin roll of Italian bread, sliced lengthwise and filled with lettuce
and cold meats, and a drink consisting of milk beaten up with
flavoring and ice cream. Sentence 3(a) illustrates the usage of
Rhode Island and southeastern Massachusetts, while sentence

---

1. These two verbs are synonymous in this particular context but not in
other contexts, where we might have to use *went into* as a synonym for
*entered*.

3(b) illustrates that of the Philadelphia region. Elsewhere the sandwich might have been called a *submarine*, a *poor boy*, or a *hero* and the drink a *frappe* or a *malt*. Each is "correct" in its own area, but if used in another area might lead to a failure of communication.

The sentences in group 4 illustrate **educational** or **social variety** in language. Sentence 4(a) is educated usage of a rather informal sort (*contradict* would be more formal than *talk back to*). Sentence 4(b), with its double negative and its rather slangy use of *lip* to mean "insolence," is uneducated or vernacular English. Once again each is "correct" in the area of its own applicability.

The sentences in group 5 illustrate **functional** or **stylistic variety** in language. Sentence 5(a) is definitely formal in style, and would be appropriate to an official report. It would be more likely to appear in writing than in speech; if spoken it would sound as if it were being read aloud from a prepared document rather than improvised. Sentence 5(b), on the other hand, is much less formal. It uses the contraction *I'll* instead of the formal, rather bookish *I shall*. The two-part verbs *ask for* and *go ahead* are less formal than *solicit* and *proceed*. It uses the all-purpose preposition *on*, very common in conversational style, instead of the more precise *about*. The whole tone of the sentence suggests that it is appropriate to speech between persons who know one another or to informal written discourse such as a personal letter or memo. It is, however, no less *correct* than 5(a). The choice between these two synonymous sentences is one of appropriateness to the context and situation. In a friendly, chatty letter, 5(a) would seem very stiff, while in an official report 5(b) would seem too casual and offhand.

These three types of linguistic variety—regional, social, and functional—are characteristic of all languages, though in general the more widespread the distribution of a language and the more complex the society which it serves, the greater is the variety. Regional variety is the inevitable consequence of the use of a language by geographically separated communities differing in natural and perhaps social environment and not in close intercommunication. Social variety is characteristic of any society where there are class differences marked by economic, political, educational, or occupational contrasts—which in effect means any normal society, in contrast to artificially maintained homogeneous groups living in circumscribed communities, like cloistered monks or the Amish of Pennsylvania. Functional variety is harder to assign to specific natural causes; it is apparently associated with the human habit of setting apart certain types of activity from others and marking the separation by outward signs such as costume, etiquette, and ritual. Even the most primitive societies customarily have special kinds of costume, behavior, and language for religious occasions and often for political occasions. In its extreme form, functional variety may extend even to the use of an entirely different language for certain especially marked functions, as in the use of Latin on college diplomas and—until recently, at any rate—in the Roman Catholic ritual of the Mass.

Whatever the causes of variety in usage, it is a fact about language to be faced and understood. People sometimes deplore it, on the ground that it may impair communication and lead to misunderstanding and prejudice. And indeed it does. It is natural to be suspicious of those who speak differently from us, and to feel at home with those whose language is like our own. On the other hand, it would be a dull world indeed if everybody wore the same clothes, ate the same food, and spoke the same language in just the same way on all occasions. The old saying that variety is the spice of life certainly applies to language. But variety brings with it a responsibility, especially for the educated. The educated man is not bound within the limits of one regional variety and one formal style of usage. He is able to use many styles himself, and to read and interpret the clues which others unconsciously furnish him in their speech. He has risen above narrow prejudice against varieties of language other than those he customarily uses himself, to the point where he can savor the vigor of the vernacular, the elegance of good formal style, and the pungency of regional dialect. He is linguistically cosmopolitan.

## 3. Regional Variety in English

In the 1500 years of its history as a separate language, English has changed from the speech of a few thousand Germanic tribesmen living close together on the island of Britain to a world language spoken by nearly 300,000,000 native speakers living in large or small groups on every continent of the earth. Even in its earliest stage it had differing regional dialects, as we saw in Chapter Three. In spite of the strong standardizing influence of a common writing system and, more recently, universal education, easy intercommunication, and close economic and political ties, a great deal of regional variety still exists, partly because of the many different geographical, climatic, economic, and social conditions under which speakers of English live. We would certainly not expect a Scottish shepherd, a London bus conductor, a Maine fisherman, an Alabama sharecropper, a Wyoming cowboy, and a Sydney longshoreman to use the same language, any more than we would expect them to eat the same food, discuss the same subjects, or wear the same clothes. Nor, in spite of the mobility of our world and the availability of telephones, radios, and television, do ordinary people who live so far apart have much opportunity to communicate with one another. The easy and constant intercommunication which is so characteristic of the twentieth-century world involves a relatively small percentage of the population—government officials, business men, journalists, professional men, the military. Most of these people customarily speak educated English, and they read and write more than do the less educated and less prosperous plain folk who stay in a small community and talk mostly with their neighbors. The result, as one would expect, is that a great deal more regional variety exists in uneducated than in educated speech. An educated man, whether he comes from Scotland, England, Australia, South Africa, Canada, or the United States, has no difficulty communicating with other educated men from any of these regions. He will notice differences of pronunciation and some variation in vocabulary, but almost none in grammar. Except for a few minor variations in spelling and vocabulary, his written language will be indistinguishable from that of educated English speakers anywhere.

Linguists call regional varieties of a language **dialects** of that language. The branch of linguistic study concerned with dialects is **dialectology**. No value judgment is implied by the label **dialect**; it is simply a useful descriptive term. But it is not easy to define. For one thing, the habit of naming dialects after geographical regions encourages the notion that there are boundaries between regional dialects as clear and sharp as political boundaries like state lines or topographical features like rivers and mountain ranges. The truth is that dialect areas usually shade gradually and imperceptibly into one another, so that a continuous sequence of small changes may be observed as one moves across the countryside. The fact that we may speak of "New England dialect" does

not mean that a major difference marks the speech of near neighbors on opposite sides of the New York-Connecticut line. What it
does mean is that this line more or less runs along the middle of a
rather broad transition area and that speakers at a distance of
twenty or thirty miles on either side of the line will have many
contrasting features in their speech.

Instead of speaking of sharply marked dialect boundaries which
can be drawn on a map like national or state lines, dialectologists
speak of **bundles of isoglosses.** An **isogloss** is a line marking the
limit of distribution of a single feature of language, such as the
use of *grinder* to describe a kind of sandwich, or the pronunciation of /r/ in *barn*. It is usually possible to draw these lines fairly
sharply on the basis of interviews with a sampling of the native
speakers in an area of transition. But even an isogloss may be
rather fuzzy. Where, for instance, is the isogloss for /r/ in *barn*
to be put if the same speaker sometimes says /ba:n/ and sometimes /barn/, or if two speakers in the same household—husband
and wife, for example—differ in their usage? It is physically impossible for a dialectologist to interview everybody in the vicinity
of his suspected isogloss. He must depend on a very small sample,
carefully chosen to be as representative as possible.

In general it may be said that no two isoglosses follow exactly
the same course. But when a number of them come close together
for all or part of their length, they constitute a **bundle.** The
average course of the isoglosses in a bundle may then be considered as a new dividing line, somewhat more theoretical and
abstract. If the isoglosses constituting the bundle describe closely
similar features, the new line is simply a more generalized isogloss. If the isoglosses marking the limit of non-pronunciation of
/r/ in *barn, cork, church*, and *cured* lie close together, the resulting bundle can be generalized as the isogloss marking the limit of
"r-lessness" in the position between vowel and final consonant.
Should this bundle in turn lie close to the generalized line for *car,
pure, fear*, and *snore*, an even more general isogloss for the limit
of the absence of postvocalic /r/ could be drawn.

If, on the other hand, a bundle consists of isoglosses representing different kinds of linguistic elements, the bundle may be said
to mark a **dialect boundary.** Note that since the isoglosses making
up the bundle will not exactly coincide, the dialect boundary
must be considered either as the whole area between the outer-
most isoglosses on both sides or as an abstract line running down

the middle of that area. In either case, what the dialectologist puts down on his map is to a considerable degree the result of his own judgment.

Let us take as an example the dialect of Boston. Both those who speak this dialect and those who do not are conscious of its differences from other varieties of American English, and it has many features that mark it off from the speech of the rest of New England. Yet when the isoglosses are plotted, it becomes difficult to draw a line setting off Boston speech precisely. If one travels west from the center of the city, he encounters before long the line marking the western limit of [a], the so-called "broad *a*," in *glass*. Some thirty miles farther west he comes to the isogloss marking the limit of r-lessness in *thirty*. Another ten miles or so further he reaches the boundary between rounded [ɒ] and unrounded [a] in *rod*. Next he comes to the limit of r-lessness in *barn*. Finally, having reached the Berkshires in western Massachusetts, he comes to the end of the broad-*a* pronunciation of *calf*. By now he is certainly well out of the Boston dialect area. But when did he cross the line? Was it when he encountered postvocalic /r/ in *thirty*, or not until he encountered it in *barn*? When the broad /aː/ of *glass* gave way to the more fronted /æ/, or not until the same change occurred in *calf*? The answer is, of course, that no line exists. What does exist is a transition area fifty or sixty miles wide, across which the characteristic features of Boston dialect drop off one by one (see map). If he had gone north or south, he would have crossed fewer isoglosses, since he would be traveling parallel to the main north-south trend of the isoglosses in this area.

People usually think of regional dialect differences in terms of pronunciation, and speak of a Boston, Oxford, Southern, or Brooklyn "accent." Actually, as the examples already cited show, the differences may be in any of the subsystems of language—in phonology, morphology, syntax, lexicon, semantics, even graphics (as in the British *-our* spellings of words like *honor*). The phonological features are the most obvious, since they strike the ear at once and affect even very short utterances, but the other differences are no less important.

**Phonological differences** are of three principal kinds: in allophones, in phonemic distribution, and in phonemic inventory. Two dialects may have the same number of phonemes, distributed

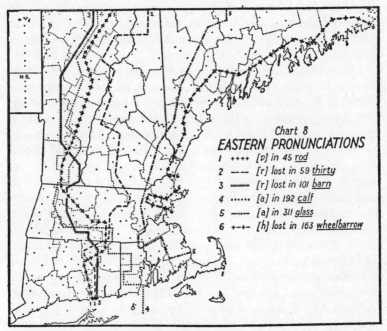

Chart 8
EASTERN PRONUNCIATIONS
1 ++++ [ɒ] in 45 rod
2 —— [r] lost in 59 thirty
3 ⏦⏦⏦ [r] lost in 101 barn
4 ······ [a] in 192 calf
5 —··— [a] in 311 glass
6 +–+– [h] lost in 163 wheelbarrow

From *Handbook of the Linguistic Geography of New England* by Hans Kurath, reprinted by permission of the American Council of Learned Societies.

in the same way, but differing in their actual phonetic realization
—their pronunciation. Such differences are below the phonemic
level and therefore do not appear in a phonemic transcription.
For example, many speakers in Rhode Island, in New York City,
and in other areas of the English-speaking world use the dental
stops [t̪] and [d̪] in words where speakers from other areas use
the dental fricatives /θ/ and /ð/. These dental stops contrast with
the alveolar stops /t/ and /d/, so that the speakers of these dialects never confuse *three* and *tree* or *there* and *dare* (though
speakers of other dialects may think they do). Therefore they
have the same number of phonemes distributed in the same way
as do those who use dental fricatives instead of dental stops.

One must observe the whole phonological structure of two
dialects before determining whether certain differences are allophonic or phonemic. There are dialects, such as the less educated
speech of Jamaica, which simply lack the phonemes /θ/ and /ð/
entirely and use /t/ and /d/ in all places where other dialects use
/θ/ and /ð/. The difference now is one of phonemic inventory;

these dialects have two fewer phonemes than the majority of English dialects do, and therefore for them many pairs of words, such as *tree* and *three*, which contrast in other dialects, are homophones.

Differences in phonemic distribution may occur when two dialects have the same number of phonemes but use different phonemes in the same word. *Tomato* is a case in point: those who say /təmá:to:/ do not do so because they have no /e:/ phoneme, since they pronounce *potato*/pəté:to:/; likewise the /təmé:to:/speakers pronounce *vibrato* as /vibrá:to:/. The difference is one of choice of phoneme for this particular syllable. Other well known examples are *economics* with /e/ or /i:/ in the first syllable, *either* and *neither* with /i:/ or /ay/, and *catch* with /e/ or /æ/. Sometimes differences of phonemic distribution may affect whole classes of words. Many Canadian speakers have the diphthong /əw/ where other dialects have /aw/ or /æw/, while speakers in Philadelphia have this diphthong in words like *boat* and *road*; a Philadelphian's pronunciation of *a boat* will sound very much like *about* to a Canadian. We have already given an example of difference of phonemic inventory in citing the case of Jamaican and other dialects which entirely lack the phonemes /θ/ and /ð/. A contrary example is Scots, many varieties of which have as an added phoneme the velar fricative /x/ (pronounced much like the German sounds spelled *ch*) in words like *night* and *loch*, pronounced as /next/ and /lɔx/. This phoneme has no counterpart in other dialects of English, so that Scots has contrasts, as between *right* and *rite*, that do not occur in other dialects. It is obvious that difference in phonemic inventory of necessity implies difference of phonemic distribution.

**Grammatical differences** between regional varieties of English are much less common than differences of pronunciation. Particularly on the level of educated speech, the grammar of English is much the same throughout the English-speaking world. But since there are rather extensive grammatical differences between social dialects in all regions, it is important when we compare the grammar of different regions to be sure that we are dealing with the same social level in each region. A case in point is the varying solutions to the problem of the second person singular pronoun.

In older stages of English, there were a singular pronoun *thou* (OE *þū*) and a plural *you* (OE *ēow*). These were distributed strictly on the basis of the number of the referent—*thou* for a single person addressed, *you* for a group of two[2] or more persons addressed. But during the Middle English and Early Modern English periods, English went through a process that also affected most other European languages about the same time. The plural form came to be used as a polite form for addressing a single person, and the singular thus was used only with intimates and inferiors. In the standard dialect the process went even farther, so that by the end of the eighteenth century *you* was general for both the singular and plural and the *thou* forms were not used at all except in the formal language of prayer. The result was a certain amount of ambiguity, usually but not always resolved by the nonlinguistic context of the utterance. In effect, a gap opened up in the pronoun system which various regional and social varieties of English filled in various ways. One solution was simply to retain the old singular form; this was done by the ordinary spoken dialects of the north and west of England. A more common solution was to treat *you* as a general second person pronoun unmarked for number and originate a marked plural form which could be used when ambiguity might otherwise result. Americans are familiar with the Southern *you all*, a marked plural form used in all levels of spoken English throughout the South. Another plural form was made by adding the plural noun inflection to *you* to produce *youse* /yu:z/, with an unstressed variant /yəz/. This is used by many speakers in the northern United States in the same way that Southerners use *you all*. But the two forms cannot be exactly matched, since *youse* has never gained acceptance in educated speech, which still lacks an unambiguous plural form. When it is necessary to indicate the number of *you* to avoid ambiguity, northern Americans solve the problem syntactically by following the pronoun with a plural noun such as *people*, *men*, *children*, or, on a more colloquial level, *guys*. The situation can be represented by a simple diagram:

### Marked second-person Plural Pronouns

|  | *Northern* | *Southern* |
|---|---|---|
| *Educated* | you (men, etc.) | you all |
| *Uneducated* | youse | you all |

2. In its oldest stages, English had a separate pronoun, a dual, for two persons addressed. This went out of use in the early Middle English period.

Other regional solutions to this problem, also confined to un-educated speech, are *together* (County of Norfolk in England) and *'mongst you* (eastern shore of Maryland and Virginia). But the southern United States remains the only region where a local form is standard for educated as well as uneducated speech.

Regional grammatical differences are thus much more prevalent on the uneducated level and in informal or colloquial style than in educated written English. They may be morphological or syn-tactic. A frequent form of morphological difference is in the past tense forms of verbs, where older strong forms like *holp* and *clomb* have survived in certain regions while in educated speech the ana-logical regular forms *helped* and *climbed* have been adopted.[3] The regional distribution of these forms is sometimes very clearly marked, as in nonstandard past forms of *see*. In Engand, the non-standard form in the North, the Northwest Midlands, and the Southwest is the analogical regular form *seed*. In the East Midlands and most of the Southeast, including London, the plain form *see* prevails, while in the Southwest Midlands and the county of Kent, the past participle form *seen* is used. These three varieties have a regional distribution in America as well: *see* in New England and New York State, *seen* in the Midlands, and *seed* alternating with *seen* in the South.[4] In both countries the standard form *saw* is used by educated speakers everywhere.

One morphological—and graphic—difference between standard British and standard American usage is in the past forms of verbs like *dream*, *lean*, *leap*, and *spell*. American usage favors regular forms *dreamed*, *leaned*, *leaped*, and *spelled*, while British favors

| British | | American | |
|---------|---------------|----------|---------------|
| Spelling | Pronunciation | Spelling | Pronunciation |
| dreamt | /dremt/ | dreamed | /driːmd/ |
| leant | /lent/ | leaned | /liːnd/ |
| spelt | /spelt/ | spelled | /speld/ |
| lept | /lept/ | leaped | /liːpt/ ∼ /lept/ |
| crept | /krept/ | crept | /krept/ |
| peeped | /piːpt/ | peeped | /piːpt/ |

3. On the regional distribution of nonstandard verb forms, see E. Bagby Atwood, *A Survey of Verb Forms in the Eastern United States* (Ann Arbor: University of Michigan Press, 1958).

4. For nonstandard forms of *see*, see Atwood, *Survey*, p. 20 and Fig. 17; also W. Nelson Francis, "Some Dialectal Verb Forms in England," *Orbis* 10:1-14 (1961).

forms with an often irregular /t/ ending and a vowel change from /i:/ to /e/. On many verbs of this type, however, the two agree.

Dialectologists have paid less attention to syntax than to other forms of linguistic variety, and syntactic variation of any notable sort is largely restricted to substandard, uneducated speech. But some minor contrasts between British and American usage may be noted. Many of these involve verb-phrase syntax, especially in interrogative and negative transformations. Americans almost always form the negative and interrogative of the full verb *have* (not the auxiliary) with *do*, while Britons often use inversion and postverbal *n't*:

| American | British |
|---|---|
| Do you have any bread? | Have you (got) any bread? |
| I don't have any money. | I haven't (got) any money. |

I have even heard *haven't to* used as the negative of the catenative verb *have to*: when I was testing the ripeness of some fruit in an English market, the market woman said "You haven't to touch the fruit!" Americans would express this prohibition by *you mustn't* or *you're not supposed to*, while *you don't have to* would mean "it's not necessary to, you needn't."[5]

Another use of *have*—the causative use—shows regional variety in America. In the North and North Midland, the usage is without a following *to*: *I'll have him write you*. South of the Mason-Dixon line, the *to* is frequently preferred: *I'll have him to write you*. A regional verb phrase of particular interest is *might could*, which appears in uneducated speech and in that of many educated speakers in the South and up through central Pennsylvania. Since, as we saw in Chapter Two, the standard verb-phrase pattern permits no auxiliary before a modal, this is a major deviation from standard syntax. So, for the same reason, is the phrase *hadn't ought* as a negative of *ought*, widely used in the northern United States and Canada.

**Lexical differences** of a regional sort, though perhaps less immediately noticeable than differences of pronunciation, are those most frequently talked about by laymen. They have also been used

5. A similar contrast affects the interrogative forms. In a recent British detective story, the detective, represented as a gentleman and a speaker of RP (the language of the Establishment), asks, "Have I to get into that thing?"

extensively by dialectologists in establishing dialect boundaries. Since they are commonly single items, not systematically related to one another, they tend to produce rather widely scattered isoglosses. Thus in phonology we would expect the isoglosses marking the absence of postvocalic /r/ in various environments, such as *barn*, *bard*, *car*, *board*, and *hurt*, to lie close together and form a fairly tight bundle. But we should have no such expectation about the regional names for familiar objects like frying pans, seesaws, and sawhorses. Words are often borrowed from one region to another as single items: a term such as *cruller*, for a certain kind of doughnut, can spread over a wide area without changing the overall lexical pattern. It is much harder to borrow a phoneme or a phonemic distribution.

Nevertheless, lexical isoglosses often do fall into rather close bundles, which may coincide with dialect boundaries established by phonological features. Two such bundles, identified by the American dialectologist Hans Kurath, divide the Atlantic seaboard of the United States into the three areas which Kurath called Northern, Midland, and Southern (see map, p. 239). The line between Northern and Midland runs diagonally northwestward across central New Jersey and due west across Pennsylvania some distance south of the New York line. The line between Midland and Southern runs close to the Pennsylvania-Maryland line and then turns south along the Blue Ridge mountains. Some of the lexical isoglosses establishing these lines may be seen in the maps in Kurath's *A Word Geography of the Eastern States*.[6]

Examples of regional lexical variety, such as the contrasting railroad terms of America and Britain, have already been given. Some lexical contrasts of this sort, such as the *whiffletree* : *singletree* contrast that separates the American North from the Midland and South, are old; others, like the regional terms already cited for submarine sandwich and milk shake, are recent. In spite of the standardizing forces of travel, military service, and the nationwide advertising and distribution of products, not to mention network radio and television, new local terms continue to arise, and old ones persist. But it is undoubtedly true that the amount of regional variety in vocabulary, especially in terms commonly written or commercially widespread, is decreasing. The southern American housewife who encounters *lima beans* and *green beans* in the

6. Ann Arbor: University of Michigan Press, 1949, Figs. 5-7, 15, and 16.

frozen-food department of her local supermarket is likely to give up her native *butter beans* and *snap beans* even in the family circle, so that her children may grow up without knowing these regionalisms.

## 4. Major Regional Types of English

The major regions where English is spoken are of three kinds, fundamentally different in their general linguistic situation and particularly in the amount of local variation within them. First is the homeland—the British Isles—where the language has been in widespread, though not universal use,[7] for about 1500 years. Then come the regions colonized during the seventeenth and eighteenth centuries, in which English almost completely replaced the native languages, as well as the other European languages that had taken a foothold. To this group belong the United States, the Dominions of Canada, Australia, and New Zealand, and the Union of South Africa. The third group comprises those areas where English became the language of government and commerce but did not replace the native languages in everyday use. India is the largest such area; also important are African countries like Nigeria, Ghana, Sierra Leone, Kenya, and Rhodesia. All of these are polyglot areas in which English is the only common language, learned as a second language by members of the professional and governing classes, many of whom received university education in England.

**British English.** As might be expected, the English of the British Isles shows greater diversity than that of any other area. In the first place there are three varieties of standard English, two of them regional though generally accepted everywhere. The most important of these is **Received Standard,** often called **Received Pronunciation** (abbreviated RP), though its features extend to matters other than phonology. This is the language of the Establishment—the public schools and universities, the Church of England, the civil service, and the City. At least until World War II, anyone who wished to make his way in any of these circles had to

7. The Celtic languages, Irish, Welsh, Gaelic, Manx, and (until about 1800) Cornish are the native languages in various parts of the British Isles, though nowadays virtually all native speakers of these languages can also speak English.

learn RP if he was not fortunate enough to have it as his native speech. So essential an attribute of the upper classes was it that Bernard Shaw could base his comedy *Pygmalion* (later made into the musical comedy *My Fair Lady*) on the notion that a Cockney flower-girl could be made acceptable in high society if she learned to speak RP.

In spite of some minor variations, especially associated with age groups, all versions of RP share a large number of features which add up to what Americans call an English or Oxford accent. In pronunciation, some of these are the absence of /r/ except before or between vowels, the /a:/ pronunciation of words like *ask, half, can't* (but not *cant*), the diphthongization of the vowel of *boat* to /əw/ or even /ew/, and the use of /a/ as the vowel of *but, rub,* and other "short-*u*" words.

Alongside RP, and equally acceptable at least to their own speakers, are the two regional standards: Scots, and Irish English. Scots, of which there are many local dialects, descends from the Northern dialect of Middle English. During the seventeenth and eighteenth centuries Scotsmen who went south to take part in governmental or other activities in England attempted to learn educated London English, the ancestor of RP. More recently, however, with the growth of national pride and patriotism, educated Scotsmen, even those pursuing careers outside Scotland, continue to use characteristic Scots pronunciation as well as grammar and vocabulary.

The English of Ireland, especially that of members of the laboring and servant classes who migrated to England or America, has often been made fun of as an "Irish brogue." But the pronunciation of educated middle and upper class Irish people constitutes a regional standard fully accepted in Ireland and to a considerable degree elsewhere. Such prominent Irishmen as George Bernard Shaw and William Butler Yeats preserved their Irish pronunciation, though in their writings they used characteristic Irish grammar and vocabulary only when portraying Irish people. Like American English, Irish English goes back in its origins to the English of the seventeenth century, and it preserves many features of seventeenth-century phonology that have been changed in RP. Notable among these are the retroflex /r/ after vowels, the /e:/ vowel in words like *meat* and *bean*, which have /i:/ in RP,[8] and the /ɛ:/ vowel in

---

8. This pronunciation is now old-fashioned and dying out.

words like *mate* and *bane*, where RP has /e:/ or /ey/. This produces the following contrasts:

| Spelling | RP | Irish |
|---|---|---|
| meet | /mi:t/ | /mi:t/ |
| meat | /mi:t/ | /me:t/ |
| mate | /me:t/ | /mɛ:t/ |

Below the level of educated standard, the English of Britain shows great diversity, greater than that of all the rest of the English-speaking world. At the level of uneducated and unsophisticated rural speech, the diversity, already great in Middle English, has tended to increase, at least until the last twenty years or so. The widespread mixing of young men from different parts of England during World War II and the recent great increase of radio and television have reduced the number of speakers who use only their regional dialect. Most people in Britain, even those whose natural daily speech is an extreme version of a local rustic dialect, are capable of speaking some version of English approaching near enough to standard English so that communication with speakers of RP or of other regional dialects is not too difficult. This does not necessarily mean that the local dialects are changing or disappearing; it simply means that dialect speakers are acquiring more linguistic versatility. The large majority of them are bidialectal.

Although rather large differences, especially in pronunciation, may occur from county to county or even from village to village in many parts of England, it is possible to group the local dialects into eight main regional classes, as shown on the map (p. 236). Scottish dialects cover the English-speaking areas of Scotland and dip below the border into the northwestern county of Cumberland. The English of the Highlands is a variety of "school English," learned as a second language by native speakers of Gaelic. Northern English dialects show considerable variation between the extremes of Lancashire on the west coast and the "Geordie" speech of Northumberland in the east. The old Midland area, already divided into East and West Midland in Middle English, now shows a three-way division between West Country, Central Midland, and East Anglian. The South shows the split, going back to Old English times, between Southwest (sharing many features with West Country) and Southeast. London speech, well known as Cockney, is in a class by itself. It varies considerably from one part of metropolitan

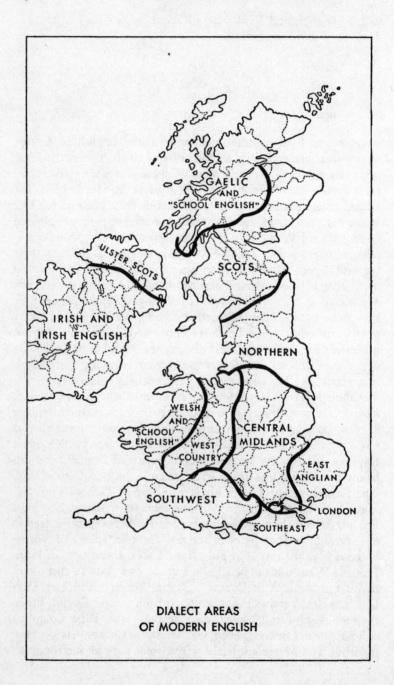

DIALECT AREAS
OF MODERN ENGLISH

London to another, though recent study has shown that the claim of Shaw's Professor Higgins to be able to locate a Londoner by his speech within two miles, or sometimes within two streets, would nowadays be much exaggerated.[9]

*Thus* The features that distinguish these various areas affect all principal aspects of language. Examples of vocabulary items are Scottish *ken* for "know," Northern *beck* contrasting with Scottish *burn* and Midland *brook*, and East Anglian *mawther* for "girl." Grammatical differences include features like the survival of the second person singular pronoun *thou* in Northern and Southwestern, considerable variety in other personal pronouns like the feminine forms *hoo*, *shoo*, *she*, and *her* (as subject) as one moves south from Lancashire to the Southwest, and great diversity in the forms of the strong verbs and of the verb *be*. In phonology, the phonemic and allophonic variations affecting /r/ are notable, including the Scottish trill, the Northumbrian "burr" (a uvular /r/ like that of German), the strong retroflexion of West Country and Southwestern, and the absence of postvocalic /r/ in most of the Central Midlands, East Anglia, and the Southeast including London. It is possible to place a dialect speaker in one of the main regions on the basis of the distribution and pronunciation of his /r/ phoneme alone.

**American English.** The English of the United States derives primarily from British English, both standard and dialectal, of the seventeenth century, when the principal settlements along the Atlantic Coast were made. Like Irish English, it has been more conservative, in some respects at least, than the language of the homeland. Phonological features like the use of the post-vocalic /r/,/æ/ rather than /a:/ in words like *ask*, and the central unround /a/ rather than the back round /ɔ/ in the "short-*o*" words like *hot* and *rod* go back to late seventeenth-century British English and are still preserved in some of the local dialects of Great Britain, though they have changed in RP. Some American speech, notably that of Boston, has followed RP in some of these changes, but every natural American dialect is clearly distinguishable from standard British English in pronunciation.

The differences in grammar between American and British English, some of which have already been noted, mostly affect col-

9. See G. B. Shaw, *Pygmalion*, Act I; also Eva Sivertsen, *Cockney Phonology* (Oslo, 1960), pp. 2-4.

USAGE AND VARIETY IN ENGLISH

loquial style rather than the more formal varieties. In written English they disappear entirely. It is possible to read an entire book, provided it has no realistic dialogue, without coming on a grammatical clue to the nationality of its author. He is much more likely to give himself away by vocabulary, since many items contrast, especially in specialized areas like railroading and automobiles. Even here, however, the close intercommunication and mutual influence of Englishmen and Americans during and since World War II has led to an exchange of words and word uses. For example, the British have just about given up their term *wireless* in favor of the American *radio*, while Americans increasingly use the British *aircraft* instead of the American *airplane*. Sometimes both the British and American terms exist side by side, often with a stylistic distinction. In America specialized moving-picture houses, often those showing mostly foreign films, are likely to use the term *cinema*, which has lost its British connotations for most urban Americans. Conversely, though ordinary Britons still go to the *pictures*, the *films*, or, more colloquially, the *flicks* rather than the *movies*, they freely use the American term *movie star*.

On both the educated and the vernacular level, American speech shows considerable regional variety, especially in the older settlements east of the Mississippi. The three major areas, Northern, Midland, and Southern, can be further subdivided according to both phonological and lexical features (see map). The Northern area is divided by a bundle of isoglosses running north and south in the vicinity of the Connecticut River. The resulting areas are Eastern or Coastal New England and Inland Northern, the latter extending across New York state, northern Pennsylvania, Ohio, Indiana, and Michigan. Metropolitan New York, like metropolitan London, is a distinctive area to itself, sharing some features with New England and deriving others from the languages of immigrants from other parts of the world that have settled there. The Midland area has three main subdivisions. Eastern Midland, whose focus is Philadelphia, extends roughly to the Allegheny Mountains west of the Susquehanna River. West Midland extends westward in a narrowing wedge from the Alleghenies to the Mississippi. South Midland reaches from West Virginia and southern Ohio and Indiana all the way to Texas; in its southerly regions it shares many features with Southern. The Southern region also can be subdivided: the speech of Tidewater and Piedmont Virginia, for example, differs in many ways from that of the Delta area of Mississippi and Louisiana.

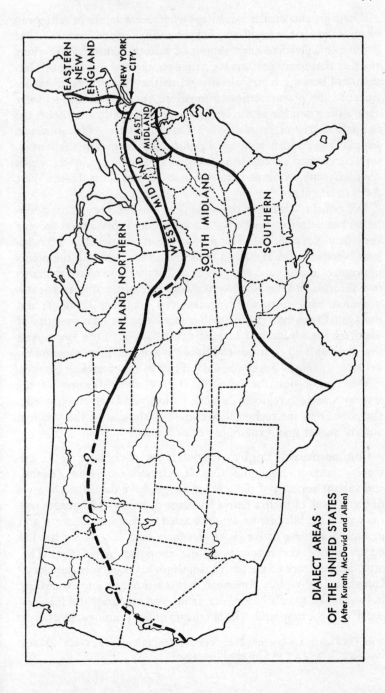

DIALECT AREAS
OF THE UNITED STATES
(After Kurath, McDavid and Allen)

There are also smaller local areas where some factor of settlement or migration has brought with it special linguistic phenomena. One is the Pennsylvania Dutch region of eastern Pennsylvania, where the fact that many persons are native speakers of a dialect of German and become bilingual only when they go to school has influenced the pronunciation, intonation, vocabulary, and to some extent the grammar of the local variety of English. Another is the Sea Island area of coastal South Carolina, where African slaves, having little contact with any English speakers except a few overseers, developed a creole or mixed dialect, known as Gullah, which contains many words and grammatical features derived from West African languages.[10]

West of the Mississippi the settlement is too recent and the population has been too mobile for distinctive local dialects to become very firmly established. The predominant varieties have been Inland Northern and West and South Midland, reflecting the points of origin of the original pioneers as well as the more recent migrants to California and the Northwest. More recently, however, the migration of both whites and Negroes from Arkansas, Oklahoma, and the Gulf Coast into California has introduced several varieties of Southern speech into the linguistic melting pot of the West. And the situation will continue to change as long as the population remains as mobile as it is in the second half of the twentieth century.

We cannot describe here the distinguishing features of the several American regional dialects; various accounts, ranging from the popular to the technical, are listed at the end of this chapter, and the reader may explore these for himself.

**Commonwealth English.** English is the official language of the three important Dominions, Canada, Australia, and New Zealand, and variant versions of the mother tongue have developed in each of them. In all of them a native language or group of languages was spoken by the inhabitants who preceded the English colonists, and in each case these native languages have been largely superseded except among the remnants of the aboriginal population. The principal influence of the native languages has been on vocabulary. Canadian English, like American, has taken over many American Indian words, especially for flora, fauna, and topographical features peculiar to the new land. The languages of the primitive Australian

10. On Gullah, see Lorenzo Dow Turner, *Africanisms in the Gullah Dialect* (Chicago: University of Chicago Press, 1949).

bushmen have contributed some words to Australian English, a few of which, like *boomerang*, have become part of the general English vocabulary. The same can be said of the Maori language of New Zealand. Canada differs from the other two dominions in the fact that English competes with another European language, French, over a large part of its most populous area. In spite of an official policy of bilingualism, however, English remains the dominant language.

The political, economic, and cultural ties of these Dominions with the home country have remained stronger than have those of the United States, and for this reason among others their versions of English have deviated less. The educated speech of New Zealand, for example, is very close to that of England. The fact that the earlier settlers in Australia were transported criminals means that the variety of English that developed there was strongly affected by substandard and dialectal British English. Canadian English, on the other hand, has been much influenced, both in pronunciation and in vocabulary, by its proximity to the United States. Unlike American English, these varieties of Commonwealth English have not been extensively studied by dialectologists. But with the increasing independence of the dominions, their growing stature in the family of nations, the development of national literatures, and the encouragement of linguistic study at their great universities, we may expect to know more about them in the future.

The English of South Africa presents a special case. The majority of the European settlers in the various areas which were formed into the Union of South Africa were not British but Dutch. Their speech, called Afrikaans, has always been more widely used than English, and with the complete separation of South Africa from the British Commonwealth, the use of English is declining. In pronunciation, South African English has always been strongly influenced by British English, so that educated speakers are often indistinguishable from native speakers of RP. Many Afrikaans words have been borrowed, and some of them, such as *trek*, have become part of the general English vocabulary.

**English as a Second Language.** English has been a language of worldwide distribution and major political importance since the eighteenth century. But with the emergence of the United States as a world power in the last generation, the prestige of English as a second language has increased greatly. From the point of view of linguistic variety, which is our present concern, we should recognize that two differing kinds of circumstances affect the type of English which is learned as a second language by those who are not native speakers.

In the first place, there is what may be called **school English**. As the name indicates, this is English taught in school to those who are not native speakers, often by teachers who themselves are not native speakers. A principal reason for teaching English in the schools is that it is the official or unofficial common language of a country whose citizens speak two or more different native tongues. India is an older example of this situation. Under British rule, English was taught in the schools to Indian boys destined to become civil or military officials, or who for some other reason belonged to the group whose position and interests brought them into frequent contact with the relatively small group of British officials and merchants. When India became an independent country with Dominion status in the British Commonwealth, English continued to be an indispensable language for intercommunication among speakers of the three hundred or so different languages native to the Indian subcontinent. Hindi is now the official language of India and was legally supposed to supersede English in 1965, though extensive civil disturbances in that year forced the government to effect a compromise in which other Indian languages were given parallel status. But for at least another generation it will be necessary for members of the government to know English. It is still being taught in the schools; in fact there is a rather strong movement in India today to improve the teaching of English and to make use of the new techniques of language teaching developed by American and British linguists and language teachers.

Other countries where English is either the official language or a second language of major importance are the Philippines, Malaysia, Ceylon, and newly independent African nations like Nigeria, Ghana, and Kenya. Nor should we forget that within the borders of the major English-speaking countries there are groups that are not native speakers of English but first learn it when they go to school. Among these are Welsh and Gaelic speakers in Britain; Puerto Ricans, Mexicans, Indians, and various immigrant groups in

America; Indians, French Canadians, and European immigrants in Canada.

In the past, school English was chiefly taught as a written literary language, and the books read were often classics such as Shakespeare and Dickens. As a result, those who learned English this way were unable to distinguish between various stylistic and historical varieties, so that they made inappropriate use of formal and often archaic vocabulary and grammar. The British gave the name "Babu English" to this often amusingly stilted and literary variety of the language (*babu* is a Hindu title which the British used to mean "minor official, clerk"). More recently, however, attention has been given to teaching the spoken language and colloquial style, using the modern methods which are used for teaching other foreign languages. The particular variety of English taught depends chiefly on the historical and political affiliations of the country concerned, as well as the availability of native speakers of English as teachers or trainers of teachers. American English, once avoided as an undesirable variety of the language, is now being taught all over the world because American linguists, teachers, administrators, and funds are available to help with the tremendous task of furnishing millions of non-native speakers with a functional command of English. American universities, foundations, and government agencies—especially the Peace Corps—now carry on extensive English-teaching operations in such far-flung places as Afghanistan, Turkey, Tanganyika, the Philippines, and Egypt.

In contrast to school English—whether the old-fashioned literary type or the more modern colloquial type—are those varieties of English which have grown up without governmental or educational sponsorship as common modes of communication between speakers of various languages. These are the **pidgin** and **creole** languages. **Pidgin English** developed in the British trading area in the Far East and the South Pacific; it is basically a simplified form of English, whose limited vocabulary and less complex grammar make it easy to learn but restrict its range principally to the basic commercial intercommunication for which it developed. There are several varieties of Pidgin in different parts of Australia, Melanesia, and mainland Asia. A creole, on the other hand, is a dialect which draws not only its vocabulary but also its phonology and grammar from two or more different languages. The creoles of Jamaica or of Sierra Leone, for example, mix features from English and various African languages in a way that makes them unintelligible to speakers of other varieties of English. They are probably best thought of not as varieties of English at all, but as new hybrid languages. They are learned not only as a second language but by many as their native speech. A brief example of Jamaican in a roughly phonemic transcription will show how far it departs from other varieties of English[11]

> 'aa 'rait. 'wen di re'puort tek 'chaaj a di 'distrik dat ba'bia'buo 'kil di 'bwai 'mada, di 'bwai 'stepmə̃da nou wi ha fi 'tiek di 'bwai, a 'likl 'biebi, an 'riez im. so di 'bwai 'duon 'nuo dat im 'baan 'mada iz 'ded. im 'kliemz 'dat 'liedi az im 'mada, di 'wan huu 'riez im 'nou. di 'bwai 'riez tu a 'standaad tel im 'riich 'skuul 'iej. di 'bwai 'goiŋ a 'skuul. him 'goiŋ a 'skuul, in 'goiŋ a 'skuul, in 'goiŋ a 'skuul, tel 'him an i 'ada 'skuul'miet-dem bigin 'kwaril wid 'wan a'nada.

This passage has been glossed by its editor, David De Camp, as follows:

> All right. When the report take charge of the district that Babiabuo kill the boy's mother, the boy's stepmother now will have to take the boy, a little baby, and raise him. So the boy don't know that his born mother is dead. He claims that lady as his mother, the one who raise him now. The boy raise to a standard until he reach school age. The boy going to school. He going to school, he going to school, he going to school, until he and the other schoolmates begin quarrel with one another.

## 5. Social and Educational Varieties of English

We have already noted that there are social varieties of English, differing in pronunciation, grammar, and vocabulary. These are the natural modes of speech of people who differ in education and in the positions they occupy in the social system. It is here, even more than in regional variation, that value judgments are most likely to be made. Specifically, the dialect of educated people who occupy positions of influence and responsibility is commonly called "good English" and that of people lower on the educational and social scale "bad English." Let us briefly investigate the implications of these terms.

11. From "Babiabuo," in R. B. Le Page and David De Camp, *Jamaican Creole* (London: Macmillan, 1960), p. 167.

Applied to language, the adjective *good* can have two meanings: (1) "effective, adequate for the purpose to which it is put" and (2) "acceptable, conforming to approved usage." The first of these is truly a value judgment of the language itself. In this sense the language of Shakespeare, for example, is "good English" because it serves as a highly effective vehicle for his material. On the other hand, the language of a poorer writer, which does not meet adequately the demands put upon it, might be called "bad English." The second meaning of *good* is not really a judgment of the language itself but a social appraisal of the persons who use it. An expression like *I ain't got no time for youse* may be most effective in the situation in which it is used, and hence "good English" in the first sense. But most people, including those who naturally speak this way, will call it "bad English" because grammatical features like *ain't, youse*, and the double negative construction belong to a variety of English commonly used by people with little education and low social and economic status.

This second meaning of the terms *good English* and *bad English* is much more common than the first. It is easier, no doubt, to identify a dialect by certain overt items of grammar and vocabulary than it is to estimate the effectiveness of a specific sample of language. Furthermore, the notion that the language of social and educational inferiors is "bad" has been extensively taught in schools, so that even those who speak it naturally often get the idea that there is something intrinsically wrong with their language, usually without clearly understanding why. Others, of course, alter their language to make it conform more nearly to what they have been taught to consider "good." In effect, they adopt a social dialect appropriate to a higher position on the educational and social scale.

It is unfortunate that these two notions—effectiveness and social prestige—have both come to be expressed in the same terms, as value judgments of the language itself. They are not necessarily connected. What is called "bad English" in the usual sense may be highly effective in the appropriate context. Conversely, language which is socially and educationally impeccable may be most ineffective, as anyone who has listened to a dull speech can testify. It is true that on the whole the language of the more educated is likely to be more effective, since it has a larger vocabulary and somewhat more complex grammar and hence is capable of finer and more subtle shades of meaning as well as finer effects of rhythm and tone. But unless these resources are used skillfully they do not necessarily produce better language from the point of view of effectiveness. On the other hand, writers like Mark Twain, Ring Lardner, and William Faulkner have shown that vernacular or uneducated English can be used with great effectiveness in literature.

As with other kinds of variation, social levels of English shade gradually into one another. But we can recognize three main levels. At the top is **educated** or **standard English**; at the bottom is **uneducated English,** and between them comes what H. L. Mencken called the **vernacular.** [12] These have in common the larger part of their grammar, pronunciation, and basic vocabulary but are marked by significant differences in all three areas.

**Educated** or **Standard English** is that naturally used by most educated people who fill positions of social, financial, and professional influence in the community. Some people learn it as their native speech, if they come from families that already belong to this social class. Others acquire it in the course of their schooling and later by conscious or unconscious imitation of their associates. Control of standard English does not, of course, guarantee professional, social, or financial success. But it is an almost indispensable attribute of those who attain such success.

In addition to its social importance, educated English is on the whole a more flexible and versatile instrument than the other social varieties. As the language of the professions and the learned disciplines, it is called on to express more complex ideas, for which it has developed an extensive vocabulary. Its grammar, too, is more complex, and it uses longer sentences with more levels of subordination. This does not mean that it presents greater difficulties to the listener or reader, provided he is familiar with its vocabulary and grammar. But the fact that it is often used to express complicated and difficult material means that, unskillfully used, it can be vague or obscure. When its resources of vocabulary and grammar are overexploited in the expression of simple ideas, it may become the inflated jargon sometimes called "gobbledygook."

> With regard to personnel utilizing the premises after normal working hours, it is requested that precautions be observed to insure that all windows and doors are firmly secured and all illumination extinguished before vacating the building.

12. H. L. Mencken, *The American Language*, 4th ed. (New York: Alfred A. Knopf, 1937), p. 417.

This is obviously only a much elaborated expression of the request that can be more simply and effectively stated:

> If you work late, be sure to lock th.. doors and windows and turn off the lights when you leave.

In the first sense of the phrase "good English," this translation is good and the gobbledygook which it translates, though it contains no errors of grammar or usage, is incredibly bad.

The British version of standard English, RP, is the same for all speakers regardless of their place of origin. In America, however, there is no such thing as a single standard form of American English, especially in pronunciation. The nearest thing to it is the speech of anonymous radio and television announcers, which one linguist has aptly called "network English."[13] In contrast to the well known individual commentators, who are allowed to use their native regional pronunciation, the network announcers all use a common version of English which is in most features that of the Inland Northern area.

Because of its nationwide use, network English is an acceptable standard form everywhere. But it is not always a prestige dialect. Educated speakers in Boston, New York, Philadelphia, Richmond, Charleston, Atlanta, or New Orleans usually use the dialects of their own regions in educated form. The last five Presidents of the United States are a good example of the diversity of pronunciation to be found in standard American English. President Johnson speaks the educated South Midland speech of Texas. President Kennedy's Boston speech, with its lack of postvocalic /r/ and its intrusive /r/ at the end of words like *Cuba*, was very distinctive. President Eisenhower's speech was a good illustration of the Middle Western variety sometimes called General American. It betrayed his Kansas origin in spite of a military career that took him to many parts of the English-speaking world. President Truman retained many of the South Midland features of his native Missouri, and President Roosevelt spoke the educated version of New York City speech, somewhat modified by his Harvard education and New England connections. Although most of these men had long careers in politics and frequently addressed nationwide

13. William A. Stewart, in a discussion of the problem of teaching standard English to nonstandard speakers, Bloomington, Indiana, August 1964.

audiences, each of them used the educated version of his native regional dialect.

**Vernacular English** is the variety naturally used by the middle group of the population, who constitute the vast majority. Their schooling extends into or through secondary school, with perhaps a year of college or technical school. They occupy the lesser white-collar jobs, staff the service trades, and fill the ranks of skilled labour. Many of these jobs require considerable verbal skill and have extensive occupational vocabularies. Vernacular speakers, when "talking shop," characteristically show considerable control of technical vocabulary and relatively complex grammar.

Just as jargon and gobbledygook are the result of overpretentious style in standard English, so the **hyperurbanism** or **hyperform** is in the vernacular. A hyperurbanism is a usage which results from the overcorrection of one of the supposedly "bad" (*i.e.* nonstandard) features of the vernacular. For example, the usage of pronoun case in the vernacular differs from that of standard English in several respects, one being that a pronoun subject when coordinated with another pronoun or with a noun may be in the objective case:

| | |
|---|---|
| *vernacular:* | Him and Joe went. |
| *standard:* | Joe and he went. |
| *vernacular:* | You and me can do it. |
| *standard:* | You and I can do it. |

The native speaker of the vernacular who aspires to speak standard learns to change this use of the objective case to the standard subjective. But this change often leads to uncertainty about pronoun case in coordination constructions elsewhere than as subject. The vernacular speaker who has learned that *you and me* is incorrect as subject is likely to be suspicious of it anywhere, so he says *between you and I*, which is just as much a violation of standard grammar as *you and me can do it*.

This is not the place for an extended discussion of the features which distinguish the vernacular from standard educated English. Many of them are identified and discussed in handbooks and dictionaries of usage, a few of which are listed at the end of this chapter. Since the vernacular shades gradually into educated standard, many of these items characterize only the varieties of vernacular nearest to uneducated English. Many points of usage which are condemned as nonstandard by handbooks actually represent **divided usage**; that is, they are accepted and used by some standard English speakers but rejected by others. Sometimes the division is regional: a form or construction which is vernacular or uneducated in one region may be standard in another. An example is the use of *like* in such sentences as *It looks like it might rain* and *He acts like he's hungry*. This usage, condemned as nonstandard by most handbooks, is certainly standard in England and in the American South in all but the most formal style. In the American North and Midland it is probably to be classed as vernacular. At least, a recent advertising slogan that used *like* in this way stirred up considerable discussion and condemnation among those who feel responsible for protecting standard English from vernacular encroachments. In fact, some aspirants to standard "correctness" avoid the use of *like* as a subordinator entirely, replacing it with *as* in sentences like *He drove as a crazy man*. This hyperurbanism throws away the nice semantic distinction between the prepositions *like* and *as*, as in the following:

He is acting *like* a lawyer in this affair.
He is acting *as* a lawyer in this affair.

The implication of the first is either that he is not a lawyer at all or that his lawyerlike behavior is inappropriate or unwelcome. In the second, no such judgment is implied; the sentence merely states that in the affair in question his participation is limited to the role of lawyer. It is frequently the effect of a hyperurbanism to gain a supposed (but spurious) "correctness" at the expense of precision. It thus becomes an example of "bad English" in the first sense discussed above. If preciseness in communication is an important quality of language, which certainly few will deny, the hyperurbanism that blurs preciseness in the interest of a fancied correctness is a greater linguistic offense than the nonstandard vernacular usage which is accurate and clear.

The vernacular is very much with us and presumably always will be. It is the stratum of English where there develop many new features of grammar, pronunciation, and vocabulary which are ultimately accepted into standard usage. In a democratic society like that of America, it is an essential medium of communication even for the educated, who must at least understand and accept its usage, though they do not necessarily have to speak it. In fact, if they can speak it only with conscious and obvious effort, educated speakers should avoid it, for people are quick to take offense at what they consider patronizing. But those native speakers of the vernacular who have also acquired a command of educated standard English should not lose control of the vernacular, since a native command of it can be of great value on many occasions.

A practical illustration is the case of the university professor of English, a native speaker of educated English, who needed a rare part for his car. He consulted a colleague who had at one time been a garage mechanic and spoke the appropriate form of the vernacular. The colleague told him where to telephone to inquire for the part, but added "You'd better let me do the phoning; it'll cost you twice as much if you do it."[14]

**Uneducated English** is that naturally used by people whose schooling is limited and who perform the unskilled labor in country and city. Certain grammatical features, such as the double or multiple negative (which was standard in Chaucer's English) and the use of *them* as a plural demonstrative, are common to most regional varieties. But in other respects uneducated English shows much regional variety in all its features. An uneducated speaker may find that he has difficulty making himself understood outside his home region. Such features as past-tense *holp* for *helped* and *drug* for *dragged* have clear-cut regional distribution.[15] Likewise regional differences of pronunciation, which, as we have seen, exist on all levels, are much greater in uneducated speech. The same is true of vocabulary; the local words and expressions which more educated speakers avoid (though they may consider them picturesque and use them occasionally for special effect) persistently survive in uneducated speech. For this reason dialectological investigations like the Linguistic Survey of England often confine themselves almost wholly to uneducated, preferably illiterate, informants.[16]

Uneducated English doesn't often get into writing, since its users

14. This anecdote is told of himself by Professor J. J. Lamberts of Arizona State University.

15. Atwood, *Survey*, pp. 9f, 16f.

16. Harold Orton and Eugen Dieth, *Survey of English Dialects* (Leeds: E. J. Arnold & Son, Ld., 1962), pp. 14-17, 44. In the Linguistic Atlas of the United States and Canada, however, three types of informants—representing roughly what we have called uneducated, vernacular, and educated English—are used. See Hans Kurath, *Handbook of the Linguistic Geography of New England* (Washington: American Council of Learned Societies, 1939), pp. 41-44.

have little occasion to write and may be semiliterate or even wholly illiterate.[17] In literary writing, uneducated speakers are often marked as such by attempts to represent their pronunciation by distorted spelling, including a liberal use of eye dialect (see p. 214). But a truly skillful use of uneducated English in literature suggests the level of the speaker without resorting to the rather cheap device of eye dialect. Notice in the following passage from William Faulkner's great novel *As I Lay Dying* how the nature of the speaker—an uneducated Mississippi farmer—is indicated by grammar and vocabulary, without any attempt to illustrate pronunciation at all.

> It was nigh toward daybreak when we drove the last nail and toted it into the house, where she was laying on the bed with the window open and the rain blowing on her again. Twice he did it, and him so dead for sleep that Cora says his face looked like one of these here Christmas masts that had done been buried a while and then dug up, until at last they put her into it and nailed it down so he couldn't open the window on her no more. And the next morning they found him in his shirt tail, laying asleep on the floor like a felled steer, and the top of the box bored clean full of holes and Cash's new auger broke off in the last one. When they taken the lid off they found that two of them had bored on into her face.
>
> If it's a judgment, it aint right. Because the Lord's got more to do than that. He's bound to have. Because the only burden Anse Bundren's ever had is himself. And when folks talks him low, I think to myself he aint that less of a man or he couldn't a bore himself this long.[18]

Here the markers of uneducated regional dialect are such grammatical items as the verb phrase *had done been buried* and the double negative in *couldn't open the window on her no more*, the lexical item *toted*, and idioms like *talks him low* and *he aint that less of a man*.

The uneducated English of this sample contrasts with the following passage from the same novel, representing the English of a country doctor from the same region:

17. C. C. Fries, in preparing his *American English Grammar* (New York: Appleton-Century-Crofts, 1940), found a plentiful source of uneducated written English in letters written to a government bureau whose constituents included many uneducated speakers.

18. From *As I Lay Dying*, by William Faulkner, p. 68. Copyright 1930 and renewed 1957 by William Faulkner. Reprinted by permission of Random House, Inc.

When Anse finally sent for me of his own accord, I said "He has wore her out at last." And I said a damn good thing, and at first I would not go because there might be something I could do and I would have to haul her back, by God. I thought maybe they have the same sort of fool ethics in heaven they have in the Medical College and that it was maybe Vernon Tull sending for me again, getting me there in the nick of time, as Vernon always does things, getting the most for Anse's money like he does for his own. But when it got far enough into the day for me to read weather sign I knew it couldn't have been anybody but Anse that sent. I knew that nobody but a luckless man could ever need a doctor in the face of a cyclone. And I knew that if it had finally occurred to Anse himself that he needed one, it was already too late.[19]

There are items here which are not educated standard—*wore* as past participle, for example. But the general level of the English is educated colloquial, quite different from that of the previous passage. Note especially the grammatical complexity of the last sentence.

The speaker who is confined to uneducated English finds himself under a great handicap if he wishes to improve his position in society. This is true even in his own region; it is doubly so when he moves to another dialect area, where he may find not only that his speech is a liability when it comes to getting a good job, but even that he can't make himself understood at all. Furthermore, in an age when more and more of the unskilled tasks are being done by machines, the number of jobs available to persons unable to use any but uneducated English gets smaller every year. The geographical and social mobility of our people presents a great problem to the schools, one of whose tasks is to help students acquire a kind of language which will be an asset to them rather than a handicap. The problem is especially acute in the Northern cities which have had a large influx of uneducated people from the South. It is encouraging to observe that linguists, especially dialectologists, are being called on to help with this problem. The idea is getting about that the speaker of uneducated English is better served if an attempt is made not to "correct" his language and eradicate his "bad language habits," but to extend his linguistic range and versatility by helping him acquire a new dialect that is socially more acceptable. Some educators are even experimenting with the techniques de-

19. *As I Lay Dying*, p. 37.

veloped for teaching foreign languages, in order to emphasize that the task is the positive one of learning something new rather than the negative one of eliminating something bad. Already the results of tentative efforts of this sort are showing promise.

Helping speakers of uneducated English to a command of the vernacular or of standard English is only part of the problem, of course. There must be other kinds of training, and above all there must be tangible evidence that the effort will be worth while; otherwise motivation will be lacking, and without motivation learning is impossible. But in this area the informed student and teacher of language can certainly be of great social usefulness.

## 6. Functional Variety in English

Whether his natural speech is educated, vernacular, or uneducated, no person uses the same kind of language for every occasion. Within the regional and educational variety of language which he speaks, he has different **functional varieties,** sometimes called **styles** or **registers,** appropriate to the occasion, the size of the group spoken to, the degree of familiarity within the group, and even the subject discussed. Selecting the proper style for a given occasion and shifting from one to another as the circumstances change are not primarily linguistic decisions, but social ones. Learning to make such decisions quickly and accurately is part of the process of socialization that we all must go through. Some people become more skillful at it than others; no doubt a large element in the complex of personal traits known as "getting along with people" is the ability to appraise a situation or a person and select the appropriate style on the basis of a few clues.

Preschool children usually have only one style, especially if their experience of the world has been confined chiefly to family and playmates of the same social level. When they go out into the larger world, they learn that not all adults are to be addressed in the same way as parents and other relatives. Much of this they learn for themselves; some of it is taught them by parents and teachers. Although people often find the direct and familiar sayings of children amusing, these sayings are often the result of inappropriate style, which parents and teachers correct with such admonitions as "You mustn't speak to the headmaster like that." By the early teens the lesson is usually well learned and the child has at least three working styles—one for his peers, one for parents and other adults he knows well, and one for strangers—the minimal stylistic repertory needed for normal social life.

For educated adult speakers, Martin Joos has identified and named five styles, each suited to a particular kind of occasion and characterized by certain features which identify it to the listener.[20] The central and, in a sense, unmarked style Joos calls **consultative.** In this style we open a conversation with a stranger; it is safe for that purpose because it will neither offend him by unsolicited intimacy nor throw him off by undue formality. It is also the appropriate style for a discussion of more or less serious matters by a relatively small group; it pays listeners the compliment of assuming that they are interested and serious and hence do not need to have their interest aroused by either the elaborate figurative language of the formal style or the slang and occasional profanity of the casual style. As Joos says,

> The diction is kept in accurate balance with the requirements: the pronunciation is clear but does not clatter, the grammar is complete but for an occasional anacoluthon [mixed construction], the semantics is adequate without fussiness.[21]

It is obviously a style whose major purpose is communication, with a minimum of the social, esthetic, and emotional overtones that characterize other styles.

The **casual style** is that appropriate to easy conversation among acquaintances and friends, except when the seriousness of the occasion or the subject calls for the consultative. In pronunciation it makes much use of elided and slurred forms like /gɔ́nə/ for *going to* and /wáčə dúːin/ for *what are you doing.* Its sentences are often elliptical, even telegraphic, dropping redundant grammatical and semantic features in the interest of directness and brevity, as in *Coming tonight?* for *Are you coming tonight?* and *Joe here?* for *Is Joe here?* Depending on the speaker, it may include slang and occasional profanity. In America, at least, it makes use of first names more often than titles and surnames. Since it is not used to convey very serious or complex information (even close friends shift to consultative for that), it makes considerable use of general-purpose, semantically nearly empty words and phrases like *gimmick, thing-*

20. Martin Joos, *The Five Clocks* (Bloomington: Indiana University Research Center in Anthropology, Folklore, and Linguistics, 1962).
21. *The Five Clocks*, p. 24.

*umajig*, and *nice*. Its deficiencies in communicative power are often acknowledged by frequent interpolation of phrases like *you know*, *I mean*, *as a matter of fact*, and *actually*. When written, as in informal friendly letters, it uses contractions like *won't* and *can't*, abbreviations and clippings like *Dr.* or *doc* for *doctor* and the dash as a general-purpose punctuation mark. It is the style most commonly used by school and university students except in class, where they usually shift to consultative.

People who habitually use casual style where the situation normally calls for consultative are considered "refreshing" or "fresh" depending on the attitude of the person making the appraisal. On the other hand an occasional shift to casual style, either in writing or in speech, may produce a desirable special effect. A teacher who habitually uses it in class usually loses the respect of his students, who feel they are being patronized. But if in a particular emergency he can switch from the consultative *I'd like you students to be quiet* to the casual *Shut up, you chaps*, he may get the quiet he wants. Some writers, particularly humorists, are adept at exploiting the surprise value of a casual sentence in a consultative or formal context:

> One reason the Ford anatomy was never reduced to an exact science was that, having "fixed" it, the owner couldn't honestly claim that the treatment had brought about the cure. There were too many authenticated cases of Fords fixing themselves—restored naturally to health after a short rest. Farmers soon discovered this, and it fitted nicely with their draft-horse philosophy: "Let 'er cool off and she'll snap into it again." [22]

Here the basically formal literary style is enlivened by the lapse into the casual in the last sentence. Such mixing of styles demands great skill if its effect is to be surprise and pleasure rather than mere inappropriateness.

The **intimate style** is used by people who know each other so well and whose relationship is so close that each can predict the other's reactions to a given situation with accuracy a large part of the time. It thus serves chiefly to maintain contact and corroborate the accuracy of each speaker's judgment of the other's reactions. Much of this communication is carried on by other than linguistic

22. E. B. White and Richard L. Strout, "Farewell, My Lovely!" in *The Second Tree from the Corner* (New York: Harper & Brothers, n.d.), p. 38.

means—between intimates a raised eyebrow, a shrug of the shoulders, or a groan can serve as well as or better than verbal expression. Grammar is reduced to a minimum; utterances are typically very short; there may be long periods of silence that in any of the other styles would be interpreted either as rudeness or as a desire to end the conversation. Vocabulary, too, is much reduced, and the words that are used often have special meanings deriving from some shared experience which the world outside the intimate group (usually but not always a pair) does not know about. Pronunciation, too, may be altered; an intimate pair may use a broad form of regional dialectal pronunciation, even though one or both of them are not native speakers of that dialect. Words are slurred and clipped, accidental mispronunciations may be purposedly preserved. Sometimes the intimate message may be carried by intonation alone, and the segmental phonology filled out with nonsense sounds or syllables. Everything about the intimate style serves to emphasize the close familiarity of the speakers and the resulting ability to reduce redundancy to a minimum. In terms of the discussion with which this chapter began, the conservative forces of society are virtually absent, which allows free play to arbitrariness.

As has already been observed, the parties to an intimate conversation are usually a pair: husband and wife, siblings (especially identical twins), lovers. But any small group who are thrown into close and frequent contact and who do not have to maintain social distance because of differences of status may develop an intimate style to be used at least in the area of their greatest common interest and application. The small crew of a boat on a long ocean voyage, an athletic team, a string quartet, a high-wire balancing act—any group where there must be complete cooperation, mutual trust, and a high degree of specialized skill—any of these, however separate their private lives may otherwise be, almost inevitably develops a laconic, stripped-down style, augmented by minute gesture and aided by empathetic understanding, that to the outsider seems almost telepathic. But unless the group is small—not more than four or five—various kinds of social complexity enter in to make the intimate style inappropriate.

When intimates wish to communicate information about something outside the very restricted range to which intimate style is appropriate, they shift to casual or even consultative style. For this reason, intimate style does not often get written down. The act of writing, relatively laborious as it is, usually is the result of the desire to convey some kind of new information to whoever is going to read the product. A love letter is, of course, an exception; its primary purpose is usually simply to communicate the fact that the writer's feelings about the reader have not changed since the last time he was able to communicate this information in person. For this reason, people outside the intimate pair usually find love letters either unintelligible or comic. Letters such as those of Abelard and Héloise or of Keats to Fanny Brawne convey much more than this basic information, and therefore range far beyond the intimate style, often to the level of formal literary style.

One famous example of intimate style in writing is the "little language" that Jonathan Swift occasionally lapsed into in his *Journal to Stella*. This journal was in the form of a series of letters, with almost daily entries, written to two women, Esther Johnson (Stella), who was an intimate correspondent and often a companion of Swift's for thirty years, and her companion, Rebecca Dingley. Although most of the *Journal* consists of an account of Swift's busy life as an important though unofficial member of the Tory administration, he occasionally interpolates an intimate passage like this:

Poor Stella, won't Dingley leave her a little day-light to write to Presto? Well, well, we'll have day-light shortly, spight of her teeth; and zoo must cly Lele and Hele, and Hele aden. Must loo minitate pdfr, pay? Iss, and so la shall. And so leles fol ee rettle. Dood mollow.[23]

A good deal of this becomes clear when we see that it represents a kind of phonemic substitution similar to "baby-talk," with *l* used in place of *r*, and *d* in place of *g*. Also characteristic of intimate style is the use of pet-names—*Stella* for Miss Johnson and *Presto* for himself—and of cryptic abbreviations like *pdfr* (according to Swift's editor, this last was pronounced "Podefar" and stood for either *Poor Dear Foolish Rogue* or *Poor Dear Fellow*).

The three styles so far discussed have in common the fact that they are primarily conversational; they imply the presence and participation of another beside the speaker. The participation, especially in consultative style, may be no more than signaling at brief intervals that one is paying attention, which may be done by brief oral attention-signals (*yes, unh-hunh*) or, when the two

23. Jonathan Swift, *Journal to Stella*, edited by Harold Williams (Oxford: Clarendon Press, 1948), vol. I, p. 210.

parties can see each other, by unobtrusive gestures. But tl . listener is usually expected to become a speaker in his turn, and he knows the signals that mark the places where he can begin speaking without causing a rude interruption. When written, the consultative, casual, and intimate styles suppose a specific reader or small group of readers who would respond in this way if present, and are more or less expected to answer letters addressed to them.

In contrast, the other two styles, the **formal** of expository discourse and the **frozen** of literature, are not conversational but informative and discursive. The hearer or reader is not given the opportunity to intervene, to ask questions, to make comments, or to indicate his lack of comprehension. Instead of the give and take of the conversational situation, the user of formal style—the lecturer, preacher, newscaster, judge, or legislator speaking on the floor (not in committee)—is alone before an audience. Without benefit of the "feedback" that is available to the conversationalist, he is obliged to hold his audience's attention on the one hand by making sure that he is understood and on the other by avoiding boresome explicitness or repetition.

The grammar of formal style is more closely organized and less tolerant of loose or mixed constructions. The vocabulary is more ample than that of the conversational styles, with a wider range of nearly synonymous words and phrases, though large areas of vocabulary—slang, for example—are ruled out except for special effects which actually constitute lapses into the conversational mode. Pronunciation is meticulous; slurring and contractions are avoided, and tactical features like disjuncture, stress, and intonation are carefully observed. The general pattern of organization avoids backtracking, second-thought interpolation, and repetition in varied terms, all of which are characteristic of conversation. The result is to place a much heavier burden of thought and planning upon the formal speaker or writer. As Joos puts it:

Formal text therefore demands advance planning. Consultative speakers never plan more than the current phrase, and are allowed only a limited number of attempts to return to their muttons before abandoning them; the formal speaker has a captive audience, and is under obligation to provide a plan for the whole sentence before he begins uttering it, an outline of the paragraph before introducing it, and a delimitation of field for his whole discourse before he embarks on it. One who does all this currently, keeping the three levels of his planning under continuous control, is correctly said to think on his feet; for clearly it calls for something other than brains, and intelligent persons do not attempt it but instead have the text all composed and written out at leisure.[24]

The formal style is thus the typical style of responsible public writing. By native speakers it is learned relatively late, if at all— usually not until the beginning of schooling and in most cases not until long after that. It has for many, perhaps most, people the qualities of a mode of language that has been learned consciously, as one learns a foreign language, rather than largely unconsciously, as one learns one's mother tongue. The range of competence of its users is greater than that of users of the conversational styles, from the virtuosity of a Churchill to the inept and platitudinous fumblings of a poor after-dinner speaker. Most of the effort in a typical English writing class is concerned with increasing the students' skill in formal style. And rightly so: the central mode of written language for the educated man in our society is formal educated standard English. Most people must learn this in school.

What Joos calls **frozen** style is primarily the style of literature, at least in the broad sense of the word. In this sense, literature can be defined as those samples of language which the whole community or a segment of it values to the point of wishing to preserve their exact expression as well as their content. Once the words have been arranged, they are set or frozen into an unchangeable pattern (though the author himself may exercise the privilege of changing them). This definition would not satisfy the literary critic, who usually would like to include an esthetic criterion in his definition. Nor is it a value judgment. Not all literature is good, by any standard of measurement including its use of language. But all literature does have the quality of rigidity of language.

A piece of literature is a **text**. A good deal of literary scholarship is exerted in the task of making sure that the texts of literary works, especially those that are highly valued, are made available to readers in a form that most accurately represents the author's wishes. The story of Hamlet, Prince of Denmark, can be told in many ways, even that of the comic book. But these are not Shakespeare's play, which must be presented in the language he wrote, as nearly as a modern editor can discover it. In this case the editor's problem is compounded by the fact that the text was frozen in several forms,

24. *The Five Clocks*, p. 26.

260 USAGE AND VARIETY IN ENGLISH

the most important of which are the first two quartos and the first folio. The text the editor produces will not be identical with any of these, but it will represent his best judgment of what Shakespeare intended the play to be, word by word.

Not all literature is frozen in printed form. Societies that have no writing system may have a large body of oral literature, which is memorized in its frozen form and passed down from generation to generation by oral transmission. This method of transmission allows changes and variations to creep into the text, especially as the language itself changes; but, for all that, oral texts remain remarkably constant for generations, even centuries. Members of preliterate societies usually have better trained memories than literate people, and they insist that a text be repeated in the exact words in which they first heard it. The same is true of children before they learn to read, as anyone knows who has read a familiar story to a child and been corrected for the smallest departure from the text. Even in highly literate cultures like our own, at least a small body of literature is passed on by oral transmission—folk songs and nursery rhymes particularly. But we normally expect a frozen text to be available in print, and we customarily read it privately and silently. The literary experience thus becomes a detached and individual one; the solitary reader and the solitary writer do not know each other and never meet except through the medium of the printed page. At least until the modern vogue for recorded readings of their own works by writers, especially poets, such features of the spoken language as intonation have had to be supplied by the reader solely on the evidence of the printed text before him. The burden of communication is carried almost wholly by grammar and vocabulary, with some help from graphic convention or originality.

The great advantage of the frozen style, especially in written form, is that it is freed from the pressures of time which exert very powerful influence on the conversational styles. A writer may spend a lifetime perfecting one poem or novel, if he chooses. A reader, likewise, may reread and study a frozen text as often as he wants to, finding new meanings each time.

Not all the texts that society wants to preserve in their exact language come under the more usual definitions of literature. Some of them, such as scriptures and liturgies, are important to the maintenance of religion. Political documents like treaties and laws must be treated as texts alterable only through elaborate procedures resulting in an acceptable new text: witness the Constitution of the United States and its amendments. Contracts, agreements, bonds, deeds, and other such legal documents follow set formulas which must not be changed lest their binding force be lost. Ceremonies such as weddings, initiations, and the awarding of academic degrees are accompanied by frozen texts, so familiar that people seldom stop to analyze their meaning but simply take them as customary parts of accepted rituals. These are all special types of frozen style, in which the basic meaning of the language is heavily overlaid with interpretation and customary understanding. It is naïve to assume that even the most intelligent and gifted reader of English can extract "the real meaning" from such documents as the Constitution or the New Testament simply by reading the text alone. What these documents mean in our society can only be discovered by prolonged study of other documents devoted to their interpretation.

Joos has succinctly summarized the primary functions of the five styles:

> Good intimate style fuses two personalities. Good casual style integrates disparate personalities into a social group which is greater than the sum of its parts, for now the personalities complement each other instead of clashing. Good consultative style produces cooperation without the integration, profiting from the lack of it. Good formal style informs the individual separately, so that his future planning may be the more discriminate. Good frozen style, finally, lures him into educating himself, so that he may the more confidently act what rôle he chooses.[25]

## 7. In Conclusion

When we take into account the three dimensions of variation—regional, social, and functional—which we have discussed here and the many possibilities within each of them, the number of varying modes in which English can be spoken or written becomes very large. As a crude measure, if we multiply seven regional varieties by three social levels and the result by five stylistic varieties, we get a theoretical figure of a hundred and five possibilities in American English alone, ranging from Eastern New England standard formal (as in President Kennedy's inaugural address) to Coastal Southern

25. *The Five Clocks*, p. 27.

uneducated casual. Not all of these possibilities are realized, of course, but on the other hand there are many gradations possible even within these categories. In the face of such a profusion of differing versions of English, where are we to locate that convenient abstraction, the "English language"? And what is our obligation as native speakers of English? Must we learn all these many varieties, or can we restrict ourselves to a few? Are we entitled to make value judgments about them, or must we accept them all as equally valid? How, in the face of this complexity, are we to know what is "good English"?

The aim of this chapter and of this book as a whole has been to supply or suggest answers to these questions as well as to many more that may be asked about language. The over-all answer is a simple one: the more you know about language, the better you are equipped to use it well yourself and to judge others' use of it. Judgments based on knowledge and fact are sounder than those based on ignorance and prejudice. It is not claimed here that this book will necessarily make you a better speaker, listener, writer, or reader, nor that competence in these skills is dependent on knowing what is here set forth about the English language. What is claimed is that if the information in this book—a tiny fragment of what there is to know about English—enlists your interest sufficiently to make you a lifelong student of the fascinating complexities of English, you will be a better user of the language as a result of that interest and study. Which leads us to a final attempt to characterize the attitude toward language that marks the liberally educated man.

Above all the educated man is characterized by linguistic versatility. He is in command of one version of standard English, usually that which is appropriate to his native region. He can write with skill the written formal style which is common to all regions. But he also can handle all the other styles, from the frozen of literature to the intimate of family life. He can understand and accept the vernacular of his own and other regions and appreciate it when it is used skillfully. He usually can use the vernacular himself without condescension or affectation. He understands the language of the uneducated and appreciates its pungencies while recognizing the stereotyped and poverty-stricken way in which it is usually used. He can savor regional variety and enjoy a dispassionate discussion of its many features. He knows how to use dictionaries and other linguistic reference works so as to avail himself of the vast stores of information they contain. But he is also an observer of language in all its manifestations, and he ultimately becomes his own judge and arbiter of questions of usage.

With this versatility and judgment come confidence in his own practice and freedom from the linguistic anxiety that troubles the incompletely educated. In short, like the skilled craftsman in any other line, he knows his medium, his materials, and his tools, and handles them with the skill born of knowledge and self-confidence. Every sentence he speaks or writes is a token of his respect for man's greatest invention—his language.

## Exercises

I. Study the map on page 227, then answer the following questions:

(a) In what order would the isoglosses be crossed if one traveled southwest instead of due west?

(b) There is a small quadrangle where the isoglosses indicate that the native speaker would have the following features:

[a] rather than [ɒ] in *rod*
[r] lost in *thirty*
[r] lost in *barn*.

Find this quadrangle. Which pronunciation of calf would you expect to find in this location: (1) with [a], (2) with [æ]?

(c) What differences would you expect to encounter if from the center of this quadrangle you moved—(1) 10 miles south? (2) 10 miles east?

II. Find an informant, preferably an older person with relatively little education, who is a lifetime resident of your community and get him to supply his own native words to fill in the blanks in the following sentences:

(a) The time for stopping work for the day is ——————.

(b) What do you call something to eat between meals? ——————.

(c) The men you work with are your ——————.

(d) What do you call an iron plate that cakes are baked on over a fire? ——————.

(e) Reddish brown insects, with feelers and a tail like a pair of pincers, are ——————.

(f) The room where you keep your food is the ——————.

(g) When it is 11:45, we can say it is a quarter —————— twelve.

(h) In June, school —————— for the summer.

*(i) A person who uses his left hand for most things is*
————————.

*If you came from a different part of the country than your
informant, supply your own words to fill the blanks. Check your
findings against those of* Survey of English Dialects, *ed. Harold
Orton, et al. (Leeds: E. J. Arnold & Son, 1962-. The volumes
covering your area may not yet be published.)*

*III. Mark Twain put the following note, headed "Explanatory," at the
beginning of* Huckleberry Finn:

> In this book a number of dialects are used, to wit: the Missouri
> negro dialect; the extremest form of the backwoods Southwestern
> dialect; the ordinary "Pike County" dialect; and four modified vari-
> eties of this last. The shadings have not been done in a haphazard
> fashion, or by guesswork; but painstakingly, and with the trust-
> worthy guidance and support of personal familiarity with these
> several forms of speech.
>
> I make this explanation for the reason that without it many readers
> would suppose that all these characters were trying to talk alike and
> not succeeding.

*Name at least one speaker of each of the dialects mentioned, and find
some of the characteristics of his speech that differentiate it from that
of other dialect speakers in the book.*

*IV. Advertisers sometimes make their slogans memorable by purpose-
ly using slightly irregular, non-standard, or even ungrammatical expressions. Example:* "X cigarettes travel the smoke farther." *Collect
some examples of this from printed or oral advertising and point out
the questions of usage involved.*

*V. The blank in a sentence like* I'm pretty clever, ————— I? *is filled
in various ways by speakers of standard, vernacular, and uneducated
English. Try this sentence on as varied a cross-section of speakers as
you can find, noting the regional origin and educational level of each
informant. Do you find any speakers who have no way of filling the
blank but feel they must recast the sentence?*

*Change the pronoun first to* he *and then to* they *and try the resulting
sentences with the same informants. Comment on the results.*

*Look up* ain't *in the* Oxford English Dictionary *and in* Webster's
Third New International Dictionary. *What bearing does the discussion
there have on the point of usage dealt with in this exercise?*

*VI. Submit the following sentences to a number of educated
speakers of English and ask them to comment on their correctness:*

Due to the rain, the picnic was postponed.
It looks like there will be a successful moon flight soon.

My brother is a better athlete than me.
The data about the problem is insufficient.
Everybody should bring their own lunch.
I have trouble with those kind of problems.
The weather looks sort of threatening.

*Do the informants agree on any or all of the sentences? Under what circumstances, if any, would you use each of these expressions?*

*Make a detailed study of one of these points of usage, consulting the Oxford English Dictionary if it is available to you and any other reference books you can find. Collect examples also from speech and from printed material. Then write a careful statement about it which would be suitable for an up-to-date textbook for school English classes.*

*VII. Supply the educated standard English equivalents for the following items from the Faulkner passage on page 251:*

| | |
|---|---|
| nigh toward | broke |
| toted | taken |
| laying | aint |
| had done been buried | folks talks him low |
| no more | that less of a man |
| clean full | couldn't a bore |

*Rewrite the passage in standard colloquial English. What is lost by this "translation"? In what sense can the passage as Faulkner wrote it be called "correct"?*

# For Further Reading

*On Dialects and Dialectology*

Brook, G. L., *English Dialects*. London: André Deutsch, 1963.
McDavid, Raven I., Jr., "The Dialects of American English," in W. Nelson Francis, *The Structure of American English*. New York: The Ronald Press, 1958. Ch. 9.
McIntosh, Angus, *Introduction to a Survey of Scottish Dialects*. Edinburgh: Thomas Nelson and Sons Limited, 1961. Chapters 1-3 are of general dialectological interest.
Turner, G. W., *The English Language in Australia and New Zealand*. London: Longmans, Green & Co., Ltd., 1966.

*On Usage and Style*

Enkvist, Nils Erik, John Spencer and Michael J. Gregory, *Linguistics and Style*. London: Oxford University Press, 1964.

Joos, Martin, *The Five Clocks*. Bloomington: Indiana University Research Center in Anthropology, Folklore, and Linguistics, 1962.

Quirk, Randolph, *The Use of English*. London: Longmans, Green and Co., Ltd., 1962.

Strevens, P. D., "Varieties of English," in *Papers in Language and Language Teaching*. London: Oxford University Press, 1965.

Warburg, Jeremy, "Some Aspects of Style," in *The Teaching of English*, ed. Randolph Quirk and A. H. Smith. London: Oxford University Press, 1964.

*Dictionaries and Lexicography*

*Webster's Third New International Dictionary of the English Language*. Springfield, Mass.: G. & C. Merriam Company, 1961.

Murray, James A. H., *et al.*, ed., *The Oxford English Dictionary*. [Revised edition of *A New English Dictionary on Historical Principles*, 1884-1928.] Oxford: Clarendon Press, 1933. 12 vols. and Supplement.

Sledd, James H., and Gwin J. Kolb, *Dr. Johnson's Dictionary: Essays in the Biography of a Book*. Chicago: University of Chicago Press, 1955.

# INDEX

Note: Page numbers of references to terms defined in the text are given in bold face.